THE COMPLETE BOOK OF BABY

NAMES

Traditional and modern

Other titles of interest from Foulsham:

BEFORE BABY ARRIVES
YOUR BABY EQUIPMENT
YOUR BABY'S DEVELOPMENT
BABY TOYS THAT BUILD SKILLS

THE COMPLETE BOOK OF BABY

NAMES

Traditional and modern

HILARY SPENCE

foulsham
LONDON • NEW YORK • TORONTO • SYDNEY

foulsham

Bennetts Close, Cippenham, Berks SL1 5AP

ISBN 0–572–01643–3

Copyright © 1993 W. Foulsham & Co. Ltd.

Printed in Great Britain by St Edmundsbury Press Ltd.,
Bury St Edmunds, Suffolk.

Girls

Abagael See **Abigail**

Abbe See **Abigail**

Abbey See **Abigail**

Aberah See **Avera**

Abia [Arabic]
'Great'.

Abigael See **Abigail**

Abigail [Hebrew]

'Father rejoiced'. Also the 18th century name for a maidservant.
(Ab, Abbey, Abbie, Abby, Gael, Gail, Gale, Gayl)

Abijah [Hebrew]
'God is my father'.

Abisha See **Abijah**

Abra [Hebrew]
'Mother of multitudes'.

Acacia [Greek]
The symbol of immortality and resurrection.

Acantha [Greek]
'Thorny'.

Accalia [Latin]
'Foster mother of Romulus and Remus, founders of Rome'.

Ada [Teutonic]
'Prosperous and joyful'. A popular name in Victorian times.
(Adda, Addie, Addy, Aida, Eda)

Adabela See **Adabelle**

Adabelle [Combination Ada/Belle]
'Joyous and beautiful'.
(Adabel, Adabela, Adabella)

Adah [Hebrew]
'The crown's adornment'. One who gives added lustre to the most eminent position.

Adalia [Teutonic]
An early Saxon tribal name, the origin of which is not known.

Adaline See **Adelaide**

Adamina [Latin]
'From the red earth'. Fem. of Adam.
(Addie, Addy, Mina)

Adar [Hebrew]
'Fire'. Name sometimes given to Jewish daughters born in the sixth month of the Jewish year which is known by the same name.

Adara [Greek]
'Beauty'.

Addi See **Adelaide**

Addia See **Ada**

Addie See **Adamina**

Addula [Teutonic]
'Noble cheer'.

Adela See **Adelaide**

Adelaida See **Adelaide**

Adelaide [Teutonic]
'Noble and kind'. A gracious lady of noble birth. A name popular in Britain in the early 19th century, in compliment to Queen Adelaide of Saxe Meiningen, Consort to

King William IV.
(Adaline, Adela, Adele,
Adelia, Adelina, Adelind,
Adeline, Adila, Dela,
Della, Edeline, Edelina)

Adele See **Adelaide**

Adelia See **Adelaide**

Adelicia [Teutonic]
'Noble cheer'.

Adelina See **Adelaide**

Adelind See **Adelaide**

Adelinda [French]
'Noble, sweet'.

Adeline See **Adelaide**

Adelle See **Adelaide**

Adelphia [Greek]
'Sisterly'. The eternal
friend and sister to
mankind.
(Adelfia, Adelpha)

Aderyn [Welsh]
'Bird'.

Adiba [Arabic]
'Cultured'.

Adila [Arabic]
'Equal, like'.

Adilah [Arabic]
'Honest'.

Adima [Teutonic]
'Noble, famous'.

Adina [Hebrew]
'Voluptuous'. One of ripe,
mature charm.
(Adena)

Adnette [French from Old
German]
'Noble'.

Adolfina See **Adolpha**

Adolpha [Teutonic]
'The noble she-wolf' Fem.
of Adolf. The noble
matriarch who will
sacrifice everything,
including life, for her
young.
(Adolfa, Adolfina,
Adolphina)

Adoncia [Spanish]
'Sweet'.

Adonia [Greek]
'Beautiful goddess of the
resurrection'. The eternal
renewal of youth.

Adora [Latin]
'Adored and beloved gift'.

Adorabella [Combination
Adora/Bella]
'Beautiful gift'.

Adorée See **Adora**

Adorna [Latin]
'Adorned with jewels'.

Adria See **Adrienne**

Adriana See **Adrienne**

Adrienne [Latin]
'Dark lady from the sea'.
Fem. of Adrian. A dark,
mysterious lady.
*(Adria, Adriana, Adriane,
Adrianna, Adrianne,
Hadria)*

Aelda See **Aldora**

Aeldra See **Aldora**

Aerona [Welsh]
'Like a berry'.
(Aeronwen)

Aeronwen See **Aerona**

Afraima [Arabic, Hebrew]
'Fruitful'.

Africa [Celtic]
'Pleasant'. Twelfth-
century queen of the Isle
of Man.
*(Afrika, Africah, Afrikah,
Affrica)*

Afton [Old English]
'One from Afton'.

Agace See **Agatha**

Agalia [Greek]
'Brightness'.

Agata See **Agatha**

Agatha [Greek]
'Good'. One of impeccable
virtue.
*(Ag, Agata, Agathe,
Agathy, Aggie, Aggy)*

Agathe See **Agatha**

Agathy See **Agatha**

Agave [Greek]
'Illustrious and noble'.

Aggie See **Agatha**

Aglaia [Greek]
'Splendour'.

Agna See **Agnes**

Agnella See **Agnes**

Agnes [Greek]
'Pure, chaste, lamblike'.
The untouchable virgin.
*(Aggie, Agna, Agnella,
Annais, Annis, Ines, Inez,
Nessa, Nessie, Nessi,*

Nesta, Neysa, Ina, Ynes,
Ynez)

Agneta See **Agnes**

Agnola See **Agnes**

Agrippa [Latin]
'Born feet first'.

Agueda See **Agatha**

Ahuda [Hebrew]
'Praise; sympathetic'.

Aidan [Gaelic]
'Little fire'. A girl with
bright red hair.

Aiden See **Edana**

Aigneis See **Agnes**

Aiko [Japanese]
'Little love, beloved'.

Aila See **Aileen**

Ailee See **Aileen**

Aileen [Greek]
A derivative of 'Helen', q.v.
(Aleen, Alene, Aline,
Eileen, Elene, Ilene, Iline,
Illene, Illona, Illeana,
Ilona, Isleen)

Ailey See **Aileen**

Aili See **Aileen**

Ailsa [Old German]
'Girl of cheer'.
(Aillsa, Ailssa, Ilsa)

Ainslee See **Ainsley**

Ainsley [Gaelic]
'From one's own meadow'.

Ainslie See **Ainsley**

Aisha [African]
'Life'.
(Asha, Ashia, Asia)

Aisha [Arabic]
'Living'.

Aisleen [Gaelic]
'The vision'.

Akasuki [Japanese]
'Bright helper'.

Akili [Tanzanian]
'Wisdom'.
(Akela, Akeyla, Akeylah)

Alain See **Alana**

Alaine See **Alana**

Alameda [Spanish]
'Poplar tree'.

Alameda [Spanish]
'Poplar grove'.

Alana [Celtic]
'Bright, fair one'. A term
of endearment used by
the Irish.
*(Alain, Alanna, Alayne,
Alina, Allene, Allyn, Lana,
Lane)*

Alanah See **Alana**

Alarica See **Alarice**

Alarice [Teutonic]
'Ruler of all'. Fem. of
Alaric.
(Alarica, Alarise)

Alberta [Teutonic]
'Noble and brilliant'. Fem.
of Albert. A nobly born
and highly intelligent girl.
Popular name in Victorian
times in compliment to the
Prince Consort.
*(Albertina, Albertine,
Allie, Berta, Berte, Bertie,
Elberta, Elbertine)*

Albertina See **Alberta**

Albertine See **Alberta**

Albina [Latin]
'White Lady'. One whose
hair and colouring is of the
very fairest.
*(Albinia, Alvina, Aubina,
Aubine)*

Albinia See **Elvira**

Alcina [Greek]
'Strong minded one'. The
legendary Grecian lady
who could produce gold
from stardust; one who
knows her own mind.
(Alciana, Alcinette)

Alcinette See **Alcina**

Alda [Teutonic]
'Wise and rich'.
(Eada, Elda)

Aldara [Greek]
'Winged gift'.

Aldora [Anglo-Saxon]
'Of noble rank'.
(Aelda, Aeldra)

Alegria [Spanish]
'Happiness'.

Alejandra See **Alexandra**

Alejandrina See **Alexandra**

Aleria [Latin]
'Eagle like'.

Alessandra See **Alexandra**

Aleta See **Alida**

Aletha See **Alice**

Alethea See **Alice**

Aletta [Latin]
'Winged, birdlike'.

Alexa See **Alexandra**

Alexandra [Greek]
'The helper of mankind'.
Popular name in early
20th century in
compliment to Queen
Alexandra.
(*Alex, Alexa, Alexine,
Alexis, Alix, Lexie,
Lexine, Sandy, Sandra,
Zandra*)

Alexandrina See
Alexandra

Alexina See **Alexandra**

Alexine See **Alexandra**

Alexis See **Alexandra**

Alfie See **Alfreda**

Alfonsine [Teutonic]
'Noble and ready'. Fem. of
Alphonse.
(*Alphonsina, Alphonsine,
Alonza*)

Alfreda [Teutonic]
'Wise Counsellor'. Fem. of
Alfred. A name popular in
Anglo-Saxon times, but
one which died out after
the conquest.
(*Alfie, Allie, Elfreda,
Elfreida, Elfrieda, Elfrida,
Elva, Elga, Freda*)

Alice [Greek]
'Truth'. A name
popularised in the mid
19th century, when it was
much used by the Royal
Family.
(*Alicia, Alicea, Aletha,
Alethea, Aliss, Alithia,
Allys, Alyce, Alys, Alisa,
Alissa, Allis, Aleece, Alla,
Allie, Ally, Elissa, Elisa,
Elke*)

Alicia See **Alice**

Alida [Latin]
'Little winged one'. A girl
who is as small and lithe
as the woodlark.
(*Aleda, Aleta, Alita, Leda,
Lita*)

Alika See **Alice**

Alima [Arabic]
'Learned in music and
dancing'.

Alina See **Alana**

Alisha See **Alice**

Alison [Combination Alice/
Louise]
'Truthful warrior maid'.
*(Alie, Allie, Allison,
Allson, Lissie, Lisy)*

Aliss See **Alice**

Alix See **Alexandra**

Aliya [Arabic]
'Sublime, exalted'.
[Hebrew]
'Ascend'.

Aliyah See **Aliya**

Alla See **Alice**

Alleen See **Alana**

Allegra [Latin]
'Cheerful'. As blithe as a
bird.

Allegra See **Alegria**

Allson See **Allison**

Allsun See **Alison**

Allyce See **Alice**

Allys See **Alice**

Allyson See **Alison**

Alma [Latin]
'Cherishing spirit'. Name
popularly given to girls
after the battle of Alma, in
the Crimean War.

Almeda [Latin]
'Pressing toward the goal'.

Almeta See **Almeda**

Almeta [Latin]
'Ambitious'.

Almira [Arabic]
(Elma)
'Truth without question'.
*(Almeira, Almeria,
Elmira)*

Alodie [Anglo-Saxon]
'Wealthy, prosperous'.

Aloha [Hawaiian]
'Greetings'. A romantic
name from the Hawaiian
Islands.

Aloisa See **Louise**

Alonza See **Alphonsine**

Alpha [Greek]
'First one'. A suitable
name for the first baby, if
she is a girl.

Alphonsina See **Alfonsine**

Alta [Latin]
'Tall in spirit'.

Althea [Greek]
'The healer'.
(Aletha, Alethea, Altheta,
Althee, Thea)

Altheda [Greek]
'Flowerlike'.

Althee See **Althea**

Altheta See **Althea**

Alula [Latin/Arabic]
'Winged one' (Latin). 'The
first' (Arabic).
(Alloula, Allula, Aloula)

Aluma [Hebrew]
'Girl'.

Alura [Anglo-Saxon]
'Divine Counsellor'.

Alva [Latin]
'White Lady'.

Alverta See **Alberta**

Alvina [Teutonic]
'Beloved and noble friend'.
(Alvine, Vina)

Alvina See **Albina**

Alvine See **Alvina**

Alvinia See **Alvina**

Alvita [Latin]
'Vivacious'.

Alysia See **Alice**

Alyssa [Greek]
'Sane one'. The small
white flower Alyssum
derives from this name.

Alyssa See **Alice**

Alzena [Arabic]
'The woman'. The
embodiment of all
feminine charm and
virtue.

Ama [African]
'Born on Saturday'.

Amabel [Latin]
'Sweet, lovable one'. A
tender, loving, loyal
daughter.
(Amabella, Amabelle)

Amabella See **Amabel**

Amadea [Latin]
'The beloved of God'.

Amadora See **Amadore**

Amadore [Italian]
'Gift of love'.

Amala [Arabic]
'Hope'.

Amalee See **Amelia**

Amalie See **Amelia**

Amana [Hebrew]
'Faithful'.

Amanda [Latin]
'Worthy of being loved'.
(Manda, Mandie, Mandy)

Amany [Arabic]
'Aspiration'.

Amapola [Arabic]
'Flower'.

Amara [Greek]
'Of eternal beauty'.

Amarantha [Greek]
'Unfading'.

Amargo See **Amara**

Amaris [Hebrew]
'God has promised'.

Amaryllis [Greek]
'Fresh, new'.
(Amarillis, Marilla)

Amaryllis. [Greek]
'Fresh, sparkling; flower
name'.

Amata See **Amy**

Amata [Latin]
'Beloved'.

Amber [Arabic]
'Jewel'. This name had a
surge of popularity in
America and Britain in the
1940's, following the
publication of the novel
Forever Amber.

Amberly See **Amber**

Ambrosia See **Ambrosine**

Ambrosina See
Ambrosine

Ambrosine [Greek]
'Divine, immortal one'.
Fem. of Ambrose.
(Ambrosia, Ambrosina)

Ambur See **Amber**

Ameerah [Arabic]
'Princess'.

Amelia [Teutonic]
'Industrious and striving'.
*(Amalia, Amalie, Amealia,
Amelea, Ameline,*

*Amelita, Amelie, Emelina,
Emeline, Emilia, Emily,
Emmeline, Emelie, Mell,
Mellie, Milicia, Mill,
Millie)*

Amelinda [Spanish]
'Beloved and pretty'.
(Amalinda, Amelinde)

Amelinde See **Amelinda**

Ameline See **Amelia**

Amelita See **Amelia**

Amena [Celtic]
'Honest'. One of
incorruptible truth.
(Amina, Amine)

Amethyst [Greek]
The name of the semi-
precious stone which has
(it is alleged) the power to
ward off intoxication.

Amilia [Latin]
'Affable'.

Amine See **Amena**

Aminta [Greek]
'Protector'. The name of a
shepherdess in Greek
mythology.
(Amintha, Aminthe)

Amintha See **Aminta**

Amira [Arabic]
'Princess, cultivated'.
[Hebrew]
'Speech'.

Amity [Old French]
'Friendship'.

Amorette [Latin]
'Darling'.
(Amarette, Morette)

Amy [French]
'Beloved friend'.
(Aim-ee, Ami, Amie)

Ana See **Anastasia**

Anamari [Basque]
Derivation of Anna Maria.

Anastasia [Greek]
'She who will rise again'.
The very apt name of the
Grand Duchess who was
officially killed during the
Russian revolution, but
who was alleged to be still
living until a few years ago.
*(Ana, Anstice, Stacey,
Stacia, Stacie, Stacy)*

Anatola [Greek]
'Woman of the East'. Fem.
of Anatole.
(Anatolia, Anatholia)

Anatolia See **Anatola**

Ancelin [Latin]
'Fairest handmaid'.
(Celine)

Anchoret [Welsh]
'Much loved'.

Andre See **Andrea**

Andrea [Latin]
'Womanly'. The epitome of
feminine charm and
beauty.
*(Andreana, Aindrea,
Andria, Andriana, Andre,
Andree)*

Andrea See **Edrea**

Andreana See **Andrea**

Aneira [Welsh]
'Honourable'.

Anemone [Greek]
'Windflower'. The nymph
of Greek mythology who,
when pursued by the
wind, turned into the
flower, anemone.

Angela [Greek]
'Heavenly messenger'.
The bringer of good
tidings.
*(Angelina, Angeline,
Angelita, Angel, Angie)*

Angelica [Latin]
'Angelic one'. A name
often used by Medieval
writers to typify the perfect
woman.
(Angelique)

Angharad [Welsh]
'Free from shame'.

Angwen [Welsh]
'Very handsome'.

Anita [Hebrew]
'Grace'. A form of Anne,
q.v. (for continuity).
(Anitra)

Anna See **Anne**

Annabelle [Combination
Anna/Belle]
*(Annabel, Anabel,
Annabella, Annie,
Annabla, Belle, Bella)*

Annais See **Agnes**

Anne [Hebrew]
'Full of Grace'. One of the
most popular feminine

names. The name of
several British Queens
Consort and a Queen
Regnant.
*(Ann, Anna, Annetta,
Annette, Annie, Annika,
Annora, Anita, Ana, Nan,
Nana, Nanna, Nancy,
Nanette, Nanetta, Nanete,
Nanine, Nanon, Nina,
Ninette, Ninon, Hannah,
Hanna)*

Annetta See **Anne**

Annette See **Anne**

Annika See **Anne**

Annis See **Agnes**

Annissa [Arabic]
'Charming, gracious'.

Annora See **Anne**

Annunciata [Latin]
'Bearer of news'. A
suitable name for a girl
born in March,
particularly 24th March,
as it derives from the
'Annunciation' — the
announcement of the
Virgin's conception.

Annunciata See **Nunciata**

Anona [Latin]
'Yearly crops'. The Roman
Goddess of the Crops.
(Annona, Nonnie, Nona)

Anora [English]
'Light and graceful'.

Anselma [Norse]
'Divinely protected'.
(Anselme, Selma, Zelma)

Anselme See **Anselma**

Anstice See **Anastasia**

Anthea [Greek]
'Flowerlike'. One of
delicate, fragile beauty.
*(Anthia, Bluma, Thea,
Thia)*

Antoinette See **Antonia**

Antoinietta See **Antonia**

Antoni See **Antonia**

Antonia [Latin]
'Beyond price, excellent'.
Fem. of Anthony. A jewel
beyond compare.
*(Anthonia, Antoinette,
Antoni, Antonina,
Antoinietta, Antonietta,
Toinette, Toni, Netta,
Nettie, Netty)*

Antonina See **Antonia**

Anya [Hebrew]
'Grace; mercy'.
(Annia)

Aphra [Hebrew]
'Female deer'.
(Afra)

Appoline [Greek]
'Sun'.
(Apollene)

April [Latin]
'The beginning of Spring'.
The name of the first
month of the Roman
calendar and the fourth
month of the Julian
Calendar.

Ara [Greek]
'Spirit of revenge'. The
Grecian Goddess of
vengeance and
destruction.

Arabella [Latin]
'Beautiful altar'.
*(Arabelle, Arabela, Aralia,
Arbelie, Arbelia, Arbel,
Bel, Bella, Belle)*

Arabelle See **Arabella**

Aralia See **Arabella**

Aramanta [Hebrew]
'Elegant lady'.
(Araminta, Aramenta)

Aramenta See **Aramanta**

Araminta [Greek]
'Beautiful, sweet smelling
flower'.

Araminta See **Aramanta**

Arbel See **Arabella**

Arbelia See **Arabella**

Arbelie See **Arabella**

Arda See **Ardelle**

Ardath [Hebrew]
'Field of flowers'.
(Aridatha, Ardatha)

Ardatha See **Ardath**

Ardelis See **Ardelle**

Ardella See **Ardelle**

Ardelle [Latin]
'Enthusiasm, warmth'.
*(Arda, Ardella, Ardere,
Ardis, Ardine, Ardene,
Ardeen, Ardella, Ardelis,
Ardra)*

Arden [Old English]
'Eagle valley'.

Ardere See **Ardelle**

Ardine See **Ardelle**

Ardis See **Ardelle**

Ardra See **Ardelle**

Areta [Greek]
'Of excellent virtue'.
One of untarnished
reputation.
(Arete, Aretha, Aretta,
Arette)

Arete See **Areta**

Aretha See **Areta**

Aretta See **Areta**

Arezou [Persian]
'Wishful'.

Argenta [Latin]
'Silvery one'.
(Argentia, Argente)

Argente See **Argenta**

Argentia See **Argenta**

Aria [Latin]
'Beautiful melody'.

Ariadna See **Ariadne**

Ariadne [Greek]
'Holy one'. The
mythological maiden who
rescued Theseus from his
labyrinth.
(Arlana, Ariane, Ariadna)

Ariane See **Ariadne**

Aridatha See **Ardath**

Ariel See **Ariella**

Ariella [Hebrew]
'God's lioness'.
(Ariel, Ariella, Arielle)

Arilda [German]
'Hearth, home'.

Ariminta [Hebrew]
'Lofty'.

Arista [Greek]
'The best'.

Arlana See **Ariadne**

Arleas See **Arlene**

Arlen See **Arlene**

Arlena See **Arlene**

Arlene [Celtic]
'A pledge'.
*(Airleas, Arlana, Arleen,
Arlen, Arlena, Arlette,
Arletta, Arlina, Arline,
Arlyne, Herleva)*

Arletta See **Arlene**

Arlette See **Arlene**

Armelle [French from
Celtic]
'Princess'.

Armida [Latin]
'Small warrior'.

Armilla [Latin]
'Bracelet'.

Armina [Teutonic]
'Warrior maid'.
*(Armine, Arminia,
Erminie, Erminia)*

Armine See **Armina**

Arminia See **Armina**

Arnalda [Teutonic]
'Eagle-like ruler'. Fem. of
Arnold.

Arselma [Norse]
'Divine protective helmet'.

Artemisia [Greek,
Spanish]
'Perfect'.

Arva [Latin]
'Pastureland, seashore'.

Ashira [Hebrew]
'Wealthy'.

Ashley [Old English]
'From the ash tree
meadow'.

Asisa [Hebrew]
'Ripe'.

Aspasia [Greek]
'Welcome'.

Asphodel [Greek]
'The wild lily of Greece'.

Assunta [Italian]
'From the Assumption
(of Mary)'.

Asta [Greek]
'Starlike'.
(Astra)

Astera See **Asta**

Astra See **Asta**

Astrea See **Asta**

Astrid [Norse]
'Divine strength'.
(Astra)

Atalanta [Greek]
'Might bearer'. The
legendary Greek huntress.
(Atlanta, Atalante)

Atalante See **Atalanta**

Atalia See **Athalia**

Atalya [Spanish]
'Guardian'. One who
protects hearth and home.

Atara [Hebrew]
'Crown'.

Athalia [Hebrew]
'God is exalted'.
*(Atalia, Athalea, Athalie,
Athie, Attie)*

Athalie See **Athalia**

Athena [Greek]
The Greek Goddess.
(Athene, Athenee)

Athene See **Athena**

Athenee See **Athena**

Athie See **Athalia**

Atiya [Arabic]
'Gift'.

Attie See **Athalia**

Aubina See **Albina**

Aubine See **Albina**

Audie See **Audrey**

Audrey [Anglo-Saxon]
'Strong and noble'.
Derives from the Anglo-
Saxon Aethelthryth.
*(Audrie, Audry, Audie,
Dee)*

Augusta [Latin]
'Sacred and majestic'.
Popular name in Royal
and Noble families in 18th
and early 19th century.
*(Auguste, Augustina,
Augustine, Austine,
Gussie, Gusta, Tina)*

Auguste See **Augusta**

Augustina See **Augusta**

Augustine See **Augusta**

Aura [Latin]
'Gentle breeze'. A name
said to endow its owner
with gentility.
(Aure, Aurea, Auria)

Aura See **Aurelia**

Aurea See **Aurelia**

Aurel See **Aurelia**

Aurelia [Latin]
'Golden'. The girl of the
dawn.
*(Aura, Aurea, Auristela,
Aurora, Aurelie, Aurel,
Aurie, Ora, Oralia, Oralie,
Oriel, Oriole)*

Aurie See **Aurelia**

Auristela See **Aurelia**

Aurora See **Aurelia**

Aurore See **Aurora**

Ava See **Avis**

Avel [Hebrew]
'Breath'.

Aveline See **Hazel**

Aveline [Hebrew]
'Pleasant'.

Avena [Latin]
'Oatfield'. A girl with rich,
golden hair.
(Avene)

Avene See **Avena**

Avenida [Chilean]
'An avenue'.

Avera [Hebrew]
'Transgressor'.
(Aberah)

Averil [Old English]
'Slayer of the Boar'.
(Avril, Averyl, Avyril)

Avery [Old French]
'To confirm'.
(Averi)

Avi See **Avis**

Avice [French]
'Warlike'.
(Avisa, Hadwisa)

Avicia [German]
'Refuge in war'.

Avis [Latin]
'A bird'.
(Ava, Avi)

Avisa See **Avice**

Avishag [Hebrew]
'Father's delight'.

Avital [Hebrew]
'God protects'.

Aviva [Hebrew]
'Springtime'.

Avivah See **Aviva**

Avrit See **Aviva**

Awena [Welsh]
'Poetry; prophecy'.

Ayala [Hebrew]
'Deer'.

Aylwen [Welsh]
'Fair brow'.

Azalee See **Azaliea**

Azaliea [Latin]
'Dry earth'. From the
flower of the same name.
(Azalia, Azalee)

Azaria [Hebrew]
'Blessed by God'.
(Azeria, Zaria)

Azura [French]
'The blue sky'. One whose
eyes are sky blue.

Boys

Aaron [Hebrew]
'Exalted'. The brother of
Moses. *(Aron, Haroun)*

Abba [Hebrew]
'Father'.

Abbe See **Abbott**

Abbott [Anglo-Saxon]
'Father of the abbey'.
(Abbot, Abott, Abbe)

Abdel See **Abdul**

Abdi [Hebrew]
'My servant'.

Abdiel [Hebrew]
'Servant of God'.

Abdon [Hebrew]
'Servant of God'.

Abdul [Arabic]
'Son of'.

Abe See **Abraham**

Abel [Hebrew]
'Breath'. The first
recorded murder victim.

Abelard [Teutonic]
'Nobly resolute'.

Abir [Hebrew]
'Strong'.

Abiri See **Abir**

Abisha [Hebrew]
'God's gift'.

Abner [Hebrew]
'Father of light'.

Abraham [Hebrew]
'Father of multitudes'. The
original patriarch.
*(Abram, Abe, Abie, Bram,
Ibrahim)*

Abram See **Abraham**

Abran See **Abraham**

Absalom [Hebrew]
'Father of peace'.
(Absolom)

Ace [Latin]
'Unity'.
(Acey)

Acelin [French]
'Noble'.

Acelot See **Acelin**

Acey See **Ace**

Achilles [Greek]
'Swift'.

Ackerley [Anglo-Saxon]
'From the acre meadow'.

Ackley [Anglo-Saxon]
'From the oak tree
meadow'.

Ackley [Old German]
'Oak-tree meadow'.

Acton [Old English]
'Town near oak trees'.

Adair [Gaelic]
'From the oak tree near the
ford'.

Adalard [Teutonic]
'Noble and brave'.
(Adelard, Adhelard)

Adalric [Old German]
'Noble ruler'.

Adalwine See **Audwin**

Adam [Hebrew]
'Of the red earth'. The first

man, according to the
Bible.

Adamo See **Adam**

Adan See **Adin**

Adan See **Adam**

Adao See **Adam**

Adar [Hebrew]
'Fiery'.

Addison [Anglo-Saxon]
'Adam's son'.

Addy [Teutonic]
'Awesome, noble'.

Ade See **Adrian**

Adelbert See **Albert**

Adelpho [Greek]
'Brother'.

Adelric See **Adalric**

Ademar [Teutonic]
'Fierce, noble, famous'.

Ademaro See **Ademar**

Adham [Arabic]
'Black'.

Adhamh See **Adam**

Adhar [Arabic]
'Waiting'.

Adin [Hebrew]
'Sensual'.
(Adan)

Adlai [Hebrew]
'My witness, my
ornament'.

Adler [Teutonic]
'Eagle'. One of keen
perception.

Adley [Hebrew]
'The fair-minded'.

Adney [Anglo-Saxon]
'Dweller on the island'.

Adolph [Teutonic]
'Noble wolf'.
*(Adolphe, Adolphus,
Adolf, Adolfus, Ad, Dolf,
Dolph)*

Adolphe See **Adolph**

Adolpho See **Adolph**

Adolphus See **Adolph**

Adon [Hebrew]
'Lord'. The sacred Hebrew
word for God.

Adrian [Latin]
'Dark one' or 'Man from
the sea'.
(Adrien, Hadrian)

Adriano See **Adrian**

Adriel [Hebrew]
'From God's
congregation'.

Aelhaearn [Welsh]
'Iron brow'.

Aeneas [Greek]
'The much praised one'.
The defender of Troy.
(Eneas)

Aethelard See **Allard**

Afdal [Arabic]
'Excellent'.

Afif [Arabic]
'Virtuous'.

Agamemnon [Greek]
'Resolute'.

Agilard [Teutonic]
'Formidably bright'.

Agosto See **August**

Agur [Hebrew]
'Gatherer'.

Aherin See **Ahern**

Ahern [Gaelic]
'Horse lord' or 'Horse owner'.
(Aherne, Aherin, Ahearn, Hearne, Hearn)

Ahmed [Arabic]
'Most highly praised'.

Ahren [Teutonic]
'The Eagle'.

Aidan [Gaelic]
'Little fiery one'.
(Adan, Eden)

Aiken [Anglo-Saxon]
'Little Adam'.
(Aikin, Aickin)

Ailean See **Alan**

Aimery [Teutonic]
'Industrious ruler'.

Aimon [French from Teutonic]
'House'.

Ainsley [Anglo-Saxon]
'Meadow of the respected one'.

Airleas See **Arlen**

Ajax [Greek]
'Eagle'.

Akbar [Arabic]
'Great'.

Akim See **Joachim**

Akmal [Arabic]
'Perfect'.

Akram [Arabic]
'Noble, generous'.

Alabhaois See **Aloysius**

Aladdin [Arabic]
'Servant of Allah'.

Alair [Gaelic]
'Cheerful'.

Alam [Arabic]
'Universe'.

Alan [Gaelic]
'Cheerful harmony'.
(Alain, Allan, Allen, Allyn, Aland, Ailean, Ailin)

Aland See **Alan**

Alano See **Alan**

Alanson See **Alan**

Alard [German]
'Noble ruler'.

Alaric [Teutonic]
'Ruler of all'.
*(Alarick, Ulric, Ulrich,
Ulrick, Rich, Richie, Ricy,
Rick, Rickie, Ricky)*

Alastair See **Alexander**

Alasteir See **Alastair**

Alaster See **Alastair**

Alaster See **Alexander**

Alban [Latin]
'White complexion'. A
man of outstandingly fair
colouring.
*(Alben, Albin, Aubin,
Alva)*

Alberik See **Aubrey**

Albern [Anglo-Saxon]
'Noble warrior'.

Albert [Teutonic]
'Noble and illustrious'.
Name which became
popular in Britain after the
marriage of Queen Victoria
to Prince Albert of Saxe-
Coborg-Gotha.
*(Aldabert, Adelbert,
Delbert, Elbert, Ailbert,
Aubert)*

Albin See **Alban**

Alcander [Greek]
'Strong'.

Alcott [Anglo-Saxon]
'Dweller at the old
cottage'.

Aldabert See **Albert**

Alden [Anglo-Saxon]
'Old, wise friend'. One on
whom friends could rely.
*(Aldin, Aldwin, Aldwyn,
Elden, Eldin)*

Alder [Anglo-Saxon]
'At the alder-tree'.

Aldin See **Alden**

Aldis [Anglo-Saxon]
'From the old house'.
(Aldous, Aldus)

Aldo [Teutonic]
'Old, wise and rich'.

Aldric See **Aldrich**

Aldrich [Anglo-Saxon]
'Old, wise ruler'.
(Alric, Eldrich, Eldric)

Aldridge See **Aldrich**

Aldus See **Aldis**

Aldwin See **Alden**, **Alvin** or
Audwin

Alejandro See **Alexander**

Alejo See **Alexander**

Aleksandr See **Alexander**

Alem [Arabic]
'Wise man'.

Aleron [Latin]
'The eagle'.

Alessandro See **Alexander**

Alexander [Greek]
'Helper and protector of
mankind'.
*(Alastair, Allister, Alec,
Alex, Aleck, Alexis, Alick,
Alsandair, Alister,
Alasdair, Sandie, Sandy,
Sander, Saunders, Sasha)*

Alexis See **Alexander**

Alf See **Alfred**

Alfie See **Alfred**

Alfons See **Alphonso**

Alfonso See **Alphonse**

Alford [Anglo-Saxon]
'The old ford'.

Alford See **Alphonso**

Alfred [Anglo-Saxon]
'The wise counsel of the
elf'.
*(Aelfred, Ailfrid, Alf, Alfie,
Alfy, Al)*

Alfredo See **Alfred**

Alger [Teutonic]
'Noble spearman'.
(Algar)

Algernon [French]
'The whiskered one'. The
man with a moustache or
beard.
(Al, Algie, Algy)

Algie See **Algernon**

Algis [French from
Teutonic]
'Spear'.

Ali [Arabic]
'Greatest'.

Ali [Arabic]
'Noble, sublime'.

Alim [Arabic]
'Scholar'.

Alison [Anglo-Saxon]
'Son of a nobleman', or
'Alice's son'.
(Allison, Al, Allie)

Allan/Allen See **Alan**

Allard [Anglo-Saxon]
'Noble and brave'.
*(Alard, Aethelard,
Aethelhard, Athelhard,
Ethelard)*

Allister See **Alexander**

Almo [Anglo-Saxon]
'Noble and famous'.

Almund [Teutonic]
'Protection'.

Aloin See **Alvin**

Alonso See **Alphonso**

Alonzo See **Alphonso**

Aloys See **Aloysius**

Aloysius [Latin]
'Famous warrior'.
*(Aloys, Lewis, Louis,
Ludwig, Alabhaois)*

Alpheus [Greek]
'God of the river'.

Alphonse See **Alphonso**

Alphonso [Teutonic]
'Noble and ready'.
*(Alfonso, Alphonse,
Alfonse, Alphonsus,
Alonso, Alonzo)*

Alphonsus See **Alphonso**

Alpin [Early Scottish]
'Blond one'. Name borne
by the descendants of the
earliest Scottish Clan —
McAlpin.

Alric See **Aldrich**

Alric See **Ulric**

Alroy [Gaelic]
'Red-haired boy'.

Alsandair See **Alexander**

Alston [Anglo-Saxon]
'From the old village'.

Altman [Teutonic]
'Old, wise man'.

Alton [Anglo-Saxon]
'Dweller in the old town'.

Aluin See **Alvin**

Aluino See **Alvin**

Alva See **Alban**

Alvah [Hebrew]
'The exalted one'.
(Alvar)

Alvan See **Alvin**

Alvin [Teutonic]
'Friend of all' or 'Noble
friend'.
*(Alwin, Aldwin, Alwyn,
Alvan)*

Alwin See **Alvin**

Amadeo [Spanish]
'Beloved of God'.

Amadour [French from
Latin]
'Lovable'.

Amal [Arabic]
'Hope'.
[Hebrew]
'Work'.

Amand See **Amandus**

Amando See **Amandus**

Amandus [Latin]
'Worthy of love'.

Amaro [Portuguese]
'Dark, moor'.

Amasa [Hebrew]
'Burden bearer'.

Ambar [Hindi]
'Sky'.

Ambert [Teutonic]
'Shining, bright light'.

Ambler [English]
'Stable-keeper'.

Ambros See **Ambrose**

Ambrose [Latin]
'Belonging to the divine
immortals'.
*(Ambrosius, Ambroise,
Ambros, Emrys)*

Ambrosi See **Ambrose**

Ambrosio See **Ambrose**

Ambrosius See **Ambrose**

Amby See **Ambrose**

Amerigo See **Emery**

Amery See **Amory**

Amhlaoibh See **Olaf**

Amijad [Arabic]
'Glorious'.

Amil [Arabic]
'Industrious'.

Amin [Arabic, Hebrew]
'Trustworthy, honest'.

Amirov [Hebrew]
'My people are great'.

Amitan [Hebrew]
'True, faithful'.

Ammon [Egyptian]
'The hidden'.

Amnon [Hebrew]
'Faithful'.

Amon [Hebrew]
'Trustworthy'.

Amory [Teutonic]
'Famous ruler'.
(Amery)

Amos [Hebrew]
'A burden'. One used to
tackling difficult problems.

Amram [Arabic]
'Life'.

Amund [Scandinavian]
'Divine protection'.

Amyot [French]
'Beloved'.

Anand [Hindi]
'Peaceful'.

Ananias [Hebrew]
'Grace of the Lord'.

Anarawd [Welsh]
'Eloquent'.

Anastasius [Greek]
'One who shall rise again'.

Anatole [Greek]
'From the East'.
(Anatol)

Anatolio See **Anatole**

Ancel [German]
'Godlike'.

Ancell See **Ansel**

Anders See **Andrew**

Anderson See **Andrew**

Andonis See **Andrew**

Andras See **Andrew**

Andre See **Andrew**

Andreas See **Andrew**

Andrej See **Andrew**

Andrew [Greek]
'Strong and manly'. The
Patron Saint of Scotland,
St. Andrew.
*(Andreas, Andre,
Aindreas, Anders,
Andrien, Andie, Andy)*

Andrien See **Andrew**

Andris See **Andrew**

Androcles [Greek]
'Man-glory'.

Aneurin [Celtic]
'Truly golden'.
(Nye)

Ange See **Angelo**

Angell See **Angelo**

Angelo [Italian]
'Saintly messenger'.

Angus [Celtic]
'Outstanding and
exceptional man'. One of
unparalleled strength.

Angwyn [Welsh]
'Very handsome'.

Annan [Celtic]
'From the stream'.

Anniss [Arabic]
'Charming'.

Ansari [Arabic]
'Helper'.

Anscom [Anglo-Saxon]
'Dweller in the secret
valley'. An awe-inspiring,
solitary man.
(Anscomb)

Anse See **Anselm**

Ansel [French]
'Nobleman's follower'.
(Ansell)

Ansel See **Anselm**

Anselm [Teutonic]
'Divine helmet'.
*(Anse, Ansel, Anselme,
Anshelm)*

Anshar [Teutonic]
'Divine spear'.

Ansley [Anglo-Saxon]
'From Ann's meadow'.

Anson [Anglo-Saxon]
'Ann's son'.

Anstice [Greek]
'The resurrected'. One
who returns to life after
death.
(Anstiss)

Anthony [Latin]
'Of inestimable worth'. A
man without peer.
*(Antony, Antoine, Anton,
Anntoin, Antonio, Tony)*

Antin See **Anthony**

Antinous [Greek]
'Contradictory'.

Anton See **Anthony**

Antonino See **Anthony**

Antonio See **Anthony**

Antons See **Anthony**

Anwell [Celtic]
'Beloved one'.
(Anwyl, Anwyll)

Anwyl See **Anwell**

Anyon [Celtic]
'The anvil'. One on whom
all the finest
characteristics have been
forged.

Aodh [Celtic]
'Fire'.

Aodh See **Hubert**

Apollo [Greek]
'Beautiful man'.

Aquila [Latin]
'Eagle'.

Ara [Arabic]
'Rainmaker'.

Araldo See **Harold**

Archaimbaud See
Archibald

Archambault See
Archibald

Archard [Teutonic]
'Sacred and powerful'.
(Archerd)

Archer [Anglo-Saxon]
'The bowman'.

Archer See **Archibald**

Archibald [Teutonic]
'Noble and truly bold'. A
brave and sacred warrior.
*(Archimbald, Gilleasbuig,
Arch, Archie, Archer,
Archy)*

Archibaldo See **Archibald**

Archimbald See **Archibald**

Archimedes [Greek]
'Master mind'.

Arden [Latin]
'Ardent, fiery, fervent,
sincere'. One of intensely
loyal nature.
(Ardin)

Ardley [Anglo-Saxon]
'From the domestic
meadow'.

Ardolph [Anglo-Saxon]
'The home loving wolf'.
The roamer who longs
only for home.
(Ardolf)

Arel [Hebrew]
'Lion of God'.

Aretino [Greek]
'Victorious'.

Argus [Greek]
'The watchful one'. The
giant with a hundred eyes,
who saw everything at
once.

Argyle [Gaelic]
'From the land of the
Gaels'.

Aric [Anglo-Saxon]
'Sacred ruler'.
(Rick, Rickie, Ricky)

Ariel [Hebrew]
'Lion of God'.

Aries [Latin]
'A ram'. One born in April,
from the sign of the Zodiac
—Aries.

Aristotle [Greek]
'Best thinker'.

Arkady See **Archibald**

Arledge [Anglo-Saxon]
'Dweller by the lake where
the rabbit dances'.

Arlen [Gaelic]
'Pledge'.
(Airleas)

Arlie [Anglo-Saxon]
'From the rabbit meadow'.
*(Arley, Arly, Harley,
Harly)*

Arlin See **Arlen**

Arlo [Spanish]
'The barberry'.

Armand [Teutonic]
'Man of the army'. The
military man personified.
(Armin, Armond)

Armand See **Herman**

Armando See **Armand**

Armin See **Armand**

Armon [Hebrew]
'Castle'.

Armond See **Armand** or
Herman

Armstrong [Anglo-Saxon]
'Strong arm'. The tough
warrior who could wield a
battle axe.

Arnaldo See **Arnold**

Arnall [Teutonic]
'Gracious eagle'. The
nobleman who is also a
gentleman.

Arnatt See **Arnett**

Arnett [French]
'Little eagle'.
(Arnatt, Arnott)

Arney [Teutonic]
'The eagle'.
(Arnie, Arne)

Arnie See **Arney**

Arno See **Arnold**

Arnold [Teutonic]
'Strong as an eagle'.
*(Arnald, Arnaud, Arne,
Arnie, Arno)*

Arnott See **Arnett**

Arpad See **Arvad**

Artair See **Arthur**

Artemis [Greek]

'Gift of Artemis'.
(Artemas)

Arthfael [Welsh]
'Bear strength'.

Arthur [Celtic]
'The noble bear man' or
'Strong as a rock'. The
semi-legendary King of
Britain, who founded the
Round Table.
*(Aurthur, Artair, Artur,
Artus, Art, Artie)*

Artur See **Arthur**

Arturo See **Arthur**

Arundel [Anglo-Saxon]
'Dweller with eagles'. One
who lives with and shares
the keen sightedness of
the eagle.

Arvad [Hebrew]
'The wanderer'.
(Arpad)

Arval [Latin]
'Much lamented'.
(Arvel)

Arvin [Teutonic]
'Friend of the people'. The
first true socialist.

Asa [Hebrew]
'The healer'.

Asaph [Hebrew]
'Gatherer'.

Ascelin [German]
'Of the moon'.
(Aceline)

Ascot [Anglo-Saxon]
'Owner of the east
cottage'.
(Ascott)

Ashbey See **Ashby**

Ashburn [Anglo-Saxon]
'The brook by the ash
tree'.

Ashby [Anglo-Saxon]
'Ash tree farm'.

Asher [Hebrew]
'The laughing one'. A
happy lad.

Ashford [Anglo-Saxon]
'One who lives in the ford
by the ash tree'.

Ashley [Anglo-Saxon]
'Dweller in the ash tree
meadow'.
(Lee)

Ashlin [Anglo-Saxon]
'Dweller by the ash tree
pool'.

Ashok [Hindi]
'Without sadness'.

Ashton [Anglo-Saxon]
'Dweller at the ash tree
farm'.

Ashton See **Ashby**

Ashur [Semitic]
'The martial one'. One of
warlike tendencies.

Ashwani [Hindi]
'First of 27 galaxies
revolving round the
moon'.

Astrophel [Greek]
'Star lover'.

Aswin [Anglo-Saxon]
'Spear comrade'.
(Aswine)

Athanasius [Greek]
'Immortal'.

Atherton [Anglo-Saxon]
'Dweller at the spring
farm'.

Athol [Scottish]
Place name.

Atley [Anglo-Saxon]
'One who lives in the
meadow'.

Atwater [Anglo-Saxon]
'One who lives by the
water'.

Atwell [Anglo-Saxon]
'From the spring'. One
who built his home by a
natural well.

Atwood [Anglo-Saxon]
'From the forest'.
(Atwoode, Attwood)

Atworth [Anglo-Saxon]
'From the farm'.

Aube See **Aubrey**

Auberon [Teutonic]
'Noble'.
(Oberon)

Auberon See **Aubrey**

Aubert See **Albert**

Aubin [French]
'The blond one'.

Aubin See **Alban**

Aubrey [Teutonic]
'Elf ruler'. The golden

haired king of the spirit
world.

Audley [Old English]
'Prospering'.

Audric [Teutonic]
'Noble ruler'.

Audwin [Teutonic]
'Noble friend'.
*(Aldwin, Aldwyn,
Adalwine)*

Augie See **August**

August [Latin]
'Exalted one'.
*(Augustus, Augustin,
Augustine, Austen,
Austin, Aguistin,
Auguste, Gus, Gussy,
Augie)*

Augustin See **August**

Augustus See **August**

Aurelius [Latin]
'Golden friend'.

Auryn [Welsh]
'Gold'.

Austen See **August**

Avan [Hebrew]

'Proud'.
(Evan)

Avenall [French]
'Dweller in the oat field'.
(Avenel, Avenell)

Averill [Anglo-Saxon]
'Boar like' or 'Born in
April'.
*(Averil, Averel, Averell,
Everild)*

Avery [Anglo-Saxon]
'Ruler of the elves'.

Avidor [Hebrew]
'Father of a generation'.

Aviv [Hebrew]
'Spring'.

Avram See **Abraham**

Axel [Teutonic]
'Father of peace'.

Axton [Anglo-Saxon]
'Stone of the sword
fighter'. The whetstone of
the warrior's sword.

Aylmer [Anglo-Saxon]
'Noble and famous'.

Aylward [Anglo-Saxon]
'Awe inspiring guardian'.

Aylworth [Anglo-Saxon]
'Farm belonging to the awe
inspiring one'.

Aymon [Old French]
'Home'.

Ayward [Old English]
'Noble guardian'.

Azarias [Hebrew]
'Whom the Lord helps'.

Azriel [Hebrew]
'Angel of the Lord'.

Girls

Bab [Arabic]
'From the gateway'. Also used as dim. of Barbara, *q.v.*

Babette See **Barbara**

Babita See **Barbara**

Badriyah [Arabic]
'Full moon'.

Balbina [Latin]
'She who hesitates'.

(Balbine, Balbinia)

Balbine See **Balbina**

Balbinia See **Balbina**

Bambi [Latin]
'The child'. Suitable name for one of tiny stature.
(Orel)

Baptista [Latin]
'Baptized'. A name symbolic of man's freedom

from sin through Baptism.
*(Baptiste, Batista,
Battista)*

Bara See **Barra**

Barbara [Latin]
'Beautiful stranger'. The
lovely, but unknown
visitor.
*(Bab, Babb, Bas, Barbie,
Barbette, Babette, Barbra)*

Barbetta See **Barbara**

Barbie See **Barbara**

Barra [Hebrew]
'To choose'.

Basile
'Fem. of Basil'.

Basilia [Greek]
'Queenly, regal'. Fem. of
Basil.

Basima [Arabic]
'Smiling'.

Bathilda [Teutonic]
'Battle commander'.
Traditionally one who
fought for honour and
truth.
(Bathilde, Batilda, Batilde)

Bathilde See **Bathilda**

Bathsheba [Hebrew]
'Seventh daughter'.
Bathsheba was the wife of
King David in Biblical
times.

Batista [Greek]
'Baptized'.

Batsheva See **Bathsheba**

Bea See **Beata**

Beata [Latin]
'Blessed, divine one'.
Blessed and beloved of
God.
(Bea)

Beatrice [Latin]
'She who brings joy'.
*(Beatrix, Beitris, Bea,
Bee, Trix, Trixie, Trixy)*

Beatrix See **Beatrice**

Bebba [Swiss from
Hebrew]
'God's oath'.

Beckie See **Rebecca**

Beda [Anglo-Saxon]
'Warrior maiden'.

Bedelia [Celtic]
'Mighty'.
(Delia)

Behira [Hebrew]
'Brilliant'.

Bela [Slavonic]
'White'.

Belda [French]
'Beautiful lady'.

Belicia [Spanish]
'Dedicated to God'.

Belinda [Italian]
'Wise and immortal
beauty'.
*(Bella, Belle, Linda,
Lindie, Lindy)*

Beline [French, Old
German]
'Goddess'.

Belisama [Latin]
'Roman divinity like
Minerva, goddess of
wisdom, skill and
invention'.

Belita [Spanish from Latin]
'Beautiful'.

Bellanca See **Blanche**

Bellance [Italian]
'Blonde beauty'.
(Blanca)

Belle [French]

'Beautiful woman'. Can
also be used as a dim. of
Belinda and Isabelle.
(Bell, Bella, Belva, Belvia)

Belle See **Annabelle**

Bellina See **Belle**

Bellona [Latin]
'War goddess'.

Belva See **Belle**

Belvia See **Belle**

Bema [Greek]
'Fair speech'.

Bena [Hebrew]
'The wise one'. A woman
whose charm is enhanced
by wisdom.

Benedetta See **Benedicta**

Benedicta [Latin]
'Blessed one'. Fem. of
Benedict.
*(Benedetta, Benedikta,
Benita, Benoite, Bennie,
Binnie, Dixie)*

Benigna [Latin]
'Gentle, kind and
gracious'. A great lady.

Benilda [Latin]
'Well-intentioned'.

Benita [Spanish]
'Blessed'.
(Benitia)

Bennie See **Benedicta**

Benoite See **Benedicta**

Berdine [Teutonic]
'Glorious one'.

Berengaria [Teutonic]
'Spearer of bears'. A
warrior huntress of
renown.

Berenice See **Bernice**

Berna See **Bernadette**

Bernadette [French]
'Brave as a bear'.
*(Bernadina, Bernadene,
Bernadine, Bernita,
Bernardina, Bernie,
Berney)*

Bernadina See **Bernadette**

Berneen [Celtic]
'Little one, brave as a
bear'.

Berneta See **Bernadette**

Bernia [Latin]
'Angel in armour'.
(Bernie)

Bernice [Greek]
'Herald of victory'.
*(Berenice, Burnice,
Berny, Bunny, Veronica)*

Bernie See **Bernadette**

Bernita See **Bernadette**

Berri See **Beryl**

Berry See **Beverley**

Berta See **Bertha**

Bertha [Teutonic]
'Bright and shining'. The
Teutonic goddess of
fertility.
*(Berthe, Berta, Bertie,
Berty, Bertina)*

Berthe See **Bertha**

Berthilda [Anglo-Saxon]
'Shining warrior maid'.
*(Berthilde, Bertilda,
Bertilde)*

Berthilde See **Berthilda**

Bertina See **Bertha**

Bertrada See **Bertrade**

Bertrade [Anglo-Saxon]
'Shining adviser'.
(Bertrada)

Berura [Hebrew]
'Pure'.

Beryl [Greek]
'Precious jewel'. This
stone is said to bring good
fortune; therefore, the
name is also said to give
good luck to its user.
*(Beryle, Beril, Berri,
Berrie, Berry)*

Bess See **Elizabeth**

Bessy See **Elizabeth**

Beth See **Bethel**

Beth See **Elizabeth**

Bethany [Aramaic]
'House of poverty'.

Bethel [Hebrew]
'House of God'.
(Beth)

Bethena See **Bethany**

Bethesda See **Bethseda**

Bethia [Hebrew]
'Daughter of God'.

Bethina See **Bethany**

Bethinn See **Bevin**

Bethseda [Hebrew]
'House of Mercy'.
(Bethesda)

Betsy See **Elizabeth**

Betta See **Elizabeth**

Bette See **Elizabeth**

Betty See **Elizabeth**

Beulah [Hebrew]
'The married one'. The
traditional wife.
(Beula)

Beverley [Anglo-Saxon]
'Ambitious one'.
*(Beverly, Beverlie, Bev,
Berry)*

Bevin [Gaelic]
'Melodious lady'. One
whose voice is so beautiful
that even the birds will
cease singing to listen to
her.
(Bebhinn)

Bianca [Italian]
'White'.

Bibi [Arabic]
'Lady'.

Bibiana [Spanish]
Variation of Vivian.

Biddie See **Bridget**

Bienvenida [Spanish]
'Welcome'.

Bijou [Old French]
'Jewel'.

Billie [Teutonic]
'Wise, resolute ruler'.
Sometimes used as a
diminutive of Wilhelmina.
(Billy, Willa)

Billye See **Billie**

Bina [African]
'To dance'.

Bina See **Sabina**

Binah See **Bina**

Binga [Teutonic]
'From the hollow'.

Binnie See **Benedicta** or
Sabina

Birdie [Mod. English]
'Sweet little bird'.

Birjis [Arabic]
'Planet Jupiter'.

Birkita See **Bridget**

Blaine [Gaelic]
'Thin'.

Blair [Gaelic]
'Dweller on the plain'.

Blaire See **Blair**

Blaise See **Blasia**

Blake [Old English]
'Fair haired'.

Blakelee See **Blake**

Blakeley See **Blake**

Blanca See **Bellance**

Blanche [French]
'Fair and white'. A very
popular name in medieval
times when it was
supposed to endow its
user with all feminine
virtues.
*(Blanch, Blanca, Blanka,
Blinne, Blinnie, Bluinse,
Branca)*

Blanda [Latin]
'Seductive, flattering,
caressing'.

Blandina See **Blanda**

Blandine See **Blanda**

Blane See **Blaine**

Blasia [Latin]
'She who stammers'.

Blayne See **Blaine**

Blenda [German]
'Glorious, dazzling'.

Blessin [Old English]
'Consecrated'.
(Blessing)

Blinne See **Blanche**

Blinnie See **Blanche**

Bliss [Old English]
'Gladness, joy'.
(Blita, Blitha)

Blita See **Bliss**

Blitha See **Bliss**

Blodwyn [Welsh]
'White flower'.
(Blodwen)

Blondelle [French]
'Little fair one'.

Blondie See **Blondelle**

Blossom [Old English]
'Fragrant as a flower'.

Bluinse See **Blanche**

Bluma See **Anthea**

Blyth [Anglo-Saxon]
'Joyful and happy'.
(Blith, Blithe, Blythe)

Bobette See **Roberta**

Bobina See **Roberta**

Bodgana [Polish]
'God's gift'.

Bona See **Bonita**

Bonfilia [Italian]
'Good daughter'.

Bonita [Latin]
'Sweet and good'.
(Bona, Bonne, Bonnie, Nita)

Bonne See **Bonita**

Bonnibelle See **Bonita**

Bonnie See **Bonita**

Bradlee See **Bradley**

Bradleigh See **Bradley**

Bradley [Old English]
'From the broad meadow'.

Branca See **Blanche**

Brandais See **Brandy**

Brandea See **Brandy**

Brandice See **Brandy**

Brandy [Dutch]
'Brandy'.

Branwen [Welsh]
'Beautiful raven'.

Breita See **Bridget**

Brenda [Teutonic]
'Fiery' or (Irish) 'Raven'.
(Bren)

Brenna [Irish]
'Raven haired beauty'.

Bria See **Briana**

Briallen [Welsh]
'Primrose'.

Briana [Celtic]
'Strength, virtue, honour'.
(Brianna, Brienne)

Briana See **Bryna**

Bridget [Irish/Celtic]
'Strong and mighty'.
Popular name in Ireland,
where St. Bridget is
Patron Saint.
*(Brigid, Brigette, Brigida,
Brigitte, Breita, Brieta,
Brietta, Brie, Biddie,
Biddy, Bridie, Bridey,
Brydie)*

Bridie See **Bridget**

Brienne See **Briana**

Brier [French]
'Heather'.

Brieta See **Bridget**

Brigid See **Bridget**

Brigida See **Bridget**

Briony See **Bryony**

Brita See **Bridget**

Britannia See **Brittany**

Britney See **Brittany**

Britta See **Brittany**

Brittany [Latin]
'Britain'.
(Britannia)

Bronhilde See **Brunhilda**

Bronwen [Welsh/Celtic]
'White bosomed'.
(Bronwyn)

Bronya [Russian]
'Armour'.

Brook [Old English]
'Living near the brook'.
(Brooke)

Brucie [French]
'From the thicket'. Fem. of
Bruce.

Bruelle See **Brunella**

Brunella [Italian]
One with brown hair. The
true brunette.
*(Brunelle, Bruella,
Bruelle)*

Brunelle See **Brunella**

Brunetta [French]
'Dark haired maiden'.

Brunhild See **Brunhilda**

Brunhilda [Teutonic]
'Warrior heroine'.
(Brunhild, Brunhilde)

Bryana See **Briana**

Bryna [Irish]
'Strength with virtue'.
Fem. of Brian.
(Brina, Briana)

Bryony [Old English]
A twining vine.
(Briony)

Buena [Spanish]
'The good one'.
(Buona)

Bunny [English]
'Little rabbit'.

Bachir [Arabic]
'Welcome'.

Bahar [Arabic]
'Sailor'.

Bahram [Persian]
'Ancient king'.

Bailey [French]
'Steward'. The trusted
guardian of other men's
properties.
(Baillie, Baily, Bayley)

Bainbridge [Anglo-Saxon]
'Bridge over the white
water'.

Baird [Celtic]
'The minstrel'. The
ancient bard.
(Bard)

Balbo [Latin]
'The mutterer'.

Baldemar [Teutonic]
'Bold, famous prince'.

Balder [Norse]
'Prince'. The god of Peace.
(Baldur, Baldhere)

Baldric [Teutonic]
'Princely ruler'.
(Baudric)

Baldwin [Teutonic]
'Bold, noble protector'.
(Baudouin, Balduin)

Balfour [Gaelic]
'From the pasture'.

Ballard [Teutonic]
'Strong and bold'.

Balraj [Hindi]
'Strongest'.

Balthasar [Greek]
'May the Lord protect the
King'.
(Belshazzar)

Bancroft [Anglo-Saxon]
'From the bean field'.

Banning [Gaelic]
'The little golden haired
one'.

Banquo [Gaelic]
'White'.

Barak [Hebrew]
'Flash of lightning'.

Baram [Hebrew]
'Son of the nation'.

Barclay [Anglo-Saxon]
'Dweller by the birch tree
meadow'.
(Berkeley, Berkley)

Bard See **Baird**

Barde See **Baird**

Barden [Old English]
'One who lives near the
boar's den'.

Bardo See **Bartholomew**

Bardo [Danish]
'Short for Bartholomew'.

Bardolf [Anglo-Saxon]
'Axe wolf'.
*(Bardolph, Bardolphe,
Bardulf, Bardulph)*

Bardon [Anglo-Saxon]
'Barley valley'.

Bardrick [Anglo-Saxon]
'Axe ruler'. One who lived
by the battle axe.
(Baldric, Baldrick)

Barend [Dutch]
'Firm bear'.

Bari [Arabic]
'The maker'.

Barker [Old English]
'Birch tree'.

Barlow [Anglo-Saxon]
'One who lives on the
barren hills'.

Barnaba See **Barnaby**

Barnabe See **Barnaby**

Barnabus See **Barnaby**

Barnaby [Hebrew]
'Son of consolation'.
*(Barnabas, Barney,
Barny)*

Barnard See **Bernard**

Barnes [Old English]
'Bear'.

Barnet See **Bernard**

Barnett [Anglo-Saxon]
'Noble leader'.
(Barnet)

Barney See **Barnaby**

Barnum [Anglo-Saxon]
'Nobleman's house'.
Dwelling place of the
princely.

Baron [Anglo-Saxon]
'Noble warrior'. The
lowest rank of the peerage.
(Barron)

Barr [Anglo-Saxon]
'A gateway'.

Barret [Teutonic]
'As mighty as the bear'.
(Barrett)

Barris [Celtic]
'Barry's son'.

Barry [Gaelic]
'Spearlike'. One whose
intellect is sword-sharp.
(Barrie)

Bart See **Bartholomew**

Bartel See **Bartholomew**

Barth See **Bartholomew**

Barthel See **Bartholomew**

Barthelmey See
Bartholomew

Barthol See **Bartholomew**

Bartholomeo See
Bartholomew

Bartholomeus See
Bartholomew

Bartholomew [Hebrew]
'Son of the furrows;
ploughman'. One of the
twelve apostles.
*(Bartel, Barthelmey,
Bartolome, Bartley,
Bardo, Barth, Barthol,
Bart, Bat, Parlan)*

Bartie See **Barton**

Bartlett See **Bartholomew**

Bartley [Anglo-Saxon]
'Bartholomew's meadow'.

Bartley See **Bartholomew**

Bartolome See
Bartholomew

Barton [Anglo-Saxon]
'Barley farmer'.

Bartram [Old German]
'Bright raven'.

Baruch [Hebrew]
'Blessed'.
(Barrie, Barry)

Baruilai [Hebrew]
'Man of iron'.

Basam [Arabic]
'Smiling'.

Base See **Basil**

Basil [Greek]
'Kingly'. St. Basil the
founder of the Greek
Orthodox Church.
*(Basile, Basilio, Basilius,
Vassily)*

Basilio See **Basil**

Basilius See **Basil**

Basilyr [Arabic]
'Insight'.

Baudowin See **Baldwin**

Baudric See **Baldric**

Baxter [Teutonic]
'The baker of bread'.
(Bax)

Bay See **Bayard**

Bayard [Anglo-Saxon]
'Red haired and strong'.
The personification of
knightly courtesy.
(Bay)

Baylor [Anglo-Saxon]
'Horse trainer'.

Beach See **Beacher**

Beacher [Anglo-Saxon]
'One who lives by the oak
tree'.
(Beecher, Beach, Beech)

Beagan [Gaelic]
'Little one'.
(Beagen)

Beal [French]
'The handsome'. In the
form 'Beau' used to
identify the smart, well
dressed, personable men
of the 17th and early 18th
centuries.
(Beale, Beall, Beau)

Beaman [Anglo-Saxon]
'The bee keeper'.

Beasley [Old English]
'Field of peas'.

Beathan See **Benjamin**

Beattie [Gaelic]
'Public provider'. One who
supplies food and drink for
the inhabitants of a town.
(Beatie, Beaty, Beatty)

Beau See **Beal**

Beaufort [French] 'Beautiful stronghold'. The name adopted by the descendants of the union of John of Gaunt and Katharine Swynford.

Beaumont [French] 'Beautiful mountain'.

Beauregard [Old French] 'Beautiful in expression'.

Beck [Anglo-Saxon] 'A brook'. *(Bec)*

Bede [Old English] 'A prayer'.

Bedell [Old English] 'Messenger'.

Beecher See **Beacher**

Behram [Persian] 'Mythological figure'.

Behzad [Persian] 'Noble'.

Belden [Anglo-Saxon] 'Dweller in the beautiful glen'. *(Beldon)*

Bellamy [French] 'Handsome friend'.

Belshazzar See **Balthasar**

Belton [Old French] 'Beautiful town'.

Beltran [German] 'Brilliant'.

Bemus [Greek] 'Platform'.

Ben See **Benjamin**

Bendick See **Benedict**

Bendix See **Benedict**

Benedetto See **Benedict**

Benedict [Latin] 'Blessed'. One blessed by God. *(Bendix, Benito, Benoit, Benot, Bengt, Benedic, Benedick, Benedix, Bennet, Bennett, Ben, Benny, Dixon)*

Benedicto See **Benedict**

Benedikt See **Benedict**

Bengt See **Benedict**

Beniah [Hebrew] 'Son of the Lord'.

Beniamino See **Benjamin**

Benito See **Benedict**

Benjamin [Hebrew]
'Son of my right hand'.
The beloved youngest
son.
*(Beathan, Ben, Bennie,
Benjy, Benny)*

Benjie See **Benjamin**

Bennet See **Benedict**

Bennett See **Benedict**

Benoit See **Benedict**

Benoni [Hebrew]
'Son of my sorrow'. The
former name of the
Biblical Benjamin.

Benot See **Benedict**

Benroy [Hebrew]
'Son of a lion'.

Benson [Hebrew]
'Son of Benjamin'.

Bently [Anglo-Saxon]
'From the farm where the
grass bends'.
(Bentley)

Benton [Anglo-Saxon]
'From the town on the
moors'.

Benyamin See **Benjamin**

Berard See **Bernard**

Béraud [French]
'Strong leader'.

Beraut See **Béraud**

Berenger [Teutonic]
'Bear, spear'.

Beresford [Anglo-Saxon]
'From the barley ford'.

Berg [Teutonic]
'The mountain'.

Berg See **Burgess**

Berger [French]
'The shepherd'.

Berger See **Burgess**

Berk See **Burke**

Berkeley See **Barclay**

Bern See **Bernard**

Bernard [Teutonic]
'As brave as a bear'. A
courageous warrior.
*(Bernhard, Barnard,
Barnet, Barnett, Bern,
Burnard, Bearnard,
Barney, Barny, Bernie,*

Berny)

Bernardo See **Bernard**

Bernie See **Bernard**

Bert See **Albert, Bertram, Egbert, Herbert, Berthold**

Berthold [Teutonic]
'Brilliant ruler'.
(Bertold, Berthoud, Bert, Bertie)

Berton [Anglo-Saxon]
'Brilliant one's estate'.
(Burton, Burt, Bertie)

Bertram [Anglo-Saxon]
'Bright raven'.
(Bartram, Bertrand)

Bertrand See **Bertram**

Bertrando See **Bertram**

Bertwin [Teutonic]
'Bright friend'.

Berty See **Albert**

Berwick [Old English]
'Barley grange'.

Berwin [Teutonic]
'Warrior friend'.

Bevan [Welsh]
'Son of a noble man'.
(Beaven, Beavan, Beven)

Beverley [Anglo-Saxon]
'From the beaver meadow'.
(Beverly)

Bevis [French]
'Fair view'.
(Beavais)

Bhagat [Arabic]
'Joy'.

Bibiano [Spanish]
Var. of Vyvyan.

Bickford [Anglo-Saxon]
'Hewer's ford'.
(Bick)

Bienvenido [Spanish]
'Welcome'.

Bildad [Hebrew]
'Beloved'.

Bing [Teutonic]
'Kettle shaped hollow'.

Bion [Greek]
'Life'.

Birch [Anglo-Saxon]
'At the birch tree'.
(Birk)

Birk See **Birch**

Birkett [Anglo-Saxon]
'Dweller by the birch
headland'.
(Birket)

Birley [Anglo-Saxon]
'Cattle shed in the field'.

Birney [Anglo-Saxon]
'Dweller on the brook
island'.

Birtle [Anglo-Saxon]
'From the bird hill'.

Bishop [Anglo-Saxon]
'The Bishop'.

Bjorn [Scandinavian]
'Bear'.

Black [Anglo-Saxon]
'Of dark complexion'.

Blade [Anglo-Saxon]
'Prosperity, glory'.

Blagden [Anglo-Saxon]
'From the dark valley'.

Blagoslav [Polish]
'Good glory'.

Blaine [Gaelic]
'Thin, hungry-looking'.
(Blain, Blayn, Blayne)

Blair [Gaelic]
'A place' or 'From the
plain'.

Blaise [Latin]
'Stammerer' or 'Firebrand'.
(Blase, Blayze, Blaze)

Blake [Anglo-Saxon]
'Of fair complexion'.

Blakeley [Anglo-Saxon]
'From the black meadow'.

Blakey [Anglo-Saxon]
'Little fair one'.

Bland [Latin]
'Mild and gentle'.

Blandford See **Blanford**

Blane See **Blaine**

Blanford [Anglo-Saxon]
'River crossing belonging
to one with grey hair'.
(Blandford)

Blaze See **Blaise**

Bliss [Anglo-Saxon]
'Joyful one'. One who
always sees the cheerful
side.

Blythe [Anglo-Saxon]
'The merry person'.

(Blyth)

Boaz [Hebrew]
'In the Lord is strength'.
(Boas, Boase)

Bob See **Robert**

Bobbie See **Robert**

Boden [French]
'The herald'. The bringer
of news.

Bogart [Teutonic]
'Strong bow'.

Bogdan [Polish]
'God's gift'.

Bolton [Old English]
'Manor farm'.

Bonamy [French]
'Good friend'.

Bonar [French]
'Good, gentle and kind'.

Bonaro [Italian, Spanish]
'Friend'.

Bond [Anglo-Saxon]
'Tiller of the soil'.

Bondie See **Bond**

Bondon See **Bond**

Boniface [Latin]
'One who does good'.

Booker [Anglo-Saxon]
'Beech tree'.

Boone [Norse]
'The good one'.

Boonie See **Boone**

Boot See **Booth**

Booth [Teutonic]
'From a market' or
'Dweller in a hut' or
'Herald'.
*(Both, Boothe, Boot,
Boote)*

Bord See **Borden**

Borden [Anglo-Saxon]
'From the valley of the
boar'.

Borg [Norse]
'Dweller in the castle'.

Boris [Slavic]
'A fighter'. A born warrior.

Bosley [Old English]
'Grove of trees'.

Boswell [French]
'Forest town'.

Bosworth [Anglo-Saxon]
'At the cattle enclosure'.

Both See **Booth**

Botolf [Anglo-Saxon]
'Herald wolf'.
(Botolph, Botolphe)

Boucard [French,
Teutonic]
'Beech tree'.

Bouchard See **Boucard**

Bourke See **Burke**

Bourne [Anglo-Saxon]
'From the brook'.
*(Bourn, Burn, Burne,
Byrne)*

Bow See **Bowie**

Bowen [Celtic]
'Descendant of Owen'. A
proud Welsh name borne
by descendants of the
almost legendary Owen.

Bowie [Gaelic]
'Yellow haired'.

Boyce [French]
'From the woods'. A
forester.

Boycie See **Boyce**

Boyd [Gaelic]
'Light haired'. The blond
Adonis.

Boyden [Celtic]
'Herald'.

Boyne [Gaelic]
'White cow'. A very rare
person.

Brad See **Bradley**

Bradan See **Braden**

Bradburn [Anglo-Saxon]
'Broad brook'.

Brade See **Braden**

Braden [Anglo-Saxon]
'From the wide valley'.

Bradford [Anglo-Saxon]
'From the broad crossing'.

Bradley [Anglo-Saxon]
'From the broad meadow'.
(Bradly, Brad, Lee)

Bradney See **Bradley**

Bradshaw [Old English]
'Large virginal forest'.

Brady [Gaelic]
'Spirited one' or 'From the
broad island'.

Brage [Nordic]
'Norse god of poetry'.

Braham [Hindi]
'Creator'.

Brainard [Anglo-Saxon]
'Bold as a raven'. One who
knows not fear.
(Brainerd)

Bram See **Abraham** or
Bran

Bramwell [Anglo-Saxon]
'From the bramble bush
spring'.

Bran [Celtic]
'Raven'. The spirit of
eternal youth.
(Bram)

Brand [Anglo-Saxon]
'Firebrand'. The grandson
of the god, Woden.

Brander [Norse]
'Sword of fire'.

Brandon [Anglo-Saxon]
'From the beacon on the
hill'.

Brandt See **Brand**

Brandyn See **Brandon**

Brannon See **Brandon**

Brant [Anglo-Saxon]
'Fiery one' or 'Proud one'.

Brantley See **Brand**

Brawley [Anglo-Saxon]
'From the meadow on the
hill slope'.

Braxton [Anglo-Saxon]
'Brock's town'.

Bren See **Brendan**

Brendan [Gaelic]
'Little raven' or 'From the
fiery hill'.
(Brendon)

Brendis See **Brendan**

Brendon See **Brendan**

Brennan See **Brendan**

Brent [Anglo-Saxon]
'Steep hill'.

Brett [Celtic]
'Native of Brittany' or
'From the island of
Britain'. One of the
original Celts.
(Bret)

Brew See **Brewster**

Brewster [Anglo-Saxon]
'The brewer'.

Brian [Celtic]
'Powerful strength with
virtue and honour'. Brian
Boru the greatest Irish
king.
*(Briant, Brien, Bryan,
Bryant, Brion, Bryon)*

Briand [French]
'Castle'.

Briano See **Brian**

Briant See **Brian**

Brice [Celtic]
'Quick, ambitious and
alert'. *(Bryce)*

Bridger [Anglo-Saxon]
'Dweller by the bridge'.

Brigg See **Brigham**

Brigham [Anglo-Saxon]
'One who lives where the
bridge is enclosed'.

Brinsley [Anglo-Saxon]
'Brin's meadow'.

Britt See **Brett**

Brock [Anglo-Saxon]

'The badger'.
(Broc, Brockie, Brok)

Brockie See **Brock**

Brockley [Anglo-Saxon]
'From the badger
meadow'.

Broderic See **Roderick**

Broderick [Anglo-Saxon]
'From the broad ridge' or
'Son of Roderick'.
(Broderic)

Brodie [Gaelic]
'A ditch'. *(Brody)*

Bromley [Anglo-Saxon]
'Dweller of the broom
meadow'.

Bronislav [Slavonic]
'Weapon of glory'.

Bronnie See **Bronson**

Bronson [Anglo-Saxon]
'The brown haired one's
son'.

Brook [Anglo-Saxon]
'One who lives by the
brook'. *(Brooke, Brooks)*

Brooks See **Brook**

Brose See **Ambrose**

Brough See **Brougher**

Brougher [Anglo-Saxon]
'The fortified residence'.
(Brough)

Broughton [Anglo-Saxon]
'From a fortified town'.

Bruce [French]
'From the thicket'. Robert
the Bruce, Scotland's
hero-king.

Bruno [Teutonic]
'Brown haired man'.

Bryan/Bryant See **Brian**

Bryce See **Brice**

Brychan [Welsh]
'Freckled'.

Bryn [Welsh]
'Hill'.

Bryn See **Brendan**

Buck [Anglo-Saxon]
'The buck deer'. A fleet
footed youth.

Buckley [Anglo-Saxon]
'One who dwells by the
buck deer meadow'.

Budd [Anglo-Saxon]
'Herald'. The welcome
messenger.

Bundy [Anglo-Saxon]
'Free man'. An
enfranchised serf.

Burbank [Anglo-Saxon]
'Dweller on the castle hill
slope'.

Burch See **Birch**

Burchard [Anglo-Saxon]
'Strong as a castle'.
*(Burckhard, Burkhart,
Burgard)*

Burdett [French]
'Little shield'.

Burdon [Anglo-Saxon]
'One who lives by the
castle on the hill'.

Burford [Anglo-Saxon]
'Dweller at the river
crossing by the castle'.

Burgard See **Burchard**

Burgess [Anglo-Saxon]
'Dweller in a fortified
town'.
*(Bergess, Berger, Berg,
Burg)*

Burke [French]
'From the stronghold'.
*(Berk, Berke, Bourke,
Burk, Birke, Birk)*

Burkett [French]
'From the little fortress'.

Burkhart See **Burchard**

Burl [Anglo-Saxon]
'The cup bearer'. The wine
server.

Burley [Anglo-Saxon]
'Dweller in the castle by
the meadow'.
(Burleigh)

Burnaby [Norse]
'Warrior's estate'.

Burnard See **Bernard**

Burne See **Bourne**

Burnell [French]
'Little one with brown
hair'.

Burnett [Anglo-Saxon]
'Little one with brown
complexion'.

Burney [Anglo-Saxon]
'Dweller on the island in
the brook'.

Burr [Norse]
'Youth'.

Burrell [French]
'One of light brown
complexion'.

Burris [Old English]
'Of the town'.

Burt See **Burton**

Burton [Anglo-Saxon]
'Of bright and glorious
fame' or 'Dweller at the
fortified town'.
(Berton, Bert, Burt)

Busby [Norse]
'Dweller in the thicket'.

Byford [Anglo-Saxon]
'Dweller by the ford'.

Byram [Anglo-Saxon]
'Dweller at the cattle pen'.
(Byrom)

Byran See **Byron**

Byrd [Anglo-Saxon]
'Like a bird'.

Byrle See **Burl**

Byrne See **Bourne**

Byron [French]
'From the cottage' or 'The
bear'.

Girls

Cadena See **Cadence**

Cadence [Latin]
'Rhythmic'. One who is
graceful and charming.
(Cadena, Cadenza)

Cadenza See **Cadence**

Caera [Gaelic]
'Spear; ruddy'.

Cailin See **Colleen**

Caireen See **Catherine**

Cairistiona See **Christine**

Cairstine See **Christine**

Caitlin See **Catherine**

Caitrin See **Catherine**

Cala [Arabic]
'Castle'.

Calandra [Greek]
'Lark'. One who is as light
and gay as a bird.
*(Calandre, Calandria, Cal,
Callie, Cally)*

Calandria See **Calandra**

Calantha [Greek]
'Beautiful blossom'. A
woman of childlike beauty
and innocence.
*(Calanthe, Kalantha,
Kalanthe, Cal, Cally,
Callie)*

Caledonia [Latin]
'Scottish lassie'. One who
comes from the part of
Scotland known in earlier
times as Caledonia.
(Caledonie)

Caledonie See **Caledonia**

Calida [Spanish]
'Ardently loving'. A
woman capable of great
affection.

Calista [Greek]
'Most beautiful of women'.
A name for a girl thought
to be beautiful beyond the
ordinary.
(Calisto, Kallista, Kallisto)

Calisto See **Calistra**

Calla [Greek]
'Beautiful'.

Calli See **Calla**

Callidora [Greek]
'Gift of beauty'.

Callie See **Calandra**

Calligenia [Greek]
'Daughter of beauty'.

Calliope [Greek]
'The muse of poetry'.

Callula [Latin]
'Little beautiful one'.

Caltha [Latin]
'Yellow flower'.

Calvina [Latin]
'Bald'. Fem. of Calvin.
Name sometimes used in
strongly Calvinistic
families.

Calypso [Greek]
'Concealer'. The legendary
sea nymph who held
Odysseus captive.
(Kalypso)

Camala See **Camilla**

Camelia See **Camilla**

Cameo [Italian]
  'Sculptured jewel'.

Camilla [Latin]
  'Noble and righteous'. The
  name given to the young
  and beautiful handmaiden
  in pagan ceremonies.
  *(Camille, Camile,
  Camella, Camelia,
  Camellia, Cam)*

Camille See **Camilla**

Cammi See **Camilla**

Canace [Latin]
  'The daughter of the wind'.
  (Kanaka, Kanake)

Candace [Latin]
  'Pure, glittering, brilliant
  white'. One whose purity
  and virtue is beyond
  suspicion.
  *(Candice, Candida,
  Candie, Candy)*

Candice See **Candace**

Candida See **Candace**

Candie See **Candace**

Candra [Latin]
  'Luminescent'.

Candra See **Chandra**

Cantara [Arabic]
  'Small bridge'.

Capriccia See **Caprice**

Caprice [Italian]
  'Fanciful'.
  (Capriccia)

Capucine [French]
  'Cape'.

Cara [Celtic/Italian]
  'Friend' (Celtic) or
  'Dearest one' (Italian). A
  term of endearment.
  *(Cariad, Carina, Carine,
  Kara, Karine, Karina)*

Caragh [Irish]
  'Love'.

Caralie See **Cara**

Caressa See **Carissa**

Caresse See **Carissa**

Carey See **Caroline**

Cari [Turkish]
  'Flows like water'.

Cariad See **Cara**

Carilla See **Caroline**

Carina [Latin]
'Keel'.

Carina See **Cara**

Carine See **Cara**

Carissa [Latin]
'Most dear one'.
*(Caressa, Caresse,
Carisse)*

Carisse See **Carissa**

Carita [Latin]
'Beloved little one'.

Carla See **Charlotte**

Carlie See **Charlotte**

Carlin See **Caroline**

Carline See **Caroline**

Carliss See **Corliss**

Carlissa See **Corliss**

Carlotta See **Charlotte**

Carma [Sanskrit]
'Destiny'. From the
Buddhist 'Karma' — Fate.

Carmacita See **Carmen**

Carmel [Hebrew]

'God's fruitful vineyard'.
*(Carmela, Carmelita,
Carmella, Carma, Carmie,
Carmelina, Carmeline,
Melina)*

Carmela See **Carmel**

Carmelina See **Carmel**

Carmeline See **Carmel**

Carmelita See **Carmel**

Carmelita See **Carmen**

Carmella See **Carmel**

Carmen [Latin]
'Songstress'. One who has
a beautiful voice.
*(Carma, Carmia, Carmina,
Carmine, Carmita,
Charmaine, Carmacita,
Carmencita)*

Carmencita See **Carmen**

Carmia See **Carmen**

Carmie See **Carmel**

Carmina See **Carmen**

Carmine See **Carmen**

Carmita See **Carmen**

Carnation [French]
'Fresh colour'. One with
perfect features and
colouring.

Caro See **Caroline**

Carol See **Caroline**

Carola See **Caroline**

Carolina See **Caroline**

Caroline [Teutonic]
'Little woman, born to
command'. The power
behind the throne; the
hand which rocks the
cradle and rules the world.
One who is all that is
feminine, but who rules
and controls.
*(Carola, Carol, Carole,
Carolina, Carline,
Charleen, Charlene,
Charline, Sharleen,
Sharlene, Sharline, Caro,
Lina, Line)*
This name is the fem. of
Charles and can also be
used as Charlotte.

Caron See **Chéron**

Caronwen [Welsh]
'Little fair love'.

Caryl [Welsh]

'Beloved'.
(Carryl, Carys)

Caryn See **Catherine**

Caryn See **Carina**

Carys See **Caryl**

Casilda [Spanish]
'The solitary one'.
(Casilde)

Casilde See **Casilda**

Cassandra [Greek]
Prophetess ignored by
men.
(Cassandre, Cass, Cassie)

Cassie See **Cassandra**

Casta [Latin]
'Of pure upbringing'.
(Caste)

Caste See **Casta**

Caterina See **Catherine**

Catharina See **Catherine**

Cathelle See **Catherine**

Catherine [Greek]
  'Pure maiden'. The saint
  who was martyred on a
  spiked (Catherine) wheel.
  *(Caireen, Carine,
  Catharine, Catharina,
  Cathleen, Catalina,
  Caterina, Caitlin, Caitrin,
  Caryn, Catriona, Cathy,
  Cathie, Katharine,
  Katherine, Katherina,
  Katharina, Katerine,
  Kateryn, Kathryn,
  Katrine, Katrina, Kate,
  Katy, Kathy, Katie, Kit,
  Kitty)*

Cathy See **Catherine**

Ceara [Irish]
  'Spear'. A warrior who
  wielded her spear to the
  detriment of her enemies.

Cecelia See **Cecilia**

Cecile See **Cecilia**

Cecilia [Latin]
  The Patron saint of Music.
  *(Cecelia, Cecile, Cecily,
  Celia, Cecil, Cicely, Sisile,
  Sisle, Sileas, Sisley,
  Sissie, Cele, Ciel, Cissie)*

Cecily See **Cecilia**

Ceinlys [Welsh]
  'Sweet gems'.

Ceinwen [Welsh]
  'Beautiful gems'.

Ceiridwen [Welsh]
  The Goddess of Bardism
  (Ceri, Kerridwen)

Celandine [Greek]
  'Swallow' or 'yellow water
  flower'.
  (Celandon)

Celandon See **Celandine**

Cele See **Cecilia** or **Celeste**

Celene See **Selena**

Celesta See **Celeste**

Celeste [Latin]
  'Heavenly'. A woman of
  divine beauty.
  *(Celesta, Celestina,
  Celestine, Cele)*

Celestina See **Celeste**

Celestine See **Celeste**

Celestyna See **Celeste**

Celia See **Cecilia**

Celia See **Celeste**

Celie See **Selena**

Celina See **Selena**

Celina See **Celeste**

Celinda See **Selena**

Celinda See **Celeste**

Celinka See **Celeste**

Celosia [Greek]
'Burning flame'.
(Kelosia)

Cerelia [Latin]
'Spring like'. Woman of
spring-blossom beauty.
*(Cerealia, Cerellia,
Cerelie)*

Cerelie See **Cerelia**

Ceri See **Ceiridwen**

Cerian [Welsh]
'Loved one'.

Ceridwen [Welsh]
'Fair poetry'.

Cerys [Welsh]
'Love'.

Chandra [Sanskrit]
'The moon who outshines
the stars'.

*(Candra, Chandre,
Candre)*

Chantal See **Chantelle**

Chantelle [French]
'Little singer'.
(Chantal, Chantel)

Charis [Greek]
'Grace'.

Charissa See **Charity**

Charita See **Charity**

Charity [Latin]
'Benevolent and loving'.
One who gives with
generosity and affection.
*(Charissa, Charita,
Charry, Cherry)*

Charleen See **Caroline**

Charlie See **Charlotte**

Charlotta See **Charlotte**

Charlotte [Teutonic]
See Caroline.
*(Charlotta, Carlotta,
Charlie, Carlie, Carla and
all the variations of
Caroline)*

Charmaine [Latin]
'Little song'.
*(Carmen, Charmain,
Charmian)*

Charmaine See **Carmen**

Charmian See **Charlotte**

Charo See **Charlotte**

Charry See **Charity**

Charyl See **Charlotte**

Chastity [Latin]
'Purity'.

Chelsea [Old English]
'A port of ships'.

Chelsey See **Chelsea**

Chelsy See **Chelsea**

Cherida See **Cherie** or
Querida

Cherie [French]
'Dear, beloved one'. A
term of endearment.
*(Cheri, Cherida, Cherry,
Cheryl, Sheryl, Sherry,
Sherrie)*

Cherise [Old French]
'Cherrylike'.

Chéron [French]
'Beloved'.

Cherry See **Charity**

Cheryl See **Charlotte** or
Cherie

Cheslie See **Chelsea**

Chesna [Slavic]
'Peaceful'.

Chiara [Italian]
'Famous, light'

Chika [Japanese]
'Near, thousand
rejoicings'.

Chiquita [Spanish]
'Little one'. A term of
endearment for a small
girl.

Chloe [Greek]
'Fresh young blossom'.
The Greek goddess of
unripened grain.
(Cloe, Kloe)

Chloras See **Chloris**

Chlori See **Chloris**

Chlorinda See **Clorinda**

Chloris [Greek]
'Goddess of the flowers'.
(Chloras, Chlores, Chlori, Loris)

Chloris See **Clarice**

Christabel [Latin]
'Beautiful bright faced Christian'.
(Christabelle, Christabella, Kristabel, Kristabella, Kristabelle)

Christabella See **Christabel**

Christalle See **Crystal**

Christan See **Christine**

Christanta [Colombian]
'A chrysanthemum'.

Christiana See **Christine**

Christina See **Christine**

Christine [French]
'Christian one'.
(Cairstine, Cairistiona, Christina, Christiana, Christiane, Cristina, Cristine, Christian, Chrystal, Crystal, Chris, Chrissie, Chrissy, Crissie, Crissy)

Christye See **Christine**

Christyna See **Christine**

Chryseis [Latin]
'Golden daughter'.

Ciel See **Cecilia**

Cilla [French]
'The Cilla flower'.

Cinderella [French]
'Girl of the ashes'. From the fairy tale.
(Cindie, Cindy, Ella)

Cindie See **Cinderella**

Cindy See **Cynthia**

Cipressa See **Cypris**

Claire See **Clara**

Clara [Latin]
'Bright, shining girl'. One of clear, outstanding beauty.
(Clare, Claire, Klara, Clareta, Clarette, Clarine)

Clarabella [Latin/French]
'Bright, shining beauty'.
(Clarabelle, Clara, Bella)

Claramae [English]
'Brilliant beauty'.
(*Clarinda, Clorinda,*
Chlarinda, Chlorinda)

Clare See **Clara**

Claresta [English]
'The most shining one'. A
woman to outshine all
others.
(*Clarista*)

Clareta See **Clara**

Clarette See **Clara**

Clarice [French]
'Little, shining one'.
French form of Clara.
(*Clarissa, Clarisse,*
Clariss, Chloris, Chlaris)

Clarimond [Teutonic]
'Brilliant protector'.
(*Clarimonda, Clarimonde,*
Chlarimonda,
Chlarimonde)

Clarimonda See
Clarimond

Clarinda See **Claramae**

Clarine See **Clara**

Clarissa See **Clarice**

Clarista See **Claresta**

Claude See **Claudia**

Claudell See **Claudia**

Claudette See **Claudia**

Claudia [Latin]
'The lame one'. Fem. of
Claud.
(*Claude, Claudette,*
Claudina, Claudine,
Claudie, Gladys)

Claudie See **Claudia**

Claudina See **Claudia**

Claudine See **Claudia**

Clea [Literary]
A name perhaps coined by
Lawrence Durrell in The
Alexandria Quartet.

Cleantha [Greek]
'Glory-flower'.
(*Cleanthe*)

Cleanthe See **Cleantha**

Clematis [Greek]
'Sweet vine'.

Clemence [Latin]
'Merciful and kind'. One
who tempers justice with
mercy.
(*Clemency, Clementia,*

Clementina, Clementine)

Clemency See **Clemence**

Clementia See **Clemence**

Clementina See
Clemence

Clementine See
Clemence

Cleo See **Cleopatra**

Cleopatra [Greek]
'Her father's glory'. A girl
who will add lustre to her
father's name.
(Cleo)

Cleva [Old English]
'Cliff dweller'. Fem. of
Clive.

Cliantha [Greek]
'Flower of glory'.
*(Cleantha, Cleanthe,
Clianthe)*

Clio [Greek]
'She who proclaims'. The
Greek Muse of History.

Clorinda [Latin]
'Famed for her beauty'.
*(Chlorinda, Chlorinde,
Clorinde, Clarinda,
Clarinde)*

Clorinda See **Claramae**

Clotilda [Teutonic]
'Famous battle maiden'. A
warrior who fought
alongside her father and
brothers. *(Clotilde,
Clothilda, Clothilde)*

Clover [English]
'Meadow blossom'. From
the flower.
(Clovie)

Clovie See **Clover**

Clydia [Greek]
'Glorious'.

Clymene [Greek]
'Fame and renown'.

Clytie [Greek]
'Splendid daughter'. The
mythical nymph who was
turned into a heliotrope,
so that she could worship
the sun.

Cody [Old English]
'A cushion'.

Colette [Latin]
'Victorious'. A form of
Nicolette.
(Collette, Collete)

Colleen [Gaelic]
'Girl'. The name given to a young girl in Ireland.
(Coleen, Colene, Colline, Coline, Cailin)

Columba [Latin]
'The dove'. One of a peaceful disposition.
(Coline, Columbine, Columbia, Colombe, Colly)

Comfort [French]
'One who gives comfort'. One of the virtue names popular with English and American Puritan families.

Con See **Constance**

Conceptia See **Conception**

Conception [Latin]
'Beginning'.
(Conceptia, Concepcion, Conchita, Concha)

Concetta [Italian]
'An ingenious thought'.

Concha See **Conception**

Conchita See **Conception**

Concordia [Latin]
'Harmony and Peace'.
(Concordina, Concordie, Concordy)

Concordie See **Concordia**

Concordina See **Concordia**

Conrada See **Conradine**

Conradina See **Conradine**

Conradine [Teutonic]
'Bold and wise'. Fem. of Conrad.
(Conradina, Conrada, Connie)

Consolata [Latin]
'One who consoles'.
(Consolation)

Consolation See **Consolata**

Constance [Latin]
'Constant'. One who is firm and unchanging.
(Constantia, Constantina, Constanta, Constantine, Constancy, Constanza, Connie, Con)

Constancy See **Constance**

Constanta See **Constance**

Constantia See **Constance**

Constantina See
   Constance

Constantine See
   Constance

Constanze See **Constance**

Consuela [Spanish]
   'Consolation'. The Friend
   when in need.
   (Consuelo, Connie)

Consuelo See **Consuela**

Cora [Greek]
   'The maiden'. From Kore,
   the daughter of Demeter.
   *(Corella, Corett, Corette,
   Corina, Corrina, Corinna,
   Corinne, Corin, Correna,
   Coretta, Corrie, Corie)*

Corabella [Combination
   Cora/Bella]
   'Beautiful maiden'.
   (Corabelle)

Corabelle See **Corabella**

Coral [Latin]
   'Sincere' or 'From the sea'.
   (Corale, Coraline, Coralie)

Coralie See **Coral**

Coraline See **Coral**

Corazon [Spanish]
   'Heart'.

Cordelia [Welsh]
   'Jewel of the sea'. The
   daughter of Lear, the Sea
   King.
   (Cordelie, Cordie, Delia)

Cordelie See **Cordelia**

Cordie See **Cordelia**

Cordula See **Cordelia**

Corella See **Cora**

Corett See **Cora**

Coretta See **Cora**

Corey [Gaelic]
   'From the hollow'.

Corina See **Cora**

Corinne See **Cora**

Corissa [Latin/Greek]
   'Most modest maiden'.
   (Corisse)

Corisse See **Corissa**

Corliss [English]
'Cheerful and kind-
hearted'.
*(Carliss, Carlissa,
Corlissa)*

Corlissa See **Corliss**

Cornela See **Cornelia**

Cornelia [Latin]
'Womanly virtue'.
*(Cornela, Cornelle,
Cornelie, Cornie, Nela,
Nelie, Nelli)*

Cornelie See **Cornelia**

Cornelle See **Cornelia**

Cornie See **Cornelia**

Corona [Spanish]
'Crowned maiden'.
(Coronie)

Coronie See **Corona**

Correna See **Cora**

Cosetta See **Cosette**

Cosette [French]
'Victorious army'.
(Cosetta)

Cosima See **Cosina**

Cosina [Greek]
'World harmony'.
(Cosima)

Courtenay See **Courtney**

Courtney [Old English]
'From the court'.

Crescent [French]
'The creative one'.
(Crescentia, Crescenta)

Crescenta See **Crescent**

Crescentia See **Crescent**

Cresseide See **Cressida**

Cressida [Greek]
'The golden one'.
(Cresseide)

Crisiant [Welsh]
'Crystal'.

Crispina [Latin]
'Curly haired'. Fem. of
Crispin. *(Crispine)*

Cristen See **Christine**

Cristiona See **Christine**

Crystal [Latin]
'Clear'. Also form of
Christine.
(Cristal, Chrystal, Krystal)

Cynara [Greek]
'Artichoke'. A beautiful
maiden, protected by
thorns.

Cynth See **Cynthia**

Cynthia [Greek]
'Moon Goddess'. Another
name for Diana, Goddess
of the Moon, born on
Cynthos.
*(Cindy, Cyn, Cynth,
Cynthie)*

Cynthie See **Cynthia**

Cypris [Greek]
'Born in Cyprus'.
*(Cypres, Cipressa,
Cypressa)*

Cyrena [Greek]
'From Cyrene'. A water
nymph, beloved of Apollo.
*(Cyrenia, Kyrena,
Kyrenia)*

Cyrenia See **Cyrena**

Cyrilla [Latin]
'Lordly one'. Fem. of
Cyril. *(Cirilla, Cirila)*

Cytherea [Greek]
'From Cythera'. Another
name for Aphrodite.
*(Cytheria, Cytherere,
Cytherine)*

Cytherere See **Cytherea**

Cytherine See **Cytherea**

Cadby [Norse]
'Warrior's settlement'.

Cadda See **Chad**

Caddaric See **Cedric**

Caddock [Celtic]
'Keenness in battle'. An
eager warrior.

Cadell [Celtic]
'Battle spirit'.

Cadeyrn [Welsh]
'Battle king'.

Cadfan [Welsh]
'Battle peak'.

Cadman [Celtic]
'Battle man'.

Cadmus [Greek]
'Man from the east'. The
legendary scholar who
devised the Greek
alphabet.

Cadogan [Celtic]
'War'.

Cadwallader [Celtic]
'Battle leader'.

Cady [French]
dim. of Léocadie.

Caedmon [Celtic]
'Wise warrior'.

Caesar [Latin]
'Emperor'. Source of all
names meaning Emperor
— Tsar, Kaiser, Shah, etc.
(Cesare, Cesar)

Cain [Hebrew]
'The possessed'. The
original murderer.

Calder [Anglo-Saxon]
'The brook'.

Caldwell [Anglo-Saxon]
'The cold spring (or well)'.

Cale See **Caleb**

Caleb [Hebrew]
'The bold one'. The
impetuous hero.
(Cal, Cale)

Caley [Gaelic]
'Thin, slender'.

Calhoun [Gaelic]
'From the forest strip'.

Callum See **Columba**

Callum [Celtic]
'Dove'.

Calvert [Anglo-Saxon]
'Calf minder'.

Calvert See **Calvin**

Calvin [Latin]
'Bald'.
(Calvert, Calvino, Cal)

Calvino See **Calvin**

Camden [Gaelic]
'From the valley which
winds'.

Cameron [Celtic]
'Crooked nose'. The
founder of the Scottish
Clan.
(Cam, Camm)

Camey See **Cameron**

Camilo [Spanish]
'Freeborn'.

Camm See **Cameron**

Campbell [Celtic]
'Crooked mouth'. Founder
of Clan Campbell.

Candan [Turkish]
'Sincerely, heartily'.

Cannon See **Channing**

Canute [Norse]
'The knot'. Name of the
king who tried to hold
back the waves.
(Knut, Knute)

Caradoc [Celtic]
'Beloved'.

Care See **Carey**

Carey [Celtic]
'One who lives in a castle'.
(Cary)

Carl See **Charles**

Carleton [Anglo-Saxon]
'Farmers' meeting place'.
(Carlton, Carl)

Carlin [Gaelic]
'Little champion'.
(Carling)

Carling See **Carlin**

Carlisle [Anglo-Saxon]
'Tower of the castle'.
(Carlile, Carlyle, Carlysle)

Carlo See **Charles**

Carlos See **Charles**

Carmichael [Celtic]
'From St. Michael's
castle'.

Carmine [Latin]
'Song'.

Carney [Gaelic]
'Victorious'. The warrior
who never lost a battle.
(Carny, Kearney)

Carol [Gaelic]
'The champion'. The
unbeatable fighter.
(Carroll)

Carol See **Charles**

Carollan [Gaelic]
'Little champion'.

Carolus See **Carol**

Carr [Norse]
'One who dwells beside a
marsh'.
(Karr, Kerr)

Carrick [Gaelic]
'The rocky cape'.

Carroll See **Carol**

Carson [Anglo-Saxon]
'Son of the marsh-dweller'.

Carswell [Anglo-Saxon]
'The water cress grower'.

Carter [Anglo-Saxon]
'The cart driver'. One who
transports cattle and
goods.

Cartland [Celtic]
'The land between the
rivers'.

Carvell [French]
'Estate in the marshes'.
(Carvel)

Carver [Old English]
'Woodcarver'.

Carvey [Gaelic]
'The athlete'.
(Carvy)

Cary See **Carey** or **Charles**

Caryl See **Carol**

Case See **Casey**

Casey [Gaelic]
'Brave and watchful'. The
warrior who never slept.

Cash See **Cassius**

Casimir [Slavic]
'The proclaimer of peace'.
(Cass, Cassie, Cassy,
Kazimir, Kasimir)

Caspar [Persian]
'Master of the treasure'.
One trusted to guard the
most precious
possessions.
(Casper, Gaspar, Gasper)

Cassidy [Gaelic]
'Ingenuity' or 'curly-
haired'.

Cassius [Latin]
'Vain and conceited'.
Never far from a mirror.

Castor [Greek]
'The beaver'. An
industrious person.

Cathmor [Gaelic]
'Great warrior'.

Cato [Latin]
'The wise one'. One with
great worldly knowledge.

Cavan [Gaelic]
'The handsome'. The Irish
Adonis!
(Kavan)

Cavell [French]
'Little lively one'. Always
up and doing.

Cawley [Norse]
'Ancestral relic'.

Cece See **Cecil**

Cecil [Latin]
'The unseeing one'.
(Sissil)

Cecilio See **Cecil**

Cecilius See **Cecil**

Cedric [Celtic]
'Chieftain'.

Celio See **Cecil**

Cephas [Aramaic]
'Rock'.

Cerwyn [Welsh]
'Fair love'.

Chad [Anglo-Saxon]
'Warlike; bellicose'.
(Cadda, Chadda)

Chadda See **Chad**

Chaddie See **Chad**

Chadwick [Anglo-Saxon]
'Town of the warrior'.

Chaim [Hebrew]
'Life'.

Chalmer [Celtic]
'The chamberlain's son' or
'King of the household'.
(Chalmers)

Chalmers See **Chalmer**

Chan See **Channing**

Chance [Anglo-Saxon]
'Good fortune'.
(Chaunce, Chauncey)

Chancellor [Anglo-Saxon]
'King's counsellor'. A man
trusted with the highest
state secrets.
*(Chaunceler, Chaunceller,
Chanceller)*

Chandler [French]
'The candle maker'.

Chane See **Chandler**

Chaney [French]
'Oak wood'.

Channing [French]
'The canon'.

(Chan, Cannon)

Chapman [Anglo-Saxon]
'The merchant'. The
travelling salesmen of
medieval times.

Charles [Teutonic]
'The strong man'. The
personification of all that
is masculine.
*(Carl, Carlos, Carol,
Carrol, Charley, Charlie,
Chas, Carlo, Cary, Carey,
Chuck, Karl, Karol,
Tearlach)*

Charley See **Charles**

Charlton [Anglo-Saxon]
'Charles's farm'.
(Charleton)

Chas See **Charles**

Chase [French]
'The hunter'. One who
enjoys the chase.

Chatham [Anglo-Saxon]
'Land of the soldier'.

Chauncey [French]
'Chancellor; record
keeper'. Also var. of
Chance and Chancellor.
(Chancey, Chaunce)

Chauncey See **Chance**

Cheiro [Greek]
'Hand'.

Cheney [French]
'Oak forest dweller'. A
woodman.
(Cheyney)

Ches See **Chester**

Chester [Latin]
'The fortified camp'.
(Cheston, Ches, Chet)

Cheston See **Chester**

Chet See **Chester**

Chet [Thai]
'Brother'.

Chetwin [Anglo-Saxon]
'Cottage dweller by the
winding path'.
(Chetwyn)

Chevalier [French]
'Knight'.

Chevy See **Chevalier**

Cheyney See **Cheney**

Chilt See **Chilton**

Chilton [Anglo-Saxon]
'From the farm by the
spring'.
(Chelton)

Chrétien See **Christian**

Chris See **Christopher**

Christian [Latin]
'Believer in Christ; a
Christian'.
*(Chris, Christy, Christie,
Kristian, Kristin, Kit)*

Christiano See **Christian**

Christoforo See
Christopher

Christoper See
Christopher

Christoph See
Christopher

Christophe See
Christopher

Christopher [Greek]
'The Christ carrier'. The
man who carried the infant
Christ across the river.
*(Chris, Christophe, Kit,
Kester, Kris, Kriss,
Gillecirosd)*

Christophorus See
Christopher

Christy See **Christian**

Chrysander [Greek]
'Golden man'.

Chuck See **Charles**

Churchill [Anglo-Saxon]
'Dweller by the church on the hill'.

Cian [Gaelic]
'The ancient one'. One who lives long.

Cicero [Latin]
'The chick-pea'.

Cirilo See **Cyril**

Ciro See **Cyrus**

Clare [Latin]
'Famous one' (Latin) or 'Bright, illustrious' (Anglo-Saxon).
(Clair)

Clarence [Latin/Anglo-Saxon]
'Famous, illustrious one'.
(Clavance)

Clark [French]
'Wise and learned scholar'.
(Clarke)

Claud [Latin]
'The lame'.
(Claude)

Claudian See **Claud**

Claudianus See **Claud**

Claudio See **Claud**

Claus See **Nicholas**

Clavance See **Clarence**

Clay [Anglo-Saxon]
'From the clay pit'.

Clay See **Clayborne**

Clayborne [Anglo-Saxon]
'From the brook by the clay pit'.
(Clay, Claiborn, Claybourne)

Clayson See **Clayton**

Clayton [Anglo-Saxon]
'From the clay town' or 'Mortal man'.

Cleary [Gaelic]
'The scholar'.

Cleavon [Old English]
'Cliff'.

Cledwyn [Welsh]
'Blessed sword'.

Clem See **Clement**

Clemence See **Clement**

Clemens See **Clement**

Clement [Latin]
'Kind and merciful'.
*(Clemence, Clemens,
Clem, Clemmy, Clim)*

Clementius See **Clement**

Clemmy See **Clement**

Cleon [Greek]
'Famous'.

Clerk See **Clark**

Cletis See **Cletus**

Cletus [Greek]
'Summoned'.

Cleve See **Clive**

Cleve See **Cleveland**

Cleveland [Anglo-Saxon]
'From the cliff land'.

Clevey See **Cleveland**

Cliff See **Clifford**

Clifford [Anglo-Saxon]
'From the ford by the cliff'.
(Clif, Cliff)

Clift See **Clifton**

Clifton [Anglo-Saxon]
'From the farm by the cliff'.

Clim See **Clement**

Clint See **Clinton**

Clinton [Anglo-Saxon]
'From the farm on the
headland'.
(Clint)

Clive [Anglo-Saxon]
'Cliff'.
(Cleve, Cleeve, Clyve)

Clovis [Teutonic]
An early form of Lewis
(Louis) — 'Famous
warrior'.

Cluny [Gaelic]
'From the meadow'.

Cly See **Clyde**

Clydai [Welsh]
'Fame'.

Clyde [Celtic]
'Warm' (Welsh Celtic),
'Heard from the distance'
(Scots Celtic)

Clywd See **Clyde**

Cobb See **Jacob**

Coburn [Old English]
'Small stream'.

Cody [Old English]
'A cushion'.

Coel [Welsh]
'Trust'.
(Cole)

Colan See **Colin**

Colbert [Anglo-Saxon]
'Brilliant seafarer' or 'Cool
and calm'.
(Colvert, Culbert)

Colby [Norse]
'From the dark country'.

Cole See **Coleman** or
Nicholas

Coleman [Anglo-Saxon/
Celtic]
'Follower of Nicholas'
(Anglo-Saxon) or 'Keeper
of the Doves' (Celtic).
(Colman, Col, Cole)

Colin [Gaelic]
'Strong and virile' or 'The
young child' or 'Victorious
army'.
*(Collin, Colan, Cailean,
and all der. of Nicholas)*

Colis See **Collier**

Colley [Old English]
'Swarthy'.

Collier [Anglo-Saxon]
'Charcoal merchant'.
*(Colier, Colis, Collyer,
Colyer)*

Colm See **Columba**

Colman See **Coleman**

Colter [Anglo-Saxon]
'The colt herder'. A lover
of horses.

Colton [Anglo-Saxon]
'From the dark town'.

Columba [Latin]
'Dove'.
(Callum, Colum, Colm)

Colver See **Culver**

Colvert See **Colbert**

Con See **Conrad**

Conal See **Conan**

Conan [Celtic]
'High and mighty' or
'Wisely intelligent'.
*(Conal, Conant, Connall,
Connel, Con, Conn,
Kynan, Quinn)*

Conant See **Conan**

Conlan [Gaelic]
'The hero'.
(Conlin, Conlon)

Conlin See **Conlan**

Conlon See **Conlan**

Conn See **Conan**

Connel See **Conan**

Connie See **Conrad**

Connor [Old English]
'Wise aid'.

Conrad [Teutonic]
'Brave counsellor'. One
who told what was right;
not what the receiver
wanted to hear.
*(Con, Connie, Cort, Curt,
Konrad, Kort, Kurt)*

Conrade See **Conrad**

Conrado See **Conrad**

Conroy [Gaelic]
'The wise one'.

Constant See **Constantine**

Constantin See
Constantine

Constantine [Latin]
'Firm and unwavering'.
Always constant.
*(Constantin, Konstantin,
Konstantine, Constant,
Conn)*

Constantino See
Constantine

Conway [Gaelic]
'Hound of the plain'.

Coop See **Cooper**

Cooper [Anglo-Saxon]
'Barrel maker'.
(Coop)

Corbett [French]
'The raven'. From the
raven device worn by the
ancient Vikings.
*(Corbet, Corbin, Corbie,
Corby)*

Corbie See **Corbett**

Corbin See **Corbett**

Corcoran [Gaelic]
'Reddish complexion'.
(Corquoran)

Cord See **Cordell**

Cordell [French]
'Rope maker'.

Corey [Gaelic]
'Dweller in a ravine'.
(Cory)

Cormac See **Cormick**

Cormick [Gaelic]
'The charioteer'.
(Cormac, Cormack)

Cornall See **Cornelius**

Cornelius [Latin]
'Battle horn'.
*(Cornell, Cornel, Cornall,
Cornal, Neal, Neil)*

Cornell See **Cornelius**

Cort See **Conrad**

Corty See **Courtenay**

Corwin [French]
'Friend of the heart'.
(Corwen)

Corydon [Greek]
'The helmeted man'.

Cosimo See **Cosmo**

Cosme See **Cosmo**

Cosmo [Greek]
'The perfect order of the
universe'.
(Cosme, Cosimo)

Costa See **Constantine**

Court See **Courtland**

Courtenay [French]
'A place'.
*(Courtney, Court, Cort,
Cortie, Corty)*

Courtland [Anglo-Saxon]
'One who dwelt on the
court land'.
(Court)

Covell [Anglo-Saxon]
'Dweller in the cave on the
slope'.
(Covill)

Covill See **Covell**

Cowan [Gaelic]
'Hollow in the hillside'.

Coyle [Gaelic]
'Battle follower'.
(Coile)

Craddock [Celtic]
'Abundance of love'.
(Caradoc, Caradock)

Craggie See **Craig**

Craig [Celtic]
'From the stony hill'.

Crandell [Anglo-Saxon]
'Dweller in the valley of the crane'.
(Crandall)

Crane [Old English]
'Cry'.

Cranley [Anglo-Saxon]
'From the crane meadow'.

Cranog [Welsh]
'Heron'.

Cranston [Anglo-Saxon]
'From the farmstead where the cranes gather'.

Crawford [Anglo-Saxon]
'From the crow ford'.
(Crowford)

Creigh See **Creighton**

Creight See **Creighton**

Creighton [Anglo-Saxon]
'From the farm by the creek'.
(Crayton)

Crepin See **Crispin**

Crichton See **Creighton**

Crisp See **Crispin**

Crispin [Latin]
'Curly haired'. St. Crispin, the patron saint of shoemakers.
(Crispen, Crisp, Crepin)

Cristobal See **Christopher**

Cromwell [Anglo-Saxon]
'One who lives by a winding spring'. The small rivulet that twists and winds through the countryside.

Crosby [Anglo-Saxon/Norse]
'Dweller at the crossroads' (Anglo-Saxon) or 'Dweller by the shrine of the cross' (Norse).
(Crosbey, Crosbie)

Crosley [Anglo-Saxon]
'From the meadow with the cross'.

Crowford See **Crawford**

Culbert See **Colbert**

Cullen [Gaelic]
'Handsome one'.
(Cullan, Cullin)

Culley [Gaelic]
'From the woodland'.
(Cully)

Culver [Anglo-Saxon]
'Gentle as the dove,
peaceful'. The symbol of
peace.
(Colver)

Curclo See **Curtis**

Curran [Gaelic]
'The resolute hero'. One
who would die defending
the right.
*(Curren, Currey, Currie,
Curry)*

Curren See **Curran**

Currey See **Curran**

Curt See **Conrad**

Curt See **Courtney**

Curtis [French]
'The courteous one'. A
gentleman with perfect
manners.
(Curtis, Curt, Kurt)

Cuthbert [Anglo-Saxon]
'Famous and brilliant'.
One famed for his high
intellect.

Cybard [French]
'Ruler'.

Cyndeyrn [Welsh]
'Chief lord'.

Cynfael [Welsh]
'Chief metal'.

Cynfor [Welsh]
'Great chief'.

Cyngen [Welsh]
'Chief son'.

Cynric [Anglo-Saxon]
'From the royal line of
kings'.

Cynyr [Welsh]
'Chief hero'.

Cyprian [Greek]
'Man from Cyprus'. The
birthplace of Venus.
(Ciprian, Cyprien)

Cyrano [Greek]
'From Cyrene'.
(Cyrenaica)

Cyrenaica See **Cyrano**

Cyril [Greek]
'The lord'.
(Cyrill, Cyrille)

Cyrillus See **Cyril**

Cyrus [Persian]
'The sun god'. The
founder of the Persian
Empire.

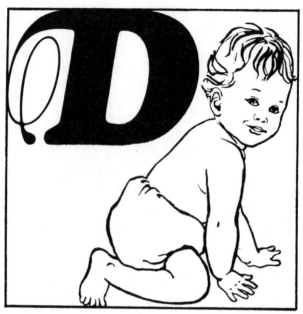

Girls

Dacey [Gaelic]
'Southerner'.

Dacia [Greek]
'From Dacia'.

Dael See **Dale**

Daffodil [Greek]
'Golden spring flower'.

Dagania [Hebrew]
'Ceremonial grain'.

Daganya See **Dagania**

Dagmar [Norse]
'Glory of the Danes'.

Dahlia
'Of the valley'. From the
flower of the same name.

Dai [Japanese]
'Great'.

Daile See **Dale**

Daisy [Anglo-Saxon]
'The day's eye'. Also a
nickname for Margaret
(Marguerite), the name of
the daisy in French.

Dale [Teutonic]
'From the valley'. An
earlier form of Dahlia.

Dallas [Gaelic]
'Wise'.

Damara [Greek]
'Gentle girl'.
(Damaris, Mara, Maris)

Damaris See **Damara**

Damia [Greek]
'Goddess of forces of
nature'.

Damita [Spanish]
'Little noble lady'.

Dana [Scandinavian]
'From Denmark'.

Danae [Greek]
Mother of Perseus.

Danella See **Danielle**

Danelle See **Danielle**

Danica [Norse]
'The morning star'.

Danice See **Danielle**

Daniela See **Danielle**

Danielea See **Danielle**

Danielle [Hebrew]
'God is my judge'. Fem. of
Daniel.
*(Danielea, Danella,
Danelle, Daniela)*

Danika See **Danica**

Danita See **Danielle**

Danuta [Polish]
'Young deer'.

Danya See **Danielle**

Danyelle See **Danielle**

Daphne [Greek]
'Bay tree'. Symbol of
victory. The nymph who
was turned into a laurel
bush to escape the
attentions of Apollo.

Dara [Hebrew]
'Charity, compassion and
wisdom'.

Daralis [Old English]
'Beloved'.

Darcia See **Darcy**

Darcie [French]
'From the fortress'. Fem.
of D'Arcy.
(D'Arcie)

Darcy [Celtic]
'Girl of dark hair'.
(Darcia, Dercy)

Dareen See **Darlene**

Darees See **Darice**

Darel [Anglo-Saxon]
'Little dear one'. Another
form of Darlene.
*(Darelle, Darrelle, Darry,
Daryl)*

Darea See **Darlene**

Daria [Greek]
'Wealthy queen'. Fem. of
Darius.

Darice [Persian]
'Queenly'.
(Dareece, Darees)

Darlene [Anglo-Saxon]
'Little darling'.
(Darleen, Darline, Daryl)

Daron [Gaelic]
'Great'.

Darry See **Darel**

Darya See **Dara**

Daryl See **Darlene**

Dasha [Russian]
'Gift of God'.

Daveen See **Davina**

Davida See **Davina**

Davina [Hebrew]
'Beloved'. Fem. of David.

Davita See **Davina**

Dawn [Anglo-Saxon]
'The break of day'. One
who lightens the
darkness.

Dayna See **Dana**

Dea [Latin]
'Goddess'.

Deane See **Dena**

Deanna See **Diana**

Debby See **Deborah**

Debor See **Deborah**

Deborah [Hebrew]
'The bee'. An industrious
woman who looks only for
what is sweet in life.
*(Debora, Debra, Debbie,
Debby)*

Decima [Latin]
'Tenth daughter'.
'Dark beauty'. Also a dim.
of Diana.

Dee See **Audrey** or **Diana**

Dee [Welsh]
'Black, dark'.

DeeAnn See **Dee**

Deel See **Dorothy**

Deerdre See **Deirdre**

Deirdre [Gaelic]
'Sorrow'. A legendary Irish
beauty — 'Deirdre of the
Sorrows'.
(Deidre)

Dela See **Adelaide**

Delcine See **Dulcie**

Delfina See **Delfine**

Delfine [Greek]
'The larkspur or
delphinium flower'.

*(Delfina, Delphina,
Delveen, Delphine)*

Delia [Greek]
'Visible'. Another name for
the Moon Goddess. Also
one who came from Delos.

Delia See **Bedelia**

Delicia [Latin]
'Delightful maiden'. 'Spirit
of delight'.

Delight [French]
'Pleasure'. One who
brings happiness to her
family.

Delilah [Hebrew]
'The gentle temptress'.
Betrayer of the Biblical
Samson.
(Delila, Dalila, Lila)

Della See **Adelaide**

Delma [Spanish]
'Of the Sea'.
(Delmar, Delmare)

Delmar See **Delma**

Delmare See **Delma**

Delora [Latin]
'From the seashore'.
(Dellora)

Delora See **Dolores**

Delores See **Dolores**

Deloris See **Dolores**

Delorita See **Dolores**

Delphine [Greek]
'Calmness and serenity'.
(Delfine)

Delta [Greek]
'Fourth daughter'. The
fourth letter of the Greek
alphabet.

Delwen [Welsh]
'Neat, fair'.

Delyth [Welsh]
'Neat, pretty'.

Demeter See **Demetria**

Demetria [Greek]
'Fertility'. The Goddess of
Fertility.
(Demeter)

Demetris See **Demetria**

Dena [Anglo-Saxon]
'From the valley'.
(Deana, Deane)

Dena See **Adina**

Denise [French]
'Wine goddess'. Fem. of
Dionysus, God of wine.
(Denice, Denys)

Denni See **Denise**

Dercia See **Darcy**

Dercy See **Darcy**

Derede [Greek]
'Gift of God'.

Derora [Hebrew]
'Brook'.

Derryth [Welsh]
'Of the oak'.

Desdemona [Greek]
'One born under an
unlucky star'. After the
heroine of Shakespeare's
Othello.
(Desmona)

Desiree [French]
'Desired one'.

Desma [Greek]
'A pledge'.

Desmona See **Desdemona**

Desta See **Modesty**

Destinee [Old French]
'Destiny'.

Deva [Sanskrit]
'Divine'. The Moon
Goddess.

Devin [Gaelic]
'Poet'.

Devona [English]
'From Devon'. Someone
born in that county, the
name of which means
'People of the deep valley'.

Devondra See **Devona**

Devora See **Deborah**

Dextra [Latin]
'Skilful, adept'.

Diahann See **Diana**

Diamanta [French]
'Diamond like'. One who
is as precious as the rarest
jewel.

Diana [Latin]
'Divine Moon Goddess'.
Roman Goddess of the
Moon and the Chase.
*(Deanna, Diane, Dianna,
Dyana, Dyanna, Dyane,
Di, Dian, Dee)*

Diandra See **Diana**

Diane See **Diana**

Diantha [Greek]
'Divine flower of Zeus'.
(Dianthe, Dianthia)

Dianthe See **Diantha**

Dianthia See **Diantha**

Didi [Hebrew]
'Beloved'.

Didiane [French]
Fem. of Didier.

Didière See **Didiane**

Dido [Greek]
'Teacher'.

Dilys [Welsh]
'Perfect'.

Dinah [Hebrew]
'Judgement'. One whose
understanding is
complete.

Dione [Greek]
'The daughter of heaven
and earth'.

Dionis See **Dione**

Dionne See **Dione**

Disa [Norse or Greek]
'Lively spirit' (Norse) or
'Double' (Greek).

Divia See **Divya**

Divya [Hindi]
'Divine, heavenly'.

Dixie [French]
'The tenth'.
(Dixey, Dixy, Dixil)

Dixie See **Benedicta**

Dixil See **Dixie**

Doanna [Combination
Dorothy/Anna]

Docie See **Endocia**

Docila [Latin]
'Gentle teacher'.

Dodi See **Doris**

Dodie [Hebrew]
'Beloved'.

Dolley See **Dorothy**

Dolly See **Dolores** or
Dorothy

Dolores [Spanish]
'Lady of Sorrow'. Deriving
from 'Our Lady of

Sorrows', which depicts
the seven sad occasions in
the Virgin's life.
*(Delores, Delora, Deloris,
Delorita, Dolly, Lola,
Lolita)*

Doloritas See **Dolores**

Domeniga See **Dominica**

Domina [Latin]
'The lady'. One of noble
birth.

Dominga See **Dominica**

Domini See **Dominica**

Dominica [Latin]
'Belonging to the Lord'.
Fem. of Dominic.
*(Dominique, Domenica,
Dominga)*

Dominique See **Dominica**

Donalda [Gaelic]
'Ruler of the world'. Fem.
of Donald.

Donata [Latin]
'The gift'.

Donna [Italian]
'Noble lady'.
(Dona)

Dora See **Dorothy** or
  Eudora

Dorcas [Greek]
  'Graceful'. A girl with the
  grace of a gazelle.

Dore [French]
  'Golden maiden'.

Dore See **Dorothy**

Doreen [Gaelic]
  'Golden girl', alternatively
  'The sullen one'.
  *(Dorene, Dorine, Dori,
  Dorie, Dory, Dora)*

Doretta See **Dorothy**

Dori See **Doreen**

Dorinda [Greek/Spanish]
  'Beautiful golden gift'.

Doris [Greek]
  'From the sea'. The
  daughter of Oceanus.
  *(Dora, Dorice, Dorise,
  Dorris, Dodi)*

Dorita See **Doris**

Dorleta [Basque]
  Name for Virgin Mary.

Dorothea See **Dorothy**

Dorothoe See **Dorothy**

Dorothy
  'Gift of God'. A form of
  Theodora.
  *(Dorothoe, Dora, Doretta,
  Dorothea, Dorothi,
  Dorthea, Dorthy, Deel,
  Dolley, Dollie, Dolly,
  Dore, Dot, Dotty,
  Theodora)*

Dot See **Dorothy**

Dotty See **Dorothy**

Douce [French]
  'Sweet'.

Douna [Slavic]
  'Valley'.

Dove [English]
  'Bird of peace'.

Doxie See **Endocia**

Druella [Teutonic]
  'Elfin vision'.
  (Druilla)

Drusilla [Latin]
  'The strong one'. One with
  patience and fortitude.

Duana [Gaelic]
  'Little dark maiden'.
  (Duna, Dwana)

Duena [Spanish]
'Chaperon'. A name given
to women of good birth
who were responsible for
the manners and morals of
the young girls in their
charge.
(Duenna)

Dulce See **Dulcie**

Dulcea See **Dulcie**

Dulciana See **Dulcie**

Dulcibella See **Dulcie**

Dulcibelle See **Dulcie**

Dulcie [Latin]
'Sweet and charming'. One
who believes that love is
the sweetest thing.
*(Dulciana, Dulcibelle,
Dulcibella, Delcine,
Dulce, Dulcea, Dulcine,
Dulcinea)*

Dulcine See **Dulcie**

Dulcinea See **Dulcie**

Durene [Latin]
'The enduring one'.

Durga [Hindi]
'Mythological figure, wife
of Siva'.

Duscha [Russian]
'Soul'.

Dwana See **Duana**

Dyane See **Diana**

Dympha See **Dymphia**

Dymphia [Latin]
'Nurse'.
(Dimphia, Dympha)

Dympna [Irish]
'Eligible'.
(Dymphna)

Dysis [Greek]
'Sunset'.

Dabert [French]
'Bright action'.

Dacey [Gaelic]
'The southerner'.
(Dacy)

Dael See **Dale**

Dag [Norse]
'Day of brightness'.

Dagan [Semitic]
'The earth' or 'The small fish'.
(Dagon)

Dagny [Teutonic]
'Fresh as day'.

Dagobert See **Dagny**

Dagwood [Anglo-Saxon]
'Forest of the shining one'.

Dahab [Arabic]
'Gold'.

Daimon [Latin]
'Guardian angel'.

Dal See **Dallas**

Dalbert [Anglo-Saxon]
'From the shining valley'.
(Delbert)

Dale [Teutonic]
'Dweller in the valley'.

Dallas [Celtic]
'Skilled' or 'From the water field'.
(Dal)

Dallis See **Dallas**

Dallon See **Dalston**

Dalston [Old English]
'From Daegal's place'.

Dalt See **Dalton**

Dalton [Anglo-Saxon]
'From the farm in the valley'.

Daly [Gaelic]
'The counsellor'.

Dalziel [Celtic]
'From the little field'.
(Dalziell)

Damek [Slavic]
'Man of the earth'.

Damian See **Damon**

Damiano See **Damon**

Damien See **Damon**

Damon [Greek]
'Tame and domesticated'.
The true friend.
(Damien)

Dana [Anglo-Saxon]
'Man from Denmark'.
(Dane)

Danby [Norse]
'From the settlement of
the Danish'.

Dane See **Dana**

Daniel [Hebrew]
'The Lord is my judge'.
*(Daniell, Danielle, Dane,
Darnell, Dan, Danny)*

Danny See **Daniel**

Dante See **Durant**

Darby [Gaelic]
'Freeman'.
(Derby)

Darcy [French]
'From the fortress'.
*(Darcie, D'Arcy, Darsey,
Darsy)*

Dare See **Darius**

Daren See **Darren**

Darien [Spanish]
A place name.

Darin See **Darren**

Dario See **Darius**

Darius [Greek]
'The wealthy man'.

Darnall See **Darnell**

Darnell [French]
'From the hidden nook'.

Darnell See **Daniel**

Daron See **Darren**

Darrell [French]
'Beloved one'.
(Daryl, Darryl)

Darren [Gaelic]
'Little great one'.

Darrick See **Derek**

Darton [Anglo-Saxon]
'From the deer forest'.

Darwin [Old English]
'Beloved friend'.

Dave See **David**

Daven See **David**

David [Hebrew]
'The beloved one'. St.
David, the patron saint of
Wales.
*(Dave, Davie, Davy,
Davis)*

Davidson See **David**

Davin [Scandinavian]
'Brightness of the Finns'.

Davis [Anglo-Saxon]
David's son.

Davis See **David**

Davon See **David**

Davorin [Slavonic]
'God of war'.

Davy See **David**

Dean [Anglo-Saxon]
'From the valley'.
(Deane, Dene)

Dearborn [Anglo-Saxon]
'Beloved child' or 'From
the deer brook'.

Decca See **Dexter**

Deck See **Dexter**

Dedrick [Teutonic]
'Ruler of the people'.

Deems [Anglo-Saxon]
'The judge's son'.

Dekkel [Arabic]
'Palm tree'.

Delaney [Gaelic]
'Descendant of the
challenger'.

Delano [French]
'From the nut tree woods'.

Delbert See **Albert**

Delling [Norse]
'Very shining one'.

Delmar [Latin]
'From the sea'.
(Delmer, Delmore)

Delmor See **Delmar**

Delmore See **Delmar**

Delwyn [Anglo-Saxon]
'Bright friend from the
valley'.
(Delwin)

Demas [Greek]
'The popular person'.

Demetri See **Demetrius**

Demetris See **Demetrius**

Demetrius [Greek]
'Belonging to Demeter'.
(Dimitri, Dmitri, Demmy)

Demmy See **Demetrius**

Demos [Greek]
'The spokesman of the
people'.

Demosthenes [Greek]
'Strength of the people'.

Dempsey [Gaelic]
'The proud one'.

Dempster [Anglo-Saxon]
'The judge'.

Den See **Dennis**

Denby [Norse]
'From the Danish
settlement'.

Denley [Anglo-Saxon]

'Dweller in the meadow in
the valley'.

Denman [Anglo-Saxon]
'Resident in the valley'.

Dennie See **Dennis**

Dennis [Greek]
'Wine lover'. From
Dionysus, the God of
Wine.
*(Denis, Denys, Dennison,
Denzil, Dion, Den,
Dennie, Denny, Deny)*

Dennison [Anglo-Saxon]
'Son of Dennis'.
(Denison)

Dennison See **Dennis**

Denton [Anglo-Saxon]
'From the farm in the
valley'.

Denver [Anglo-Saxon]
'From the edge of the
valley'.

Denzil [Cornish]
'High stronghold'.

Denzil See **Dennis**

Deodatus [Latin]
'God-given'.

Derby See **Darby**

Derek [Teutonic]
'Ruler of the people'.
*(Derrick, Derk, Dirk,
Derry)*

Derk See **Derek**

Dermot [Gaelic]
'Free man'.

Derril See **Darrel**

Derron See **Darren**

Derry [Gaelic]
'The red one'.

Derry See **Darius**

Derry See **Derek**

Derward [Anglo-Saxon]
'Guardian of the deer'.

Derwin [Anglo-Saxon]
'Dearest friend'.

Desmond [Gaelic]
'Man of the world;
sophisticated'.

Desmund See **Desmond**

Deverell [Celtic]
'From the river bank'.

Devin [Celtic]
'A poet'.

Devland See **Devlin**

Devlin [Gaelic]
'Fierce bravery'.

Dew See **Dewey**

Dewain See **Dwayne**

Dewey [Celtic]
'The beloved one'. The
Celtic form of David.

Dewitt See **De Witt**

De Witt [Flemish]
'Fair haired one'.

Dex See **Dexter**

Dexter [Latin]
'The right handed man;
dextrous'.
(Deck, Dex)

Diamond [Anglo-Saxon]
'The shining protector'.

Diarmid See **Dermot**

Diccon See **Richard**

Dick See **Richard**

Dickie See **Richard**

Dickon See **Richard**

Diego See **Jacob**

Dieter [German]
'From strong people'.

Digby [Norse]
'From the settlement by
the dyke'.

Diggory [French]
'Strayed, lost'.

Dilan See **Dylan**

Dillon [Gaelic]
'Faithful'. A true and loyal
man.

Dilly See **Dylan**

Dimitri See **Demetrius**

Dino See **Dean**

Dinsmore [Gaelic]
'From the fortified hill'.

Diomede [Greek]
'Divine ruler'.

Dion See **Dennis**

Dionisio See **Dennis**

Dionysus See **Dennis**

Dirk See **Derek**

Dixon [Anglo-Saxon]
'Son of Richard' (Dick's
son).
(Dickson)

Dixon See **Benedict**

Doane [Celtic]
'From the sand dune'.

Dodd [Teutonic]
'Of the people'.

Dolan [Gaelic]
'Black haired'.

Dolf See **Adolph**

Dolph See **Adolph**

Dom See **Dominic**

Domenico See **Dominic**

Domingo See **Dominic**

Dominic [Latin]
'Belonging to the Lord;
born on the Lord's day'.
*(Dominic, Domingo,
Dominy, Dom, Nic, Nick,
Nickie, Nicky)*

Dominik See **Dominic**

Dominy See **Dominic**

Don See **Donald**

Donahue [Gaelic]
'Warrior clad in brown'.
(Don, Donn)

Donal See **Donald**

Donald [Celtic]
'Ruler of the world'. The
founder of Clan Donald
(MacDonald).
*(Donal, Donnall, Donnell,
Don, Donn, Donnie,
Donny)*

Donalt See **Donald**

Donato [Latin]
'A gift'.

Donaugh See **Donald**

Donnell See **Donald**

Donnelly [Gaelic]
'Brave dark man'.

Donny See **Donald**

Donovan [Irish]
'Dark brown'.

Doran [Celtic]
'The stranger'.

Dorcas [Hebrew]
'From the forest'.

Dore See **Theodore**

Dorian [Greek]
'Man from Doria'.

Dory [French]
'The golden haired'.

Doug See **Douglas**

Dougal See **Douglas**

Douggie See **Douglas**

Douglas [Celtic]
'From the dark stream'.
One of the largest Scottish
clans.
*(Duglass, Dougal, Dugal,
Dugald, Doug, Douggie,
Douggy, Duggie, Duggy)*

Dow [Gaelic]
'Black haired'.

Doyle [Gaelic]
'The dark haired stranger'.

Drake [Anglo-Saxon]
'The dragon'.

Drew [Celtic]
'The wise one'. Also dim.
of Andrew.

Driscoll [Celtic]
'The interpreter'.
(Driscol)

Drostan See **Tristan**

Druce [Celtic]
  'Son of Drew'.

Drud See **Drew**

Drury [French]
  'The dear one'.

Dryden [Anglo-Saxon]
  'From the dry valley'.

Duane See **Dwayne**

Duddie See **Dudley**

Dudley [Anglo-Saxon]
  'From the people's
  meadow'.
  *(Dudly, Dud, Duddie,
  Duddy)*

Duff [Gaelic]
  'Dark complexion'.

Dugal See **Douglas**

Dugald See **Douglas**

Dugan [Gaelic]
  'Dark skinned'. The
  suntanned man.
  (Dougan, Doogan)

Duke [French]
  'The leader'.

Duke See **Marmaduke**

Duncan [Celtic]
  'Brown warrior'.
  (Dunc)

Dunham [Celtic]
  'Dark man'.

Dunley [Anglo-Saxon]
  'From the meadow on the
  hill'.

Dunmore [Celtic]
  'From the fortress on the
  hill'.

Dunn [Anglo-Saxon]
  'Dark skinned'.

Dunstan [Anglo-Saxon]
  'From the brown stone
  hill'.

Durand See **Durant**

Durant [Latin]
  'Enduring'. One whose
  friendship is lasting.
  (Durand, Dante)

Durward [Anglo-Saxon]
  'The gate keeper'. The
  guardian of the
  drawbridge.

Durwin [Anglo-Saxon]
'Dear friend'.
(Durwyn)

Dustan See **Dustin**

Dustin [Old German]
'Valiant fighter'.

Dusty See **Dustin**

Dwain See **Dwayne**

Dwayne [Gaelic/Celtic]
'The small dark man'
(Gaelic) or 'The singer'

(Celtic).
(Duane)

Dwight [Teutonic]
'The light haired one'.

Dyfan [Welsh]
'Tribe ruler'.

Dylan [Welsh]
'Man from the sea'.

Dynawd [Welsh]
'Given'.

Girls

Eadwine See **Edwina**

Earlene [Anglo-Saxon]
'Noble woman'. Fem. of
Earl.
*(Earlie, Earley, Earline,
Erlene, Erline)*

Earlie See **Earlene**

Earline See **Earlene**

Eartha [Old English]
'Of the earth'.
*(Ertha, Erda, Herta,
Hertha)*

Easter [Old English]
'Born at Easter'. The pre-
Christian Goddess of
Spring.
(Eastre, Eostre)

Eastre See **Easter**

Ebba [Anglo-Saxon]
Form of Eve, *q.v.*

Eberta [Teutonic]
'Brilliant'.

Ebony [Greek]
'A hard, dark wood'.

Echo [Greek]
'Repeating sound'. From
the Greek nymph who
pined away for love.

Eda [Anglo-Saxon/
Greek]
'Poetry' (Anglo-Saxon).
'Loving mother of many' or
'Prosperous' (Greek).
(Eada, Edda)

Eda See **Edith**

Edana [Gaelic]
'Little fiery one'. A warmly
loving child, whose ardent
nature is said to have been
bestowed by God himself.
(Aiden, Aidan, Eidann)

Ede See **Edith**

Edelina See **Adelaide**

Edeline See **Adelaide**

Eden [Hebrew]
'Enchanting'. The epitome
of all female charm.

Edina [Scottish]
Another form of Edwina,
q.v.

Edina See **Edwina**

Edith [Teutonic]
'Rich gift'.
*(Eadith, Eda, Edythe,
Eadie, Eaidie, Eady, Ede,
Edie, Edithe, Ediva,
Editha)*

Editha See **Edith**

Ediva See **Edith**

Edlyn [Anglo-Saxon]
'Noble maiden'.

Edmonda [Anglo-Saxon]
'Rich protector'. Fem. of
Edmund.
(Edmunda)

Edna [Hebrew]
'Rejuvenation'. One who
knows the secret of eternal
youth.
(Edny, Ed, Eddie)

Edny See **Edna**

Edra See **Edrea**

Edrea [Anglo-Saxon]
'Powerful and
prosperous'. Fem. of
Edric.
(Andrea, Eadrea, Edra)

Edwardina [Anglo-Saxon]
'Rich guardian'. Fem. of
Edward.

Edwina [Anglo-Saxon]
'Rich friend'.
*(Eadwina, Eadwine,
Edwine, Edina, Win,
Wina, Winnie)*

Effie [Greek]
'Famous beauty'.
(Effy)

Effie See **Euphemia**

Egberta [Anglo-Saxon]
'Bright, shining sword'.
Fem. of Egbert.
*(Egbertha, Egberthe,
Egberte, Egbertina,
Egbertine)*

Egberte See **Egberta**

Egberthe See **Egberta**

Egbertina See **Egberta**

Egbertine See **Egberta**

Eglantina See **Eglantine**

Eglantine [French]
'The wild rose'.
*(Eglantina, Eglintyne,
Eglyntine)*

Eiblin [Gaelic]
'Pleasant'.
(Eveleen)

Eileen [Celtic] See **Helen**

Eilwen [Welsh]
'Fair brow'.

Eir [Norse]
'Peace and mercy'. The
goddess of healing.

Eirena See **Irene**

Eirian [Welsh]
'Silver'.

Eiric See **Henrietta**

Eirlys [Welsh]
'Snowdrop'

Eirwen [Welsh]
'Snow-white'.

Eister See **Esther**

Ekaterina See **Catherine**

Elaine [French] See
Helen

Elana [Hebrew]
'Oak tree'.

Elata [Latin]
'Lofty, noble'. A woman of
high birth and beauty.

Elberta [Teutonic]
'Brilliant'.

Elda [Anglo-Saxon]
'Princess'.

Eldora [Spanish]
'Gilded one'. From El
Dorado, the land of gold.

Eldrida [Teutonic]
'Old and wise adviser'.
Fem. of Eldred.
(Aeldrida)

Eleanor [French]
A medieval form of Helen.
(Eleanore, Eleanora,
Elinor, Elinore, Elinora,
Eleonor, Eleonora,
Eleonore, Elnore,
Leonora, Leonore,
Lenora, Lenore, Leanor)

Eleanor See **Helen**

Eleanora See **Eleanor**

Electra [Greek]
'Brilliant one'.

Elefteria [Greek]
'Freedom'.

Eleora See **Eliora**

Eleuteria [Greek]
'Daughter of Jupiter and
Juno'.

Elfreda [Teutonic]
'Wise counsellor'. See also
Alfreda.
(Elfrida, Elfrieda,
Aelfreda)

Elga [Slav]
'Consecrated'.
(Olga)

Elga See **Alfreda**

Elga See **Olga**

Elicia See **Elysia**

Elinora See **Helen**

Eliora [Hebrew]
'God is my light'.

Elisa See **Elizabeth**

Elise See **Elizabeth**

Elise See **Elysia**

Elissa See **Elizabeth**

Elita See **Melita**

Elita [Old French]
'Chosen'.

Elizabeth [Hebrew]
'Consecrated to God'.
Isabel is another version
of this name.
(Elisabeth, Elisa, Elise,
Elissa, Eliza, Elyse, Elysa,
Elsie, Elsa, Else, Elsbeth,
Elspeth, Bess, Bessie,
Bessy, Beth, Betsy, Betty,
Betta, Bette, Betina, Liza,
Lizzy, Lizabeta, Lisbeth,
Lizbeth, Libby). And all
the various forms of
Isabel/Isabella.

Elkana [Hebrew]
'God has acquired'.

Elke See **Alice**

Ella [Teutonic]
'Beautiful fairy maiden'.
Beauty bestowed by fairies
as a birth gift. Also form of
Helen.

Ellen See **Helen**

Ellice [Greek]
'Jehovah is God'. Fem. of
Elias.
(Ellis)

Ellissa See **Elizabeth**

Elma [Greek]
'Pleasant and amiable'.

Elmina [Old German]
'Awe-inspiring fame'.

Elmira See **Almira**

Elna See **Helen**

Elnore See **Eleanor**

Elodie [Greek]
'Fragile flower'.

Eloine [Latin]
'Worthy to be chosen'.

Eloisa See **Louise**

Eloise See **Louise**
'Noble one'. Also form of
Elizabeth.

Elora [Greek]
'Light'.

Elrica [Teutonic]
'Ruler of all'.
(Ulrica)

Elsa [Old German]
'Noble'.

Elsa See **Elizabeth**

Elsbeth See **Elizabeth**

Else See **Elizabeth**

Elsie See **Elizabeth**

Elspeth See **Elizabeth**

Elswyth [Old English]
'Noble strength'.

Eluned [Welsh]
'Idol'.

Elva [Anglo-Saxon]
'Friend of the elves'.
(Elvia, Elvie, Elfie, Elvina)

Elva See **Alfreda**

Elvera See **Elvira**

Elvia See **Elva**

Elvie See **Elva**

Elvira [Latin]
'White woman'.
(Albinia, Elvera, Elvire)

Elvita [Latin]
'Life'.

Elwira See **Elvira**

Elwy [Welsh]
'Benefit'.

Elysia [Latin]
'Blissful sweetness'. From
Elysium.

Ema See **Emma**

Embla [Scandinavian]
The first woman (in Norse
mythology).

Emelda See **Emily**

Emelina See **Amelia** or
Emma

Emeline See **Emma**

Emeline See **Emily**

Emerald [French]
'The bright green jewel'.
*(Emerant, Emeraude,
Esme, Esmeralda,
Esmeralde)*

Emerande See **Emerald**

Emerant See **Emerald**

Emily See **Amelia**

Emina [Latin]
'Highly placed maiden'.
Daughter of a noble
house.

Emma [Teutonic]
'One who heals the
universe'. A woman of
command.
*(Emmeline, Emelina,
Emeline, Emelyne,
Emmaline, Ema)*

Emmalee See **Emily**

Emmalynn See **Emily**

Emmanuela [Hebrew]
'God with us'.

Emmeline See **Emma**

Emmeranne [French, Old
German]
'Raven'.

Emogene See **Imogen**

Ena [Gaelic]
'Little ardent one'. Also
dim. of Eugenia.

Ena See **Eugenia**

Endocia [Greek]
'Of spotless reputation'.
*(Docie, Doxie, Doxy,
Eudosia, Eudoxia)*

Endora [French, Old
German]
'Noble'.

Engacia See **Grace**

Engelberga See
Engelberta

Engelbert See **Engleberta**

Engelberta [Teutonic]
'Bright angel'. One of the
bright defenders of legend.
*(Engelberga, Engelbertha,
Engelberthe, Engelbert)*

Engracia [Spanish]
'Graceful'.

Enid [Celtic]
'Purity of the soul'.

Ennata [French, Greek]
'Goddess'.

Enona [Greek]
'Nymph on Mt Ida, who
married Paris'.

Enora [French, Greek]
'Light'.

Enrica [Italian]
Italian form of Henrietta,
q. v.

Eolande See **Yolande**

Ephratah [Hebrew]
'Fruitful'.

Ernaline See **Erna**

Eranthe [Greek]
'Flower of spring'.

Erda See **Eartha**

Erena See **Irene**

Erica [Norse]
'Powerful ruler'. Symbol of
royalty. Fem. of Eric.
(Erika)

Erin [Gaelic]
'From Ireland'. One born
in the Emerald Isle.

Erina See **Erin**

Erina [Gaelic]
'Girl from Ireland'.

Erlina [Old English]
'Little elf'

Erma [Teutonic]
'Army maid'.
*(Erminia, Ermina,
Erminie, Hermia,
Hermine, Hermione)*

Erme See **Irma**

Ermina See **Erma**

Erminia See **Erma**

Erminie See **Armina** or
Erma

Erna [Anglo-Saxon]
'Eagle'. Also variation of
Ernestine.
(Ernaline)

Ernesta See **Ernestine**

Ernestine [Anglo-Saxon]
'Purposeful one'.
(Erna)

Ertha See **Eartha**

Erwina [Anglo-Saxon]
'Friend from the sea'.

Esme See **Emerald**

Esmeralda See **Emerald**

Esmeralde See **Emerald**

Essa See **Esther**

Essylt [Welsh]
'Beautiful to behold'.

Esta [Italian]
'From the East'.

Estaphania [Greek]
'Crown'.

Estella See **Estelle**

Estelle [French]
'Bright star'.
*(Estella, Estrella,
Estrelita, Stella, Stelle)*

Esther [Hebrew]
'The star'.
*(Essa, Etty, Eister,
Hester, Hesther, Hetty,
Hessy)*

Estra [Anglo-Saxon]
'Goddess of spring'.

Estrelita See **Estelle**

Estrella See **Estelle**

Eswen [Welsh]
'Strength'.

Esyllt See **Isolde**

Etain [Irish]
'Shining'.

Ethel [Teutonic]
'Noble maiden'. The
daughter of a princely
house.
*(Ethelda, Ethelinda,
Etheline, Ethylyn, Ethyl)*

Ethelda See **Ethel**

Ethelinda [Teutonic]
'Noble Serpent'. The
symbol of immortality.

Ethelinda See **Ethel**

Etheline See **Ethel**

Ethylyn See **Ethel**

Etoile [French]
'Star'.

Etsu [Japanese]
'Delight'.

Etta See **Henrietta**

Etty See **Esther**

Euclea [Greek]
'Glory'.

Eudine [French, Old
German]
'Noble'.

Eudocia See **Eudosia**

Eudora [Greek]
'Generous gift'.
(Eudore, Dora)

Eudosia See **Endocia**

Eudosia [Greek]
'Esteemed'.

Eugenia [Greek]
'Well born'. A woman of a
noble family.
(Eugenie, Genie, Gene,

Gina, Gena, Ena)

Eugenie See **Eugenia**

Eula See **Eulalia**

Eulalia [Greek]
'Fair spoken one'.
(Eulalie, Eula, Lallie)

Eunice [Greek]
'Happy and victorious'.

Euphemia [Greek]
'Of good reputation'.
*(Euphemie, Effie, Effy,
Phemie)*

Euphemie See **Euphemia**

Euphrasia [Greek]
'Delight'.

Eurielle [Celtic, French]
'Angel'.

Eurwen [Welsh]
'Gold-fair'.

Eurydice [Greek]
'Broad'.

Eustacia [Latin]
'Tranquil maiden'.
'Fruitful'.
*(Eustacie, Stacey, Stacy,
Stacie)*

Eustacie See **Eustacia**

Evadne [Greek]
'Fortunate'.

Evangelina See
Evangeline

Evangeline [Greek]
'Bearer of glad tidings'.
*(Evangelina, Eva, Vangie,
Vancy)*

Evania [Greek]
'Tranquil, untroubled'.

Evania [Greek]
'Tranquil'.

Evanne See **Evania**

Evanthe [Greek]
'Lovely flower'.

Eve [Hebrew]
'Life giver'.
*(Eva, Eveleen, Evelina,
Eveline, Evelyn, Evita,
Evonne, Evie)*

Eveleen See **Eiblin** or **Eve**

Evelina See **Eve**

Evelyn See **Eve**

Everilde [French from Old German]
  'Honour in battle'.

Evie See **Eve**

Evita See **Eve**

Evonne See **Eve**

Eachan [Gaelic]
'Little horse'.
(Eacheann)

Eachan See **Hector**

Eamonn See **Edmond**

Eanruig See **Henry**

Earl [Anglo-Saxon]
'Nobleman; chief'.
*(Erle, Earle, Erl, Errol,
Early)*

Early See **Earl**

Eaton [Anglo-Saxon]
'From the estate by the
river'.

Eben [Hebrew]
'Stone'.

Ebenezer [Hebrew]
'Stone of help'.

Eberhard See **Everard**

Eberhart See **Everard**

Edan [Celtic]
'Flame'.

Edbert [Anglo-Saxon]
'Prosperous; brilliant'.

Edd See **Edwin**

Edel [Teutonic]
'The noble one'.

Edelmar [Anglo-Saxon]
'Noble and famous'.

Eden [Hebrew]
'Place of delight and
pleasure'. The original
paradise.

Edgar [Anglo-Saxon]
'Lucky spear warrior'.
*(Ed, Eddie, Eddy, Edgard,
Ned)*

Edgard See **Edgar**

Edison See **Edson**

Edlin See **Edwin**

Edlin [Anglo-Saxon]
'Prosperous friend'.

Edmondo See **Edmund**

Edmonn See **Edmund**

Edmund [Anglo-Saxon]
'Rich guardian'.
(*Edmond, Edmon,*
Edmonn, Ed, Eddie,
Eddy, Ned)

Edolf [Anglo-Saxon]
'Prosperous wolf'.

Edouard See **Edward**

Edric [Anglo-Saxon]
'Fortunate ruler'.

Edryd [Welsh]
'Restoration'.

Edsel [Anglo-Saxon]
'A prosperous man's
house' or 'Profound
thinker'.

Edson [Anglo-Saxon]
'Edward's son'.
(*Edison*)

Eduard See **Edward**

Eduino See **Edwin**

Edwald [Anglo-Saxon]
'Prosperous ruler'.

Edward [Anglo-Saxon]
'Prosperous guardian'.
(*Eduard, Ed, Eddie, Eddy,*
Ned, Neddie, Neddy,
Teddy)

Edwin [Anglo-Saxon]
'Prosperous friend'.
(*Edlin, Edd, Eddie, Eddy*)

Edwy [Old English]
'Richly beloved'.

Egan [Gaelic]
'Formidable, fiery'.

Egbert [Anglo-Saxon]
'Bright, shining sword'.
The name of the first king
of all England'.

Egerton [Old English]
'Town on ridge'.

Egon See **Egan**

Ehren [Teutonic]
'Honourable one'.

Einar [Norse]
'Warrior leader'.

Eiros [Welsh]
'Bright'.

Elaeth [Welsh]
'Intelligent'.

Elan [Hebrew]
'Tree'.

Elazar [Hebrew]
'God helps'.

Elbert See **Albert**

Elden [Anglo-Saxon]
'Elf Valley'.

Elder [Anglo-Saxon]
'One who lives by an elder
tree'.

Eldon [Anglo-Saxon/
Teutonic]
'From the holy hill'
(Anglo-Saxon) or
'Respected elder'
(Teutonic).

Eldredge See **Eldridge**

Eldrid See **Eldridge**

Eldridge [Anglo-Saxon]
'Wise adviser'.
*(Eldrid, Eldwyn, Eldwin,
Eldred)*

Eldwin [Old English]
'Old friend'.

Eldwyn See **Eldridge**

Eleazar [Hebrew]
'Helped by God'.
(Elizer, Lazarus, Lazar)

Eleutherios [Greek]
'A free man'.

Elfed [Welsh]

'Autumn'.

Elgar [Old English]
'Noble spearman'.

Elhanan [Hebrew]
'God is gracious'.

Eli [Hebrew]
'The highest'.
(Ely)

Elian [Hebrew]
'Bright'.

Elias [Hebrew]
'The Lord is God'.
*(Elihu, Elijah, Eliot,
Elliott, Ellis)*

Elidr [Welsh]
'Brass'.

Elihu See **Elias**

Elijah See **Elias**

Eliot See **Elias**

Elisha [Hebrew]
'God is my salvation'.

Elizer See **Eleazar**

Elkanah [Hebrew]
'God has created'.

Ellard [Anglo-Saxon]
'Noble, brave'.

Ellery [Teutonic]
'From the elder tree'.
(Elery, Ellerey)

Elliot See **Elias**

Ellis See **Elias**

Ellison [Anglo-Saxon]
'Son of Elias'.

Ellsworth [Anglo-Saxon]
'A farmer; lover of the
land'.

Elmer [Anglo-Saxon]
'Noble; famous'.
(Aylmer)

Elmo [Italian/Greek]
'Protector' (Italian) or
'Friendly' (Greek).

Elmore [Anglo-Saxon]
'Dweller by the elm tree on
the moor'.

Elnathan [Hebrew]
'God gives'.

Elner [Teutonic]
'Famous'.

Elrad [Hebrew]
'God is my ruler'.

Elroy [French]
'The king'. The name is
supposed to be an
anagram of *Le Roi* or it
may be from the Spanish
El Rey, either meaning
The King.

Elsdon [Anglo-Saxon]
'Hill belonging to the
noble one'.

Elson See **Ellison**

Elston [Anglo-Saxon]
'Estate of the noble one'.

Elsworth [Anglo-Saxon]
'Estate of the noble one'.

Elton [Anglo-Saxon]
'From the old farm'.

Elvis [Norse]
'All wise'. The prince of
wisdom.

Elvy [Anglo-Saxon]
'Elfin warrior'. Though
small in stature he had the
heart of a lion.

Elwell [Anglo-Saxon]
'From the old well'.

Elwin [Anglo-Saxon]
'Friend of the elves'.

Elwood [Anglo-Saxon]
'From an ancient forest'.

Ely See **Eli**

Emelen See **Emil**

Emerson See **Emery**

Emery [Teutonic]
'Industrious ruler' or
'Joint ruler'.
*(Emmery, Emory,
Emerson, Emmerich,
Amerigo, Emery, Merrick)*

Emil [Teutonic]
'Industrious'.
(Emile, Emilio, Emlyn)

Emilio See **Emil**

Emlen See **Emil**

Emlyn [Welsh]
'A border dweller'.

Emlyn See **Emil**

Emmanuel [Hebrew]
'God is with us'.
*(Emanuel, Immanuel,
Manuel, Mannie, Manny)*

Emmerich See **Emery**

Emmet [Anglo-Saxon]
'The industrious ant'.

*(Emmett, Emmit, Emmot,
Emmott, Emmy)*

Emmit See **Emmet**

Emmot See **Emmet**

Emmy See **Emmet**

Emory See **Emery**

Emry [Welsh]
'Honour'.

Emrys See **Ambrose**

Endemon [Greek]
'Fortunate'.

Endimion [Greek]
'Mythological figure, son
of Jupiter and Calyce
(nymph), so beautiful,
honest and just, Jupiter
made him immortal'.

Eneas See **Aeneas**

Engelbert [Old German]
'Bright as an angel'.

Ennis [Gaelic]
'The only choice'.

Enoch [Hebrew]
'Consecrated; dedicated;
devoted'.

Enos [Hebrew]
  'The mortal'.

Enrico See **Henry**

Enzio See **Ezio**

Ephraim [Hebrew]
  'Abounding in
  fruitfulness'.
  (Efrem, Eph)

Erasme See **Erasmus**

Erasmus [Greek]
  'Worthy of being loved'.
  (Erasme, Ras, Rasmus)

Erastus [Greek]
  'The beloved'.
  (Ras)

Erdogan [Turkish]
  'Son is born'.

Erhard [Old German]
  'Honour'.

Erhart See **Erhard**

Eric [Norse]
  'All powerful ruler'.
  'Kingly'.
  *(Erich, Erick, Erik, Rick,
  Ricky)*

Erin [Gaelic]
  'Peace'.

Erland [Anglo-Saxon]
  'Land of the nobleman'.

Erle See **Earle**

Erling [Anglo-Saxon]
  'Son of the nobleman'.

Ermin See **Herman**

Ernest [Anglo-Saxon]
  'Sincere and earnest'.
  (Ernst, Ernie, Erny)

Ernesto See **Ernest**

Ernestus See **Ernest**

Ernie See **Ernest**

Ernst See **Ernest**

Errol See **Earl**

Erskine [Celtic]
  'From the cliff's height'.

Erwin [Old English]
  'Army friend'.

Esmond [Anglo-Saxon]
  'Gracious protector'.

Este [Italian]
  'Man from the East'.
  (Estes)

Estes See **Este**

Etan See **Ethan**

Ethan [Hebrew]
'Steadfast and firm'.

Ethelbert [Teutonic]
'Noble, bright'.

Ethelred [Teutonic]
'Noble counsel'.

Etienne See **Stephen**

Euclid [Greek]
'True glory'.

Eugene [Greek]
'Nobly born'.
(Gene)

Eugenio See **Eugene**

Eugenius See **Eugene**

Eurwyn [Welsh]
'Gold-fair'.

Eusebius [Greek]
'Honourable'.

Eustace [Greek]
'Stable, tranquil' or
'Fruitful'.

Eustazio See **Eustace**

Eustis See **Eustace**

Evan [Gaelic]
'Well born young warrior'.
Also Welsh form of John.
(Ewan, Ewen, Owen)

Evaristus [Greek]
'Most excellent'.

Evelin See **Evelyn**

Evelyn [English]
A surname.

Everard [Anglo-Saxon]
'Strong as a boar'.
*(Evered, Everett,
Eberhard, Eberhart, Ev,
Eb)*

Evered See **Everard**

Everett See **Everard**

Everild See **Averill**

Everley [Anglo-Saxon]
'Field of the wild boar'.

Evner [Turkish]
'House'.

Evyn See **Evan**

Ewald [Anglo-Saxon]
'Law powerful'.

Ewart See **Edward**

Ewart See **Everard**

Ewert [Anglo-Saxon]
'Ewe herder'. One who
tended the ewes in lamb'.

Ewing [Anglo-Saxon]
'Friend of the law'.

Ezekiel [Hebrew]

'Strength of God'.
(Zeke)

Ezio [Italian]
'Aquiline nose'.

Ezra [Hebrew]
'The one who helps'.
(Esra, Ez)

Girls

Fabia [Latin]
'Bean grower'.
(Fabiana, Fabianna, Fabienne)

Fabiana See **Fabia**

Fabienne See **Fabia**

Fabrianna See **Fabrianne**

Fabrianne [Latin]
'Girl of resourcefulness'.
(Fabriane, Fabrianna, Fabrienne)

Fadilla [French]
Dim. of Francoise (see Frances).

Faida [Arabic]
'Abundant'.

Faine [Old English]
'Joyful'.

Faith [Teutonic]
'Trust in God'. One who is
loyal and true.
(Fae, Fay, Faye)

Fallon [Gaelic]
'Grandchild of the ruler'.

Fan See **Frances**

Fanchon [French]
'Free being'. A derivative of
Francoise.

Fania [Teutonic]
'Free'.

Fanny See **Frances**

Farah See **Farrah**

Farhanna [Arabic]
'Joyful'.

Farica See **Frederica**

Farica [Teutonic]
'Peaceful rule'.

Farida [Arabic]
'Unique, precious gem'.

Farideh [Persian]
'Glorious'.

Fariha [Arabic]
'Happy'.

Farrah [Middle English]
'Beautiful'.

Faten [Arabic]
'Fascinating, charming'.

Fathia [Arabic]
'My conquest'.

Fatima [Arabic]
'Unknown'.

Faun See **Fawn**

Faunia See **Fawn**

Fausta See **Faustine**

Fausta [Italian, Spanish]
'Fortunate'.

Faustina See **Faustine**

Faustine [Latin]
'Lucky omen'.
(Fausta, Faustina)

Favor [French]
'The helpful one'.
(Favora)

Favora See **Favor**

Fawn [French]
'Young deer'. A lithe, swift

footed girl.

Fawnia See **Fawn**

Fay [French]
  'A fairy' or 'A raven'
  (Irish). A fairy-like person.
  Also dim. of Faith.
  (Fae, Faye, Fayette)

Faye See **Faith**

Fayette See **Fay**

Fayina See **Fay**

Fayme [French]
  'Of high reputation'.
  Beyond reproach.

Fayre [Old English]
  'Beautiful'.

Fe [Spanish]
  'Faith'.

Feadore See **Theodora**

Fealty [French]
  'Faithful one'. One who is
  loyal to God, sovereign,
  country and friend.

Fedora See **Theodora**

Fedore See **Theodora**

Felda [Teutonic]
  'From the field'. For one

born at harvest time.

Felice See **Felicia**

Felicia [Latin]
  'Joyous one'. Fem. of
  Felix.
  *(Felice, Felicity, Felis,
  Felicie, Felise, Felicidad)*

Felicidad See **Felicia**

Felicity See **Felicia**

Feliza See **Felicia**

Fenella [Gaelic]
  'White shouldered'.
  (Finella, Fionnula)

Feodora See **Theodora**

Ferdinanda See **Fernanda**

Feride [Turkish]
  'Unique'.

Feriga [Italian, Teutonic]
  'Peaceful ruler'.

Fern [Anglo-Saxon]
  'Fernlike'.

Fernanda [Teutonic]
  'Adventurous'. One who is
  daring and courageous.
  (Ferdinanda, Fernandina)

Fernandina See **Fernanda**

Fidela [Latin]
'Faithful one'.
(Fidelia, Fidele)

Fidele See **Fidela**

Fidelia See **Fidela**

Fidelity See **Fidela**

Fifi See **Josephine**

Filipa See **Philippa**

Filma [Anglo-Saxon]
'Misty veil'. An ethereal
type of beauty.
(Pholma, Philmen)

Fiona [Gaelic]
'Fair one'.
(Fionn, Fionna)

Fionn See **Fiona**

Fionnula See **Fenella**

Fiora See **Florence**

Firoenza See **Florence**

Flanna [Gaelic]
'Red haired'.

Flavia [Latin]
'Yellow haired'.

Fleda See **Fleta**

Fleta [Anglo-Saxon]
'The swift one'.

Fleur [French]
'A flower'. French version
of Florence.
(Fleurette)

Fleurdelice [French]
'Iris or lily'.

Fleurette See **Fleur**

Flo See **Florence**

Flora See **Florence**

Florance See **Florence**

Flore See **Florence**

Florella See **Florence**

Florence [Latin]
'A flower'.
*(Flora, Flore, Floria, Flor,
Fiora, Florance, Florinda,
Floris, Florine, Firoenza,
Florencia, Florentia, Flo,
Florrie, Florry, Flossie)*

Florencia See **Florence**

Florentia See **Florence**

Florenza See **Florence**

Floria See **Florence**

Florida [Latin]
'Flowery'.

Florimel [Greek]
'Flower honey'.

Florinda See **Florence**

Florine See **Florence**

Floris See **Florence**

Florrie See **Florence**

Flossie See **Florence**

Flower [English]
The English version of
Florence.

Fonda [English]
'Affectionate'.

Fortuna See **Fortune**

Fortune [Latin]
'Fate'. The woman of
destiny.
(Fortuna)

Fossetta [French]
'Dimpled'.

Fran See **Frances**

Frances [Latin]

'Free' or 'Girl from
France'.
*(Francine, Francyne,
Francoise, Francesca,
Francisca, Fan, Fanny,
Fran, Frannie, Franny,
Francy, Frankie)*

Francesca See **Frances**

Francine See **Frances**

Franciska See **Frances**

Francoise See **Frances**

Francy See **Frances**

Frankie See **Frances**

Frannie See **Frances**

Freda [Teutonic]
'Peace'. One who is calm
and unflurried.
*(Frieda, Freida, Frida,
Friedie, Freddie)*

Freda See **Alfreda**

Frederica [Teutonic]
'Peaceful ruler'.
*(Frederika, Frederique,
Friederik, Fredericka,
Frerike, Frerika, Farica,
Freddie, Freddy)*

Frederique See **Frederica**

Freida See **Halfrida**

Frerika See **Frederica**

Freya [Norse]
'Noble goddess'. The
Norse Goddess of Love —
the Norse equivalent of the
Greek Aphrodite.

Friedie See **Freda**

Fritzi See **Frederica**

Frodis See **Fronde**

Fronde [Latin]
'Leaf of the fern'.
(Frodis, Frond)

Fulvia [Latin]
'Golden girl'. The daughter
born at high summer.

Fabe See **Fabian**

Faber See **Fabian**

Fabian [Latin]
'The bean grower' or
'Prosperous farmer'.
(Fabien, Fabe)

Fabiano See **Fabian**

Fabio See **Fabian**

Fabre See **Fabron**

Fabron [French]
'The little blacksmith'.
(Fabre, Faber)

Fadoul [Arabic]
'Honest'.

Fagan [Gaelic]
'Little, fiery one'.
(Fagin)

Fairfax [Anglo-Saxon]
'Fair haired one'.

Fairleigh See **Farley**

Fairley [Anglo-Saxon]
'From the far meadow'.

*(Farley, Fairly, Fairlie,
Farl)*

Faisal [Arabic]
'Wise judge'.

Falah [Arabic]
'Success'.

Falkner [Anglo-Saxon]
'Falcon trainer'. One who
trained the birds used in
the hunt.
*(Faulkner, Faulkener,
Fowler)*

Fane [Anglo-Saxon]
'Glad, joyful'.

Faramond [Teutonic]
'Journey protection'.

Farand [Teutonic]
'Pleasant and attractive'.
(Farant, Farrand, Ferrand)

Farant See **Farand**

Farl See **Fairley**

Farland [Old English]
'Land near road'.

Farleigh See **Farley**

Farley [Old English]
'From the bull meadow'.

Farman See **Firman**

Farnell [Anglo-Saxon]
'From the fern slope'.
(Farnall, Fernald, Fernall)

Farnley [Anglo-Saxon]
'From the fern meadow'.
(Fernley)

Farold [Anglo-Saxon]
'Mighty traveller'.

Farquhar [Celtic]
'Man; friendly'.

Farr [Anglo-Saxon]
'The traveller'.

Farrell [Celtic]
'The valorous one'.
(Farrel, Ferrell)

Farris See **Ferris**

Faust [Latin]
'Lucky, auspicious'.

Favian [Latin]
'A man of understanding'.

Fawaz [Arabic]
'Victorious'.

Faxon [Teutonic]
'Thick-haired'.

Fay [Gaelic]
'The raven'. Symbol of
great wisdom.
(Fayette)

Fayad [Arabic]
'Generous'.

Fayette See **Fay**

Fayza [Arabic]
'Victorious'.

Felice See **Felix**

Felicio See **Felix**

Felix [Latin]
'Fortunate'.
(Felice)

Felizio See **Felix**

Felton [Anglo-Saxon]
'From the town estate'.

Fenton [Anglo-Saxon]
'Dweller of the
marshland'. One who lived
by the fens.

Feodor See **Theodore**

Ferant See **Ferrand**

Ferd See **Ferdinand**

Ferdie See **Ferdinand**

Ferdinand [Teutonic]
'Bold, daring adventurer'.
*(Fernando, Fernand,
Hernando, Ferd, Ferdie,
Ferdy)*

Ferdusi [Persian]
'Paradisical'.

Fergie See **Fergus**

Fergus [Gaelic]
'The best choice'.
(Fergie, Feargus)

Ferguson See **Fergus**

Fermin [Spanish]
'Firm'.

Fernald See **Farnell**

Fernand See **Ferdinand**

Fernando See **Ferdinand**

Ferrand [French]
'One with iron grey hair'.
(Ferant, Ferrant, Ferand)

Ferris [Gaelic]
'The rock'.
(Farris)

Fidel [Latin]
'Advocate of the poor'.
(Fidele, Fidelio)

Fidelio See **Fidel**

Fielding [Anglo-Saxon]
'One who lives near the
field'.

Filbert [Anglo-Saxon]
'Very brilliant one'.
(Philbert)

Filberto See **Filbert**

Filmer [Anglo-Saxon]
'Very famous one'.
(Filmore, Fillmore)

Filmore See **Filmer**

Fin See **Finlay**

Findlay See **Finlay**

Finlay [Gaelic]
'Fair soldier'.
*(Finley, Findlay, Findley,
Fin, Lee)*

Finn [Gaelic]
'Fair haired'.

Firman [Anglo-Saxon]
'Long distance traveller'.
(Farman)

Firmin [French]
'The firm, strong one'.

Fiske [Anglo-Saxon]
'Fish'.

Fitch [Anglo-Saxon]
'The marten'.

Fitz [Anglo-French]
'Son'. Originally in the
form of Fils (French for
son) the present form was
introduced into Britain by
the Normans.

Fitzgerald [Anglo-Saxon]
'Son of Gerald'.

Fitzhugh [Anglo-French]
'Son of Hugh'.

Fitzroy [French]
'King's son'.

Flann [Gaelic]
'Lad with red hair'.

Flavian See **Flavius**

Flavius [Latin]
'Yellow haired one'.
(Flavian)

Flem See **Fleming**

Fleming [Anglo-Saxon]
'The Dutchman'.

Fletch See **Fletcher**

Fletcher [French]
'The arrow maker'.

Flinn [Gaelic]
'Son of the redhaired one'.
(Flynn)

Flint [Anglo-Saxon]
'A stream'.

Florian [Latin]
'Flowering; blooming'.
(Flory)

Flory See **Florian**

Floyd See **Lloyd**

Flynn See **Flinn**

Forbes [Gaelic]
'Man of prosperity; owner
of many fields'. The great
landowner.

Ford [Anglo-Saxon]
'The river crossing'.

Forester See **Forrest**

Forrest [Teutonic]
'Guardian of the forest'.
*(Forest, Forester,
Forrester, Forster, Foster,
Forrie, Foss)*

Forrie See **Forrest**

Forster See **Forrest**

Fortune [French]
'The lucky one'. Child of
many blessings.

Foss See **Forrest**

Foster See **Forrest**

Fowler See **Falkner**

Fran See **Francis**

Franchot See **Francis**

Francis [Latin]
'Free man'.
*(Frank, Franchot, Franz,
Frankie, Fran)*

Francklin See **Franklin**

Frank See **Francis or
Franklin**

Frankie See **Francis**

Franklin [Anglo-Saxon]
'Free-holder of property'.
He owned his own land to
use as he wished.
*(Frank, Franklyn,
Francklin, Francklyn,
Frankie)*

Franz See **Francis**

Fraser [French]
'Strawberry' or 'Curly
haired one'.
(Frazer, Frasier, Frazier)

Frayne [Anglo-Saxon]
'Stranger'.
*(Fraine, Frean, Freen,
Freyne)*

Frean See **Frayne**

Fred See **Frederick**

Freddy See **Frederick**

Frederick [Teutonic]
'Peaceful ruler'. One who
used diplomacy not war'.
*(Frederic, Fredric,
Fredrick, Friedrich, Fritz,
Frederik, Fred, Freddie,
Freddy)*

Freedman See **Freeman**

Freeland [Old English]
'From free land'.

Freeman [Anglo-Saxon]
'Born a free man'.

Freen See **Frayne**

Fremont [Teutonic]
'Free and noble protector'.

Frewin [Anglo-Saxon]
'Free, noble friend'.
(Frewen)

Frey [Anglo-Saxon]
'The lord of peace and
prosperity'. From the Old
Norse God.

Frick [Anglo-Saxon]
'Bold man'.

Fridolf [Anglo-Saxon]
'Peaceful wolf'.

Fritz See **Frederick**

Fulbert See **Fulbright**

Fulbright [Old German]
'Very bright'.
(Fulbert)

Fuller [Anglo-Saxon]
'Cloth thickener'.

Fulton [Anglo-Saxon]
'From the field' or 'Dweller
by the fowl-pen'.

Fyfe [Scottish]
'Man from Fife'.
(Fife, Fyffe)

Girls

Gabinia [French, Italian from Latin]
'Famous Roman family; name of city in central Italy'.

Gabriella See **Gabrielle**

Gabrielle [Hebrew]
'Woman of God'. The bringer of good news.
(Gabriel, Gabriella, Gabriele, Gabriela, Gaby, Gabbie)

Gabrila See **Gabrielle**

Gaby See **Gabrielle**

Gaea [Greek]
'The earth'. The Goddess of the Earth.
(Gaia)

Gael See **Abigail**

Gail See **Abigail**

Galane [French]
'Flower name'.

Galatea [Greek]
'Milky white'.

Gale See **Abigail**

Galia [Hebrew]
'God has redeemed'.

Galiena [Teutonic]
'Lofty maiden'. A tall girl of
lofty mien.
(Galiana)

Galilah [Hebrew]
Place name in Galilee.

Galina See **Helen**

Galliane See **Galane**

Garda See **Gerda**

Gardenia [Latin]
'White, fragrant flower'.

Garland [French]
'Crown of blossoms'.

Garnet [English]
'Deep red haired beauty'.
(Garnette)

Gartred See **Gertrude**

Gavrielle See **Gabrielle**

Gavrila [Hebrew]
'Heroine'.

Gay [French]
'Lively'.
(Gai, Gaye)

Gayle See **Abigail**

Gayleen See **Gail**

Gaylene See **Gail**

Gaynor See **Genevieve**

Gaynor See **Guinevere**

Gazella [Latin]
'The antelope'. One who is
graceful and modest.

Gedalia [Hebrew]
'God is great'.

Gelasia [Greek]
'Laughing water'. One
who is like a fresh and
gurgling stream.
(Gelasie)

Gelasia [Greek]
'Laughing'.

Gelasie See **Gelasia**

Gemini [Greek]
'Twin'.

Gemma [Latin]
'Precious stone'.
(Gemmel)

Gemmel See **Gemma**

Gena See **Eugenia**

Gene See **Eugenia**

Genesa See **Genesia**

Genesia [Latin]
'Newcomer'.
*(Genesa, Genisia,
Jenesia)*

Geneva [French]
'Juniper tree'. Also var. of
Genevieve.
(Genvra, Genevre)

Genevieve [French]
'Pure white wave'.
*(Genevra, Genevre,
Gaynor, Ginevra,
Jennifer, Guinevere,
Guenevere, Vanora,
Ginette)*

Genevra See **Genevieve**

Genevre See **Geneva**

Genie See **Eugenia**

Genovera See **Genevieve**

Genvra See **Geneva**

Georgana See **Georgina**

Georgeanne See **Georgina**

Georgene See **Georgina**

Georgette See **Georgina**

Georgia See **Georgina**

Georgiana See **Georgina**

Georgianna See **Georgina**

Georgina [Greek]
'Girl from the farm'. Fem.
of George.
*(Georgiana, Georgana,
Georgia, Georgene,
Georgette, Georgine,
Girogia, Georgy, Georgie)*

Georgy See **Georgina**

Geralda See **Geraldine**

Geraldina See **Geraldine**

Geraldine [Teutonic]
'Noble spear carrier'.
*(Geraldina, Gerhardine,
Geralda, Gerry, Giralda,
Jeraldine, Jeroldine,
Jerri, Jerry)*

Geranium [Greek]
'Bright red flower'.

Gerda [Norse]
'Protected one'. One who
has been strictly brought
up.

Gerda See **Gertrude**

Gerhardine See
Geraldine

Gerianna See **Geraldine**

Germaine [French]
'From Germany'.
(Germain)

Gerrilee See **Geraldine**

Gerry See **Geraldine**

Gert See **Gertrude**

Gertie See **Gertrude**

Gertruda See **Gertrude**

Gertrude [Teutonic]
'Spear maiden'. One of the
Valkyrie.
*(Gertruda, Gertrud,
Gertrudis, Gert, Gertie,
Gerty, Gerda, Trudie,
Trudy, Gartred)*

Gertrudis See **Gertrude**

Gervaise [French from
Teutonic]
'War eagerness'.

Ghislaine [French]

Giacinta See **Hyacinth**

Gianina [Hebrew]
'The Lord's grace'.

Gigi See **Gilberta**

Gilah [Hebrew]
'Joy'.

Gilberta [Teutonic]
'Bright pledge'. Fem. of
Gilbert.
*(Gilberte, Gilbertha,
Gilberthe, Gilbertina,
Gilbertine, Gigi, Gillie,
Gilly)*

Gilberte See **Gilberta**

Gilbertina See **Gilberta**

Gilbertine See **Gilberta**

Gilda [Celtic]
'God's servant'.

Gill See **Gillian**

Gillian [Latin]
'Young nestling'. Also der.
of Juliana.

(Jillian, Jill, Jillie, Gill, Gillie)

Gillie See **Gilberta** or **Gillian**

Gina See **Eugenia** or **Regina**

Ginette See **Genevieve**

Ginger See **Virginia**

Giorsal See **Grace**

Girogia See **Georgina**

Gisella See **Gisselle**

Giselle [Teutonic]
'A promise'. One who stands as a pledge for her family.
(Gisella, Gisela, Gisele)

Gita [Hindi]
'Song'.

Gitana [Spanish]
'The gipsy'.

Githa See **Gytha**

Gittle [Hebrew]
'Innocent flatterer'.
(Gittle, Gytle)

Gizela See **Giselle**

Glad See **Gladys**

Gladdie See **Gladys**

Gladine See **Gladys**

Gladys [Celtic]
'Frail delicate flower'. Celtic version of Claudia (the lame).
(Gladine, Gladis, Gladdie, Glad, Gwyladys, Gwladys, Gleda)

Gleda [Anglo-Saxon]
Old English version of Gladys.

Gleda See **Gladys**

Glenda See **Glenna**

Glenine See **Glenna**

Glenn See **Glenna**

Glenna [Celtic]
'From the valley'. One of the oldest names on record.
(Glenda, Glynis, Glenn)

Glennis See **Glenna**

Glenys [Welsh]
'Holy'.

Gloire See **Gloria**

Gloria [Latin]
'Glorious one'. An illustrious person. This name was often used of Queen Elizabeth I by her sycophantic courtiers. *(Gloire, Glori, Glory, Gloriana, Glorianna, Gloriane, Glorianne)*

Gloriana See **Gloria**

Glorianna See **Gloria**

Glorianne See **Gloria**

Glory See **Gloria**

Glynis See **Glenna**

Goda See **Guda**

Godgifu See **Godiva**

Godiva [Anglo-Saxon]
'Gift of God'. *(Godgifu)*

Golda See **Goldie**

Goldie [Anglo-Saxon]
'Pure gold'. *(Golda)*

Goldina See **Goldie**

Grace [Latin]
'The graceful one'. *(Gracia, Grazia, Gracie, Grayce, Giorsal, Engracia)*

Gracia See **Grace**

Gracie See **Grace**

Grainne [Irish]
'Love'. *(Grania)*

Grania See **Grainne**

Gratiana See **Grace**

Grazina [Italian]
'Grace, charm'.

Greer [Greek]
'The watchful mother'. The eternal matriarch. *(Gregoria)*

Gregoria See **Greer**

Greta See **Margaret**

Gretchen See **Margaret**

Grete See **Margaret**

Griselda [Teutonic]
'Grey heroine'. *(Griselde, Grishelda, Grishelde, Grishilda, Grishilde, Grizelda, Selda, Zelda)*

Griselde See **Griselda**

Grishilda See **Griselda**

Grishilde See **Griselda**

Guadalupe [Arabic]
'River of black stones'.

Guda [Anglo-Saxon]
'The good one'.
(Goda)

Gudrun [German]
'War; rune'.

Guida [Latin]
'The guide'.

Guilla See **Wilhelmina**

Guinevere [Celtic]
'White phantom'.
(Guinivere, Guenevere, Gwenhwyvar, Jennifer)

Guinevere See **Genevieve**

Gunhilda [Norse]
'Warrior maid'.
(Gunhilde)

Gunhilde See **Gunhilda**

Gussy See **Gustava**

Gustava [Scandinavian]
'Staff of the Goths'.
(Gustave, Gussie, Gussy)

Gustave See **Gustava**

Gwen See **Gwendoline**

Gwenda See **Gwendoline**

Gwendoline [Celtic]
'White browed maid'.
(Gwendolen, Gwendolene, Gwendolyn, Gwendolyne, Gwenda, Gwennie, Gwen, Gwyn, Wendy)

Gwendydd [Welsh]
'Morning star'.

Gweneira [Welsh]
'White snow'.

Gwenllian [Welsh]
'Fair, Flaxen'.

Gwennie See **Gwendoline**

Gwenonwyn [Welsh]
'Lily of the valley'.

Gwyladys See **Gladys**

Gwyn See **Gwendoline**

Gwyneth [Welsh]
'Blessed'.

Gwynne [Old Welsh]
'White or fair one'.

Gypsy [Anglo-Saxon]
'The wanderer'. See also
Gitana.

(Gipsy)

Gytha [Anglo-Saxon]
'The war like'.
(Githa)

Gabbie See **Gabriel**

Gabe See **Gabriel**

Gable [French]
'The small Gabriel'.

Gabriel [Hebrew]
'Messenger of God'. The
archangel who announced
the birth of Christ.
*(Gabe, Gabbie, Gabie,
Gabby)*

Gabriello See **Gabriel**

Gadiel [Hebrew]
'God is my fortune'.

Gaelan See **Galen**

Gage [French]
'A pledge'. The glove that
was given as an earnest of
good faith.

Gair [Gaelic]
'Short one'.

Gaius [Latin]
'Rejoiced'.

Galahad [Hebrew]
'Gilead'.

Galdemar [French, Old
German]
'Famous ruler'.

Gale [Celtic]
'The lively one'.
(Gail, Gayle)

Galen [Gaelic]
'Little bright one' or
(Greek) 'The helper'.

Gallagher [Gaelic]
'Eager helper from
overseas'.

Gallard See **Gaylord**

Galloway [Celtic]
'Man from the stranger
gaels'.
(Galway, Gallway)

Galt [Old English]
'High land'.

Galton [Anglo-Saxon]
'Lease holder of an estate'.

Galvan See **Galvin**

Galvin [Gaelic]
'Bright, shining white' or
'The sparrow'.
(Galvan, Galven)

Galway See **Galloway**

Gamalat [Arabic]
'Beautiful one'.

Gamaliel [Hebrew]
'The recompense of the
Lord'.

Gannon [Gaelic]
'Little blond one'.

Ganymede [Greek]
'Rejoicing in mankind'.

Gardiner [Teutonic]
'A gardener; a flower
lover'.
(Gardner, Gardener)

Gardner See **Gardiner**

Gare See **Gary**

Garek See **Garrick**

Gareth [Welsh]
'Gentle'.

Garey See **Gary**

Garfield [Anglo-Saxon]
'War or battle field'.

Garland [Anglo-Saxon]
'From the land of the
spears'.

Garman [Anglo-Saxon]
'The spearman'.

Garmon See **Garmond**

Garmond [Anglo-Saxon]
'Spear protector'.
(Garmon, Garmund)

Garner [Teutonic]
'Army guard; noble
defender'.

Garnet [Latin]
'A red seed; pomegranate
seed'.

Garnett [Anglo-Saxon]
'Compulsive spear man'.
He struck first and
challenged afterwards.

Garnock [Celtic]
'One who dwells by the
river alder'.

Garrek See **Garrick**

Garrett [Anglo-Saxon]
'Mighty spear warrior'.
*(Garett, Garret, Garritt,
Gerard, Garrard, Jarrett)*

Garrick [Anglo-Saxon]
'Spear ruler'.

Garroway [Anglo-Saxon]
'Spear warrior'.
(Garraway)

Garson [French]
'Young man; garrison'.

Garth [Norse]
'From the garden'.

Garton [Anglo-Saxon]
'The dweller by the
triangular shaped farm'.

Garvey [Gaelic]
'Rough peace'. Peace
obtained after victory!
(Garvie)

Garvin [Teutonic]
'Spear friend'.
(Garwin)

Garwin See **Garvin**

Garwood [Anglo-Saxon]
'From the fir trees'.

Gary [Anglo-Saxon]
'Spearman'.
(Gari, Garey, Garry)

Gaspar [Persian]
'Master of the treasure'.
One of the Magi.

*(Caspar, Casper, Gasper,
Kaspar, Kasper, Jasper)*

Gaspar See **Casper**

Gaston [French]
'Man from Gascony'.

Gaubert [Old German]
'Brilliant ruler'.

Gauderic [Old German]
'Ruler, king'.

Gavin See **Gawain**

Gawain [Celtic]
'The battle hawk'.
*(Gawaine, Gavin, Gavan,
Gaven, Gawen)*

Gayle See **Gale**

Gaylor See **Gaylord**

Gaylord [French]
'The happy noble man'.
(Gayler, Galor, Gallard)

Gaynor [Gaelic]
'Son of the blond haired
one'.

Gearalt See **Gerald**

Geary [Anglo-Saxon]
'The changeable'.
(Gearey, Gery)

Gemmel [Scandinavian]
'Old'.

Gene See **Eugene**

Geno See **John**

Geof See **Geoffrey**

Geoffrey [Teutonic]
'God's Divine peace'.
*(Godfrey, Jeffery, Jeffrey,
Jeffry, Jeffers, Jeff, Geof,
Geoff)*

Geordie See **George**

George [Greek]
'The farmer'. The Patron
Saint of England.
*(Georges, Georgie,
Geordie, Gordie, Gordy,
Georgy, Georg, Jorge,
Jorin, Joris, Jurgen,
Yorick)*

Georges See **George**

Georgie See **George**

Ger See **Gerald**

Geraint [Welsh]
'Old'.

Gerald [Teutonic]
'Mighty spear ruler'.
*(Geraud, Giraud, Gearalt,
Garold, Gereld, Gerrald,
Jereld, Jerold, Jerald,
Jerrold, Gerry, Gery,
Jerry, Ger, Jer)*

Gerard [Anglo-Saxon]
'Spear strong; spear
brave'.
*(Gerrard, Gerhard,
Gerhardt, Gearard, Gerry)*

Gerard See **Garrett**

Gerardo See **Gerard**

Geraud See **Gerald**

Gerhardt See **Gerard**

Germain [Middle English]
'Sprout, bud'.

Gerry See **Gerard**

Gervase [Teutonic]
'Spear vassal'.
*(Gervais, Jarvis, Jervis,
Jarvey, Jarv, Ger)*

Gerwyn [Welsh]
'Fair love'.

Gethin [Welsh]
'Dark skinned'.

Ghislaine [French]
'A pledge'.

Gian See **John**

Gianni See **John**

Gib See **Gilbert**

Gibson [Anglo-Saxon]
'Son of Gilbert'.

Gideon [Hebrew]
'Brave indomitable spirit'
or 'The destroyer'.

Gifford [Teutonic]
'The gift'.
(Giffard, Gifferd)

Gilbert [Anglo-Saxon]
'Bright pledge; a hostage'.
*(Gil, Gill, Gillie, Gib,
Gibb, Bert, Gilibeirt,
Gilleabart)*

Gilby [Norse]
'The pledge; a hostage'.
(Gilbey)

Gilchrist [Gaelic]
'The servant of Christ'.
(Gilecriosd)

Gilecriosd See **Gilchrist**

Giles [Latin/French]
'Shield bearer' (Latin)
or 'Youthful shaveling'
(French).
(Gilles, Gil)

Gill See **Gilbert**

Gilleabart See **Gilbert**

Gilleasbuig See
Archibald

Gillecirosd See
Christopher

Gillet [French]
'Little Gilbert'.

Gillie See **Gilbert**

Gilmer [Anglo-Saxon]
'Famous hostage'. An
eminent knight taken
captive in battle.

Gilmore [Gaelic]
'St. Mary's servant'.
(Gillmore, Gilmour)

Gilroy [Latin/Gaelic]
'The king's servant'
(Latin) or 'The red- haired
one's servant' (Gaelic).

Gino See **Ambrose**

Giorgio See **George**

Giovanni See **John**

Giraldo See **Gerald**

Girvin [Gaelic]
'Little rough one'.
(Girvan, Girven)

Gladwin [Anglo-Saxon]
'Kind friend'.

Glanville [French]
'Dweller on the oak tree
estate'.
(Glanvil)

Glen [Celtic]
'From the valley'.
(Glenn, Glyn, Glynn)

Glenden See **Glendon**

Glendon [Celtic]
'From the fortress in the
Glen'.

Glyn See **Glenn**

Glynn See **Glen**

Godart See **Goddard**

Goddard [Teutonic]
'Divinely firm'. Firm in
belief and trust in God.
(Godard, Godart, Goddart)

Godfrey See **Geoffrey**

Golding [Anglo-Saxon]
'Son of the golden one'.

Goldwin [Anglo-Saxon]
'Golden friend'.

Gomez [Spanish]
'Man'.

Goodman [Anglo-Saxon]
'Good man'.

Goodwin [Anglo-Saxon]
'Good friend; God's
friend'.
*(Godwin, Godwine,
Godewyn)*

Gordie See **Gordon**

Gordon [Anglo-Saxon]
'From the cornered hill'.
*(Gordan, Gorden, Gordie,
Gordy)*

Gorman [Gaelic]
'Small, blue eyed lad'.

Gouveneur [French]
'The Governor; the ruler'.

Gower [Celtic]
'The pure one'.

Grady [Gaelic]
'Illustrious and noble'.

Graham [Teutonic]
'From the grey lands'. One
from the country beyond
the mists.

(Graeme)

Grange See **Granger**

Granger [Anglo-Saxon]
'The farmer'.

Grant [French]
'The great one'.

Grantham [Old English]
'From the big meadow'.

Grantland [Anglo-Saxon]
'From the great lands'.

Grantley See **Grant**

Granville [French]
'Dweller in the big town'.
*(Grandville, Granvil,
Grandvil, Greville)*

Grayson [Anglo-Saxon]
'The bailiff's son'.

Greeley [Anglo-Saxon]
'From the grey meadow'.

Greg See **Gregory**

Gregor See **Gregory**

Gregorio See **Gregory**

Gregorius See **Gregory**

Gregory [Greek]

'The watchful one'.
Someone ever vigilant.
*(Greg, Gregor, Gregg,
Greiogair, Greagoir)*

Greiogair See **Gregory**

Grenville See **Grant**

Gresham [Anglo-Saxon]
'From the grazing
meadow'.

Greville See **Granville**

Griff See **Rufus**

Griffin See **Griffith**

Griffith [Celtic]
'Fierce, red haired
warrior'.
(Griffin, Gruffydd, Rufus)

Griffith See **Rufus**

Grimbald [Teutonic]
'Fierce power'.

Griswold [Teutonic]
'From the grey forest'.

Grover [Anglo-Saxon]
'One who comes from the
grove'.

Guido See **Guy**

Gunnar See **Gunther**

Gunter See **Gunther**

Gunther [Teutonic]
'Bold warrior'.
*(Gunnar, Gunner,
Gunter, Gunar, Guntar,
Gunthar)*

Gurion [Hebrew]
'Dwelling place of God'.

Gus See **August** or
Gustave

Gustave [Scandinavian]
'Staff of the Goths'.
*(Gustav, Gustaf,
Gustavus, Gus)*

Gustavo See **Gustave**

Gustavus See **Gustave**

Guthrie [Celtic]
'War serpent; war hero' or

'From the windy country'.
(Guthry)

Guy [French/Teutonic/
Latin]
'The guide' (French); 'The
warrior' (Teutonic); 'Life'
(Latin).
*(Guido, Guyon, Wiatt,
Wyatt)*

Guyon See **Guy**

Gwylim See **William**

Gwynfor [Welsh]
'Fair place'.

Gwynllyw [Welsh]
'Blessed leader'.

Gwynn [Celtic]
'The blond one'.
(Gwynn, Guin)

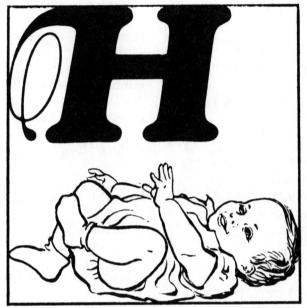

Girls

Hadria See **Adrienne**

Hadwisa See **Avice**

Hafwen [Welsh]
'Summer-beautiful'.

Hagar [Hebrew]
'Forsaken'.

Haidee [Greek]
'Modest, honoured'. A
maid renowned for her
natural modesty.

Halcyone [Greek]
'The king fisher'. The
mythological Greek who
was turned into a bird
when she drowned
herself.
(Halcyon)

Haldana [Norse]
'Half Danish'.

Haleigh See **Haley**

Halette See **Hallie**

Haley [Scandinavian]
'Hero'.

Halfrida [Teutonic]
'Peaceful heroine'. A
diplomat not a warrior.
*(Halfreida, Halfrieda,
Hallie, Frida, Freida,
Frieda)*

Hali See **Hallie**

Halima [Arabic]
'Kind, humane'.

Halimeda [Greek]
'Sea thoughts'. One who is
drawn to the sea.
(Hallie, Meda)

Halla [African]
'Unexpected gift'.

Halley See **Hallie**

Hallie See **Halfrida**

Hallie [Greek]
'Thinking of the sea'.

Halona [North American
Indian]
'Fortunate'.

Hana [Japanese]
'Flower'.

Hanako See **Hana**

Hannah See **Anne**

Happy [English]
'Happy'.

Haracia See **Horatia**

Haralda [Norse]
'Army ruler'. Fem. of
Harold.
*(Haraldina, Harolda,
Haroldina)*

Haraldina See **Haralda**

Harika [Turkish]
'Most beautiful'.

Harlene See **Harley**

Harley [Old English]
'From the long field'.

Harlie See **Harley**

Harmonia See **Harmony**

Harmony [Latin]
'Concord and harmony'.
(Harmonia, Harmonie)

Harriet See **Henrietta**

Hasna [Arabic]
'Beautiful'.

Hatsu [Japanese]
'First-born'.

Hattie See **Henrietta**

Hayfa [Arabic]
'Slender'.

Hayley [English]
From the surname.

Hazar [Arabic]
'Nightingale'.

Hazel [English]
'The hazel tree'.
(Aveline)

Heather [Anglo-Saxon]
'Flower of the moors'.

Hebe [Greek]
Goddess of Youth

Hedda [Teutonic]
'War'. A born fighter.
(Heddi, Heddy, Hedy)

Heddi See **Hedda**

Hedia [Greek]
'Pleasing'.

Heidi See **Hilda**

Helen [Greek]
'Light'. According to
tradition, the most
beautiful woman, Helen of
Troy. There are so many
variations of this name,
that it is not possible to
list them all. A
representative selection:
*(Helena, Helene, Eleanor,
Eleanore, Elinor, Elenor,
Elinore, Elinora, Elenore,
Elenora, Elaine, Elane,
Ella, Ellen, Ellyn, Ellene,
Elena, Galina, Ileane,
Ilena, Ilona, Illona, Illone,
Aileen, Aisleen, Eileen,
Isleen, Leonora, Leonore,
Lenora, Leora, Lora,
Lana, Leona, Nora,
Norah, Nell, Lena, Lina)*

Helena See **Helen**

Helga [Teutonic]
'Pious, religious and holy'.
Var. of Olga.

Helia [Greek]
'Sun'.

Helianthe [Greek]
'Bright flower; sunflower'.

Helice [Greek]
  'Spiral'.
  (Helixa)

Helixa See **Helice**

Helma [Teutonic]
  'A helmet'.
  (Hilma)

Helma See **Wilhelmina**

Heloise See **Louise**

Helsa [Danish] See
  Elizabeth

Hendrika See **Henrietta**

Henrietta [Teutonic]
  'Ruler of home and estate'.
  Fem. of Henry.
  (Harriet, Harriette,
  Harriot, Harriotte,
  Henriette, Henrika,
  Hattie, Hatty, Hettie,
  Hetty, Etta, Netta, Netie,
  Yetta, Eiric, Minette,
  Hendrika)

Henriette See **Henrietta**

Henrika See **Henrietta**

Hera [Latin]
  'Queen of the heaven'. The
  wife of the ruler of the
  Heaven, Zeus.

Herleva See **Arlene**

Hermia See **Hermione**

Hermina See **Hermione**

Herminia See **Hermione**

Hermione [Greek]
  'Of the earth'. The
  daughter of Helen of
  Troy'.
  (Hermia, Hermina,
  Hermine, Herminia)

Hermosa [Spanish]
  'Beautiful'.

Hernanda [Spanish]
  'Adventuring life'.

Herta See **Eartha**

Hertha See **Eartha**

Hesper [Greek]
  'The evening star'.
  (Hespera, Hesperia)

Hespera See **Hesper**

Hesperia See **Hesper**

Hessy See **Esther**

Hester See **Esther**

Hestia [Greek]
'A star'.

Hettie See **Henrietta**

Hetty See **Esther**

Heulwen [Welsh]
'Sunshine'.

Heutte [Old English]
'Brilliant'.
(Hughette, Hugette, Huetta)

Hiberna [Latin]
'Girl from Ireland'.
(Hibernia)

Hibernia See **Hiberna**

Hibiscus [Latin]
'The marshmallow plant'.

Hidé [Japanese]
'Excellent, fruitful, superior'.

Hilaria See **Hilary**

Hilary [Latin]
'Cheerful one'. One who is always happy.
(Hilaria, Hilaire)

Hild See **Hilda**

Hilda [Teutonic]

'Battle maid'. A handmaiden of the warriors of Valhalla.
(Heidi, Hilde, Hildie, Hild, Hildy, Heidy, Hidie)

Hildagard See **Hildegarde**

Hildegaard See **Hildegarde**

Hildegarde [Teutonic]
'Battle stronghold'.

Hildemar [Teutonic]
'Battle celebrated'.

Hildie See **Hilda**

Hildreth [Teutonic]
'Battle adviser'.
(Hildretha)

Hildretha See **Hildreth**

Hilma See **Helma**

Hina [Hebrew]
'Female deer'.

Hippolyta [Greek]
'Horse destruction'.

Holda [Norse]
'Muffled'
(Holde, Holle, Hulda)

Holde See **Holda**

Holle See **Holda**

Holly [Anglo-Saxon]
'Bringer of good luck'. The
child born during the
Christmas season.
(*Hollie*)

Honey [English]
'Sweet one'. A term of
endearment, especially in
the U.S.

Honey See **Honora**

Honi [Hebrew]
'Gracious'.

Honor See **Honora**

Honora [Latin]
'Honour'.
(*Honor, Honour,
Honoria, Honey, Noreen,
Norine, Nora, Norah,
Norrey, Norrie, Norry*)

Honoria See **Honora**

Hope [Anglo-Saxon]
'Cheerful optimism'.
Another 'virtue' name.

Horatia [Latin]
'Keeper of the hours'.
Fem. of Horace.
(*Haracia, Horacia*)

Hortense [Latin]
'Of the garden'. One with
green fingers.
(*Hortensia*)

Hortensia See **Hortense**

Hoshi [Japanese]
'Star'.

Huberta [Teutonic]
'Brilliant mind'. One with
intelligence above the
ordinary.
(*Hubertha, Huberthe*)

Hubertha See **Huberta**

Huberthe See **Huberta**

Huetta See **Heutte**

Huette [Anglo-Saxon]
'Brilliant thinker'. Fem. of
Hugh'.
(*Hugette, Huetta*)

Hugette See **Huette**

Hulda See **Holda**

Huriyah [Arabic]
'Virgin of paradise'.

Hyacinth [Greek]
'Hyacinth flower'.
(*Hyacintha, Hyacinthia,
Jacintha, Jacinthia,*

Cynthie, Cynthis, Jackie,
Giacinta)

Hyacintha See **Hyacinth**

Hyacinthia See **Hyacinth**

Hypatia [Greek]
'Highest'.

Haakon [Scandinavian]
'Noble kin'.

Haaris [Arabic]
'Vigilant'.

Habakkuk [Hebrew]
'Embrace'.

Habib [Arabic]
'Beloved'.

Hackett [Teutonic]
'The small woodsman'.
The apprentice forester.
(Hacket)

Hacon [Old Norse]
'Useful'.

Had See **Hadley**

Hadar [Hebrew]
'Ornament'.

Hadden [Anglo-Saxon]
'From the heath valley'.
(Haddan, Haddon)

Hadi [Arabic]
'Guide'.

Hadlee See **Hadley**

Hadleigh See **Hadley**

Hadley [Anglo-Saxon]
'From the heath meadow'.

Hadwin [Anglo-Saxon]
'Battle companion'.

Hafiz [Arabic]
'He who remembers'.

Hagen [Gaelic]
'The young one'.
(Hagan, Haggan, Haggen)

Haggai [Hebrew]
'Festive'.

Hagley [Anglo-Saxon]
'From the hedged
meadow'.

Hagos [Ethiopian]
'Happy'.

Haig [Anglo-Saxon]
'One who lives in an
enclosure'. Popular name
for boys during early part
of 20th century, in

compliment to the Field
Marshal Lord Haig.

Haines [Old German]
'From a vined cottage'.

Hakeem [Arabic]
'Wise'.
(Hakim)

Hako See **Hakon**

Hakon [Norse]
'From an exalted race'.
(Haakon, Hako)

Hal See **Harold, Henry**

Halbert [Anglo-Saxon]
'Brilliant hero'.

Haldane See **Halden**

Halden [Norse]
'Half Danish'.
*(Haldan, Halfdan,
Haldane)*

Hale [Anglo-Saxon]
'From the hall'.

Haley [Gaelic]
'The ingenious one'. One
with a scientific
intelligence.

Halfdan See **Halden**

Halford [Anglo-Saxon]
'From the ford by the
manor house'.

Halim [Arabic]
'Patient'.

Hall [Anglo-Saxon]
'Dweller at the manor
house'.

Hallam [Anglo-Saxon]
'One who lives on the hill
slopes'.

Halley [Anglo-Saxon]
'From the Manor House
meadow' or 'Holy'.

Halliwell [Anglo-Saxon]
'The dweller by the holy
well'.

Hallward [Anglo-Saxon]
'Guardian of the Manor
House'.
(Halward)

Halsey [Anglo-Saxon]
'From Hal's island'.
(Halsy)

Halstead [Anglo-Saxon]
'From the manor house'.
(Halsted)

Halton [Anglo-Saxon]
'From the estate on the hill
slope'.

Ham [Hebrew]
'South'.

Hamal [Arabic]
'The lamb'. A very gentle
person.

Hamar [Norse]
'Symbol of ingenuity'. A
great gift for invention.
(Hammar)

Hamdan [Arabic]
'Thankful'.

Hamid [Arabic]
'Thanking God'.

Hamil See **Hamilton**

Hamilton [Anglo-Saxon/
French]
'Sheep enclosure' (Anglo-
Saxon) or 'From the
mountain village'
(French).

Hamish See **James**

Hamlet [Teutonic]
'Little village'.

Hamlin [Teutonic]
'Small home lover'.

*(Hamelin, Hamlyn,
Hamelyn)*

Hamlin See **Henry**

Hamon [Greek]
'Faithful'.

Hanafi [Arabic]
'Orthodox'.

Hanan [Hebrew]
'Grace'.

Hananel [Hebrew]
'God is gracious'.

Handley See **Hanley**

Hanford [Anglo-Saxon]
'From the high ford'.

Hanif [Arabic]
'Orthodox, true'.

Hank See **Henry**

Hanley [Anglo-Saxon]
'From the high meadow'.
*(Handley, Henleigh,
Henley)*

Hannibal
The hero Carthage

Hanraoi See **Henry**

Hans See **John**

Hansel [Scandinavian]
'Gift from the Lord'.

Harailt See **Harold**

Harbert See **Herbert**

Harbin See **Herbert**

Harcourt [French]
'From a fortified court'.

Harden [Anglo-Saxon]
'From the valley of the
hare'.

Harden See **Harley**

Harding [Anglo-Saxon]
'Son of the hero'.

Hardwin [Anglo-Saxon]
'Brave friend'.
*(Harwin, Hardwyn,
Harwyn)*

Hardy [Teutonic]
'Bold and daring'.
(Hardey, Hardie, Hardi)

Harford [Anglo-Saxon]
'From the hare ford'.
*(Herford, Hereford,
Hareford)*

Hargrave See **Hargrove**

Hargreave See **Hargrove**

Hargreaves See **Hargrove**

Hargrove [Anglo-Saxon]
'From the hare grove'.
*(Hargrave, Hargreave,
Hargreaves)*

Hark See **Henry**

Harl See **Harley**

Harlan See **Harlon**

Harland See **Harlon**

Harley [Anglo-Saxon]
'From the hare meadow'.
*(Arley, Harden, Harleigh,
Hartley, Hartleigh, Arlie,
Harl, Hart)*

Harley See **Arlie**

Harlon [Teutonic]
'From the battle land'.
(Harland)

Harlow [Anglo-Saxon]
'The fortified hill'. An army
camp on the hillside.

Harman/Harmon See
Herman

Harold [Anglo-Saxon]
'Army commander'. A
mighty general.
(*Harald, Herold, Hereld,
Herrick, Harailt, Hal,
Harry*)

Harper [Anglo-Saxon]
'The harp player'. The
wandering minstrel.

Harris [Anglo-Saxon]
'Harold's son'.
(*Harrison*)

Harrison See **Harris**

Harry See **Harold, Henry**

Hart [Anglo-Saxon]
'The hart deer'.

Hart See **Harley**

Hartford [Anglo-Saxon]
'The river crossing of the
deer'.
(*Hertford*)

Hartley [Anglo-Saxon]
'Meadow of the hart deer'.

Hartley See **Harley**

Hartman [Teutonic]
'Strong and austere'. The
original stoic. Also
'Keeper of the stags'

(Anglo-Saxon).
(*Hartmann*)

Hartwell [Anglo-Saxon]
'Well where the deer
drink'.
(*Harwell, Hartwill,
Harwill, Hart*)

Hartwill See **Hartwell**

Hartwood [Anglo-Saxon]
'Forest of the hart deer'.
(*Harwood*)

Harve See **Harvey**

Harvey [Teutonic/French]
'Army warrior' (Teutonic)
or 'Bitter' (French).
(*Hervey, Harve, Harv,
Herve, Herv*)

Harwell See **Hartwell**

Harwill See **Hartwell**

Harwin See **Hardwin**

Harwood See **Hartwood**

Hasheem See **Hashim**

Hashim [Arabic]
'Destroyer of evil'.

Haslett [Anglo-Saxon]
'Hazel tree grove on the

headland'.
(Haslitt, Hazlett, Hazlitt)

Haslitt See **Haslett**

Hassan [Arabic]
'Handsome'.

Hastings [Anglo-Saxon]
'Son of violence'.

Havelock [Norse]
'Sea battle'.
(Havlock)

Haven [Anglo-Saxon]
'A place of safety'.

Hawley [Anglo-Saxon]
'From the hedged
meadow'.

Hayden [Teutonic]
'From the hedged valley'.
(Haydon)

Hayes [Old English]
'From the hedged forest'.

Hayward [Anglo-Saxon]
'Keeper of the hedged
field'.
(Heyward)

Haywood [Anglo-Saxon]
'From the hedged forest'.
(Heywood)

Hearne See **Ahern**

Heath [Anglo-Saxon]
'Heathland'.

Heathcliff [Anglo-Saxon]
'From the heather cliff'.
(Heathcliffe)

Hebert See **Herbert**

Heck See **Hector**

Hector [Greek]
'Steadfast, unswerving;
holds fast'.
*(Eachan, Eachann,
Eachunn, Heck)*

Heddwyn [Welsh]
'Blessed peace'.

Hedley [Old English]
'Blessed peace'.

Heinrich See **Henry**

Henderson [Old English]
'Son of Henry'.

Hendrick See **Henry**

Henley See **Hanley**

Henry [Teutonic]
'Ruler of the estate'. Lord
of the Manor.
*(Hamlin, Heinrich,
Heinrick, Hendrick,
Henri, Henrik, Eanruig,
Hanraoi, Harry, Hal,
Hank)*

Herald See **Harold**

Herb See **Herbert**

Herbert [Teutonic]
'Brilliant warrior'.
*(Harbert, Hebert,
Hoireabard, Herb, Herbie,
Bert)*

Herbie See **Herbert**

Hercules [Latin]
'Glory of Hera'.

Hereford See **Harford**

Heriberto See **Herbert**

Herm See **Herman**

Herman [Teutonic]
'Army warrior'.
*(Harman, Harmon,
Hermann, Ermin,
Armand, Herm, Hermie,
Armin, Armond, Armyn,
Hermon)*

Hermie See **Herman**

Hermon See **Herman**

Hernando See **Ferdinand**

Herold See **Harold**

Herrick [Teutonic]
'Army ruler'.

Herrick See **Harold**

Herschel [Hebrew]
'Deer'.

Herv See **Harvey**

Hervey See **Harvey**

Herwin [Teutonic]
'Lover of war; battle
companion'.

Hewe See **Hugh**

Hewett [Anglo-Saxon]
'Little Hugh'.

Heywood See **Haywood**

Hezekiah [Hebrew]
'God is strength'. Belief in
God arms this man against
all adversity.

Hiatt See **Hyatt**

Hilary [Latin]
'Cheerful and merry'.
(Hillary, Hillery, Hilaire)

Hildebrand [Teutonic]
'Sword of war'.

Hillel [Hebrew]
'Greatly praised'.

Hilliard [Teutonic]
'War guardian; brave in
battle'.
(Hillier, Hillyer)

Hillier See **Hilliard**

Hilton [Anglo-Saxon]
'From the hill farm'.
(Hylton)

Himmet [Turkish]
'Support, help'.

Hiram [Hebrew]
'Most noble and exalted
one'.
(Hyram, Hi, Hy)

Hobart See **Hubert**

Hobbard See **Hubert**

Hogan [Celtic]
'Youth'.

Hoibeard See **Hubert**

Hoireabard See **Herbert**

Holbrook [Anglo-Saxon]
'From the brook in the
valley'.

Holcomb [Anglo-Saxon]
'Deep valley'.
*(Holcombe, Holecomb,
Holecombe)*

Holden [Anglo-Saxon/
Teutonic]
'From the valley' or 'Kind'.

Holgate [Anglo-Saxon]
'Gatekeeper'.

Holger [Scandinavian]
'Faithful warrior'.

Hollis [Anglo-Saxon]
'Dweller in the holly
grove'.

Holman [Dutch]
'Man from the hollow'.

Holmes [Anglo-Saxon]
'From the island in the
river'.

Holt [Anglo-Saxon]
'From the forest'.

Homer [Greek]
'A pledge'.

Horace [Latin]
'Time keeper; hours of the
sun'.
(Horatio, Horatius, Race)

Horatio See **Horace**

Horatius See **Horace**

Horst [German]
'From the thicket'.

Horton [Anglo-Saxon]
'From the grey farm'.

Hosea [Hebrew]
'Salvation'.

Houghton [Anglo-Saxon]
'From the estate on the
cliff'.

Houston [Anglo-Saxon]
'From the town in the
mountains'.

Howard [Anglo-Saxon]
'Chief guardian'.
(Howie)

Howe [Teutonic]
'The eminent one'. A
personage of high birth.

Howell [Celtic]
'Little, alert one'.
(Hywel, Hywell)

Howie See **Howard**

Howland [Anglo-Saxon]
'Dweller on the hill'.

Hoyt See **Hubert**

Hube See **Hubert**

Hubert [Teutonic]
'Brilliant, shining mind'.
*(Hobart, Hubbard, Hoyt,
Hugh, Hube, Bert,
Hoibeard, Hugo, Hughes,
Huey, Hughy, Hughie,
Aodh, Aoidh)*

Hudson [Anglo-Saxon]
'Son of the hoodsman'.

Huey See **Hubert**

Hugh See **Hubert**

Hughes See **Hubert**

Hugo See **Hubert**

Hulbard See **Hulbert**

Hulbert [Teutonic]
'Graceful'.
*(Hulbard, Hulburd,
Hulburt)*

Humbert [Teutonic]
'Brilliant Hun' or 'Bright
home'.

(Umberto, Humbie, Bert, Bertie, Berty)

Humbie See **Humbert**

Humph See **Humphrey**

Humphrey [Teutonic]
'Protector of the peace'.
(Humfrey, Humfry, Hump, Humph)

Hunt See **Hunter**

Hunter [Anglo-Saxon]
'A hunter'.
(Hunt)

Huntingdon [Anglo-Saxon]
'Hill of the hunter'.

Huntington [Anglo-Saxon]
'Hunting estate'.

Huntly [Anglo-Saxon]
'From the hunter's meadow'.
(Huntley)

Hurlbert [Teutonic]
'Brilliant army leader'.

Hurley [Gaelic]
'Sea tide'.

Hurst [Anglo-Saxon]

'One who lives in the forest'.
(Hearst)

Hussein [Arabic]
'Little and handsome'.

Hutton [Anglo-Saxon]
'From the farm on the ridge'.

Huxford [Anglo-Saxon]
'Hugh's Ford'.

Huxley [Anglo-Saxon]
'Hugh's meadow'.

Hy See **Hiram**

Hyatt [Anglo-Saxon]
'From the high gate'.
(Hiatt)

Hyde [Anglo-Saxon]
'From the hide of land'. An old unit of measurement of land'.

Hyman [Hebrew]
'Life'. The divine spark.
(Hymen, Hymie, Hy)

Hymie See **Hyman**

Hywel See **Howell**

Hywell See **Howell**

Girls

Ian See **Ianthe**

Ianira [Greek]
'Enchantress'.

Iantha See **Ianthe**

Ianthe [Greek]
'Violet coloured flower'.
(Iantha, Ianthina, Ian,
Janthina, Janthine)

Ianthina See **Ianthe**

Ida [Teutonic]
'Happy'. Name comes
from Mount Ida in Crete,
where Jupiter is supposed
to have been hidden.
(Idalia, Idaline, Idalina,
Idelea, Idelia, Idalia,
Idella, Idalle, Idelle)

Idalia See **Ida**

Idalia [Spanish]
'Sunny'.

Idalina See **Ida**

Idaline See **Ida**

Idalle See **Ida**

Idelea See **Ida**

Idelia [Teutonic]
'Noble'.

Idella See **Ida**

Idelle See **Ida**

Idonia See **Iduna**

Idonie See **Iduna**

Iduna [Norse]
'Lover'. The keeper of the
golden apples of youth.
(Idonia, Idonie)

Ierne [Latin]
'From Ireland'.

Ignatia [Latin]
'Fiery ardour'. Fem. of
Ignatius.
(Ignacia)

Ignatia See **Iniga**

Ila [French]
'From the island'.
(Ilde)

Ilana [Hebrew]
'Tree'.

Ilde See **Ila**

Ileana [Greek]
'Of Ilion (Troy)'.

Ileana See **Aileen**

Ilena See **Helen**

Ilka [Slavic]
'Flattering'.

Illona See **Aileen**

Ilona See **Helen**

Ilse See **Elizabeth**

Iluminada [Spanish]
'Illuminated'.

Imelda [Latin]
'Wishful'.
(Imalda, Melda)

Immaculada [Spanish]
'Immaculate Conception'.

Imogene [Latin]
'Image of her mother'.
(Imogen)

Imperial [Latin]
'Imperial one'.

Ina See **Agnes**

Ines See **Agnes**

Inessa See **Agnes**

Inez See **Agnes**

Inga See **Ingrid**

Ingaberg See **Ingrid**

Ingeborg See **Ingrid**

Ingrid [Norse]
'Hero's daughter'. Child of
a warrior.
*(Inga, Inger, Ingunna,
Ingaberg, Ingeborg,
Ingebiorg, Ingibiorg)*

Ingunna See **Ingrid**

Iniga [Latin]
'Fiery ardour'.
(Ignatia)

Inocencia [Spanish]
'Innocence'.

Iola [Greek]
'Colour of the dawn
cloud'.
(Iole)

Iolanthe [Greek]
'Violet flower'.
(Yolanda, Yolande)

Iolanthe See **Violet**

Iole See **Iola**

Iona See **Ione**

Ione [Greek]
'Violet coloured stone'.
(Iona)

Iphigenia [Greek]
'Sacrifice'.

Iphigenia [Greek]
'Sacrifice'. In mythology
the daughter of the Greek
leader Agamemnon. In
one myth she was
sacrificed to a goddess; in
another she was saved.

Irene [Greek]
'Peace'. The Goddess of
Peace.
*(Eirene, Eirena, Erena,
Irena, Irina, Irenna,
Renata, Rena, Rene,
Reini, Rennie, Renny)*

Irenna See **Irene**

Ireta [Latin]
'Enraged one'.
(Iretta, Irette, Irete)

Irette See **Ireta**

Iris [Greek]
'The rainbow'. The
messenger of the Gods.

Irisa See **Iris**

Irma [Latin or Teutonic]
'Noble person' (Latin);
'Strong' (Teutonic).
*(Erma, Erme, Irmina,
Irmine, Irme)*

Irmina See **Irma**

Irmine See **Irma**

Irvetta See **Irvette**

Irvette [English]
'Sea friend'.
(Irvetta)

Isa [Teutonic]
'Lady of the iron will'. A
determined lass.

Isabeau See **Isabel**

Isabel [Hebrew]
Spanish form of Elizabeth,
q.v.
*(Isabella, Isabelle, Isobel,
Isbel, Ishbel, Ysabel,
Isabeau, Ysabeau, Ysobel,
Ysabella, Ysabelle,
Ysobella, Ysobelle, Bella,*
Belle, Bel) and the
variations of Elizabeth

Isabella See **Isabel**

Isadora [Greek]
'The gift of Isis'.
*(Isidora, Isidore, Isadore,
Dora, Dori, Dory, Issie,
Issy, Izzy)*

Isadore See **Isadora**

Isbel See **Isabel**

Isidora See **Isadora**

Isis [Egyptian]
'Supreme goddess'. The
Goddess of Fertility.

Isleen See **Aileen**

Ismena [Greek]
'Learned'.

Isoda See **Isolde**

Isola [Latin]
'The isolated one'. A
'loner'.

Isolabella [Combination
Isola/Bella]
'Beautiful lonely one'.
(Isolabelle)

Isolabelle See **Isolabella**

Isolde [Celtic]
'The fair one'.
*(Isoda, Ysolda, Ysolde,
Yseult, Iseult, Esyllt)*

Issie See **Isadora**

Ita [Caelic]
'Desire for truth'.
(Ite)

Ite See **Ita**

Iva [French]
'The yew tree'.
(Ivanna, Ivanne)

Ivanna See **Iva**

Ivanne See **Iva**

Iverna [Latin]
An old name for Ireland.

Ivonne See **Yvonne**

Ivory [Welsh]
'Highborn lady'.

Ivy [English]
'A vine'. The sacred plant
of the ancient religions.

Ian [Celtic]
'God is gracious'. See also
John.
(Iain, Iaian)

Ibrahim See **Abraham**

Icarus [Greek]
'Dedicated to the moon'.

Ichabod [Hebrew]
'The glory has departed'.

Iden [Anglo-Saxon]
'Prosperous'.

Idris [Welsh]
'Fiery Lord'.

Idwal [Welsh]
'Wall lord'.

Iestin See **Justin**

Ignace See **Ignatius**

Ignacio See **Ignatius**

Ignate See **Ignatius**

Ignatius [Latin]
'The ardent one'. A fiery
patriot.
*(Inigo, Ignace, Ignate,
Ignacio, Ignatius)*

Ignazio See **Ignatius**

Igor [Scandinavian]
'The hero'.

Ikar [Russian]
'Ancient legendary hero'.

Ike See **Isaac**

Ikey See **Isaac**

Ilia [Russian]
'Equivalent of Elias'.

Illan [Basque]
'Equivalent of Julian'.

Illtyd [Welsh]
'Ruler of a district'.

Immanuel See **Emmanuel**

Ingeborg [Scandinavian]
'Protection'.

Ingemar [Norse]
'Famous son'.
(Ingmar)

Inger [Norse]
'A son's army'.
(Ingar, Ingvar)

Inglebert [Teutonic]
'Brilliant angel'.
(Englebert, Engelbert)

Ingram [Teutonic]
'The raven' or 'The raven's son'.
(Ingraham)

Ingvar See **Inger**

Inigo See **Ignatius**

Inir [Welsh]
'Honour'.

Inness [Celtic]
'From the island in the river'.
(Innes, Innis, Iniss)

Iorweth [Welsh]
'Lord Worth'.

Iorwyn [Welsh]
'Fair lord'.

Ira [Hebrew]
'The watcher'.

Iram [Arabic]
'Mountain peak; crown of the head'.

Irfon [Welsh]
'Annointed one'.

Irvin See **Irving**

Irving [Anglo-Saxon/ Celtic]
'Sea friend' (Anglo-Saxon) or 'White river' (Welsh/ Celtic)
(Irvin, Irvine, Irwin, Erwin)

Irwin See **Irving**

Isaac [Hebrew]
'The laughing one'.
(Isaak, Izaak, Ike, Ikey, Ikie)

Isaam [Arabic]
'Noble'.

Isaiah [Hebrew]
'God is my helper'.

Isham [Anglo-Saxon]
'From the estate of the iron man'.

Ishmael [Hebrew]
'The wanderer'.

Isidore [Greek]
'The gift of Isis'.
(Isidor, Isador, Isadore,
Issy, Iz, Izzy, Izzie)

Iskander [Ethiopian]
'Equivalent of Alexander'.

Isoep See **Joseph**

Israel [Hebrew]
'The Lord's soldier'. The
warrior of god.
(Issie, Izzie)

Istvan [Hungarian]
'Equivalent of Stephen'.

Ithel [Welsh]
'Lord-generous'.

Ivan See **John**

Ivar [Norse]
'Battle archer'. The
warrior with the long bow.
(Iver, Ivor, Ives, Ivon, Ivo,
Ives, Iven)

Iven See **Ivar**

Ives [Anglo-Saxon]
'Son of the archer' or der.
of Ivar.

Ives See **Ivar**

Ivo See **Ivar**

Ivon See **Ivar**

Ivor [Welsh]
'Lord'.
(Ifor)

Ivor See **Ivar**

Iz See **Isidore**

Izzie See **Isidore**

Girls

Jacenta See **Jacinda**

Jacinda [Greek]
'Beautiful and comely'.
Also a var. of Hyacinth.
(*Jacenta*)

Jacinth See **Hyacinth**

Jacintha See **Hyacinth**

Jacinthia See **Hyacinth**

Jackie See **Hyacinth** or
Jacqueline

Jacklyn See **Jacqueline**

Jacoba [Latin]
'The supplanter'. The
understudy who is better
than the star.
(*Jacobina, Jacobine*)

Jacobina See **Jacoba**

Jacobine See **Jacoba**

Jacqueline [Hebrew]
'The supplanter'.
*(Jacqueleine, Jacquelyn,
Jacquetta, Jacketta,
Jackelyn, Jackeline,
Jackie, Jacky, Jamesina,
Jacobina)*

Jacquetta See **Jacqueline**

Jacqui See **Jacqueline**

Jade [Spanish]
'Daughter'. A mother's
most precious jewel.

Jaffa [Hebrew]
'Beautiful'.

Jagoda [Slavonic]
'Strawberry'.

Jaime [French]
'I love'.
(Jaimee, Jamie, Jamey)

Jaimey See **Jaime**

Jakinda See **Hyacinth**

Jala [Arabic]
'Clarity'.

Jalila [Arabic]
'Great'.

Jamesina See **Jacqueline**

Jamila [Muslim]
'Beautiful'.

Jan See **Jane**

Jana See **Jane**

Jane [Hebrew]
'God's gift of grace'. With
Mary the most
consistently popular girl's
name, defying fashion and
whim. A selection of
variations:
*(Jan, Jana, Janet,
Janette, Janetta, Janice,
Janina, Janna, Jayne,
Jean, Jeanne, Jeannette,
Jeanette, Jenette, Joan,
Joana, Joanna, Joanne,
Johanna, Johanne,
Juana, Juanita, Sinead,
Shena, Sheena, Sine,
Sean, Seon, Seonaid)*

Janet See **Jane**

Janetta See **Jane**

Janice See **Jane**

Janina See **Jane**

Janna See **Jane**

Janthina See **Ianthe**

Janthine See **Ianthe**

Jaquith See **Jacqueline**

Jarita [Hindi]
'Legendary bird'.

Jarmila [Slavic]
'Spring'.

Jarvia [Teutonic]
'Keen as a spear'.

Jasmin [Persian]
'Fragrant flower'.
(*Jasmina, Jasmine,
Jessamine, Jessamyn,
Jessamy, Jessamie,
Yasmin, Yasmina*)

Jasmina See **Jasmin**

Jaymee See **Jaime**

Jayne [Sanskrit]
'God's victorious smile'.
Also a var. of Jane.

Jaynell See **Jane**

Jean See **Jane**

Jeanette See **Jane**

Jemie See **Jemina**

Jemina [Hebrew]
'The dove'. Symbol of
peace.
(*Jemie, Jemmie, Mina*)

Jena [Arabic]
'A small bird'.

Jenda See **Jane**

Jeniece See **Jane**

Jennifer See **Genevieve** or
Guinevere

Jeremia [Hebrew]
'The Lord's exalted'. Fem.
of Jeremiah.
(*Jeri, Jerrie, Jerry*)

Jeri See **Geraldine** or
Jeremia

Jerri See **Geraldine**

Jerusha [Hebrew]
'The married one'. The
perfect wife.
(*Yerusha*)

Jessalyn See **Jessica**

Jessamine See **Jasmin**

Jessamy See **Jasmin**

Jessica [Hebrew]
'The rich one'.
(*Jessalyn*)

Jessie [Hebrew]
'God's grace'.

Jewel [Latin]
'Most precious one'. The
ornament of the home.

Jill See **Julia** or **Gillian**

Jillie See **Gillian**

Jinny See **Virginia**

Jinx [Latin]
'Charming spell'. One who
can enchant with her
beauty and grace.
(Jynx)

Joakima [Hebrew]
'The Lord's Judge'.
(Joachima)

Joan See **Jane**

Joana See **Jane**

Joanne See **Jane**

Jobina [Hebrew]
'The afflicted'. Fem. of
Job.
(Jobyna)

Joby [Hebrew]
'Persecuted'. A feminine
form of Job.

Jocasta [Greek]
'Shining moon'.

Joccoaa [Latin]
'The humorous one'. Girl
with a lively wit.

Jocelyn [Latin]
'Fair and just'. Fem. of
Justin.
*(Jocelyne, Joceline,
Jocelin, Joscelyn,
Joscelyne, Joscelin,
Josceline, Joslin, Josline,
Joselin, Joseline,
Joselyn, Joselyne,
Joselen, Joselene,
Josilin, Josiline, Josilyn,
Josilyne, Josilen,
Josilene, Justine,
Justina, Lyn, Lynne)*

Jodie See **Judith**

Jody See **Judith**

Joelle [Hebrew]
'The Lord is willing'.

Joette See **Josephine**

Johanna See **Jane**

Jolee See **Jolie**

Joleen See **Jolene**

Jolene [Middle English]
'He will increase'.

Joletta See **Joliette**

Jolie [French]
'Pretty'.

Joliette [French]
'Violet'.

Joly See **Jolie**

Jolyn See **Jolene**

Joni See **Jane**

Jonquil [Latin]
'Flower-name'.

Jordana [Hebrew]
'The descending'.

Joseline See **Jocelyn**

Josepha See **Josephine**

Josephina See **Josephine**

Josephine [Hebrew]
'She shall add'. Fem. of
Joseph.
*(Josepha, Josephina,
Joette, Josette, Josetta,
Jo, Josie, Fifi, Yusepha,
Yosepha)*

Josetta See **Josephine**

Josette See **Josephine**

Josie See **Josephine**

Joslin See **Jocelyn**

Jovita [Latin]
'The joyful one'. The fem.
of Jove the bringer of
jollity.

Joy See **Joyce**

Joyce [Latin]
'Gay and joyful'.
*(Joy, Joice, Joyous,
Joycelyn, Joicelin,
Joicelyn, Joycelin)*

Joyous See **Joyce**

Juana See **June**

Juanita See **Jane**

Judith [Hebrew]
'Admired, praised'. One
whose praises cannot be
sufficiently sung.
*(Juditha, Judie, Judy,
Jodie, Judy, Siobhan,
Siuban)*

Juditha See **Judith**

Judy See **Judith**

Julia [Greek]
'Youthful'. Young in heart
and mind.
*(Julie, Juliana, Juliane,
Julianna, Julianne,
Juliet, Julietta, Julina,
Juline, Jill, Juli, Sile,
Sileas)*

Juliana See **Julia**

Juliane See **Julia**

Julie See **Julia**

Juliet See **Julia**

Julietta See **Julia**

Julina See **Julia**

Juline See **Julia**

Jumanah [Arabic]
'Pearl'.

Juna See **June**

June [Latin]
'Summer's child'. One
born in the early summer.
*(Juna, Junia, Juniata,
Junette, Junine, Juana)*

Junette See **June**

Junia See **June**

Juniata See **June**

Junine See **June**

Juno [Latin]
'Heavenly being'. The wife
of Jupiter, ruler of the
heavens.

Jurisa [Slavonic]
'Storm'.

Justina See **Jocelyn**

Justine See **Jocelyn**

Jutta [Latin]
'Near'.

Jyoti [Hindi]
'Light'.

Jabez [Hebrew]
'Cause of sorrow'.

Jacinto [Spanish]
'Purple flower'.

Jack See **John**

Jackie See **John**

Jackson [Old English]
'Son of Jack'.

Jacob [Hebrew]
'The supplanter'.
*(Jacobus, Jacques,
Jamie, Jim, Jimmie,
Jimmy, Jas, Hamish,
Diego, Seamus, Shamus,
Jem, Jemmie, Jemmy,
Jock, Jocko)*

Jacobus See **Jacob**

Jacques See **Jacob**

Jael [Hebrew]
'To ascend'.

Jagger [Northumbrian]
'A carter'.

Jalaad [Arabic]
'Glory'.

Jaleel [Arabic]
'Majestic'.

Jamaal See **Jamal**

Jamal [Arabic]
'Beauty'.

James See **Jacob**

Jamie See **Jacob**

Jamil [Arabic]
'Handsome'.

Jan See **John**

Janos See **John**

Japhet [Hebrew]
'Youthful, beautiful'.

Jared [Hebrew]
'The descendant'.

Jarid See **Jared**

Jarman [Teutonic]
'The German'.
(Jerman, Jermyn)

Jaron [Hebrew]
'Sing out, cry out'.

Jaroslav [Slavic]
'Praise of spring'.

Jarrad See **Jared**

Jarratt [Teutonic]
'Strong spear'.

Jarrett See **Garrett**

Jarrod See **Jared**

Jarv See **Gervase**

Jarvey See **Gervase**

Jarvis See **Gervase**

Jas See **Jacob**

Jason [Greek]
'The healer'.

Jasper See **Gaspar**

Jasun See **Jason**

Javier See **Xavier**

Jay [Anglo-Saxon]
'Jay or crow'. Also used as
dim. for any name
beginning with J.

Jean See **John**

Jed See **Jedediah**

Jedediah [Hebrew]
'Beloved by the Lord'.
(Jed, Jedidiah, Jeddy)

Jeffers See **Geoffrey**

Jefferson [Anglo-Saxon]
'Jeffrey's son'.

Jeffrey See **Geoffrey**

Jehiel [Hebrew]
'May God live'.

Jehoshaphat [Hebrew]
'The Lord judges'.

Jem See **Jacob**

Jemmie See **Jacob**

Jeramey See **Jeremy**

Jere See **Jeremy**

Jeremiah See **Jeremy**

Jeremias See **Jeremy**

Jeremy [Hebrew]
'Exalted by the Lord'.
*(Jeremiah, Jeremias,
Jerry)*

Jermyn See **Jarman**

Jerome [Latin]
'Sacred; holy'. A man of
God.
(Jerome, Gerome, Jerry)

Jerrold See **Gerald**

Jerry See **Jeremy**

Jervis See **Gervase**

Jervoise See **Gervase**

Jesse [Hebrew]
'God's gift'. *(Jess)*

Jesus [Hebrew]
'God will help'.

Jethro [Hebrew]
'Excellent; without equal'.

Jevon See **John**

Jim See **Jacob**

Jimmy See **Jacob**

Joachim [Hebrew]
'Judgement of the Lord'.

Joaquin See **Joachim**

Job [Hebrew]
'The persecuted; the
afflicted'.

Jock See **Jacob, James** or
John

Jocko See **Jacob**

Jodel [Latin]
'Sportive'.

Jodi See **Joseph**

Jody See **Joseph**

Joe See **Joel**

Joel [Hebrew]
'The Lord is God'.
(Joe, Joey)

Joey See **Joel**

Johan See **John**

John [Hebrew]
'God's gracious gift'. The
most consistently popular
boy's name.
*(Jon, Jean, Jack, Jock,
Jevon, Jan, Janos,
Johan, Johann, Jackie,
Johnnie, Johnny, Sean,
Shawn, Shane, Sian,
Evan, Ivan, Ian, Gian,
Hans, Zane, Iain, Iaian,
Eoin, Seain, Seann)*

Johnnie See **John**

Joliet See **Julius**

Jolyon See **Julius**

Jon See **Jonathan**

Jonah [Hebrew]
'Peace'.

Jonas [Hebrew]
'Dove'. A man of peace and
tranquillity'.

Jonathan [Hebrew]
'Gift of the Lord'.
(Jon, Jonathon)

Jordan [Hebrew]
'The descending river'.
(Jordon, Jourdain)

Jorens [Norse]
'Laurel'.

Jorgen See **George**

Jorin See **George**

Jorin [Spanish, from
Hebrew]
'Child of freedom'.

Joris See **George**

Joseph [Hebrew]
'He shall add'.
*(Joe, Joey, Jose, Isoep,
Seosaidh, Josiah)*

Josh See **Joshua**

Joshua [Hebrew]
'God's salvation'. A man
saved by his belief in God.
(Josh)

Josiah See **Joseph**

Jotham [Hebrew]
'God is perfect'.

Jozef See **Joseph**

Juan See **John**

Juaud [Arabic]
'Generous'.

Judah See **Judd**

Judd [Hebrew]
'Praised; extolled'.
(Judah, Jude)

Jude See **Judd**

Jule See **Julius**

Jules See **Julius**

Julian See **Julius**

Julie See **Julius**

Julius [Latin]
'Youthful shaveling'.
*(Jules, Julian, Joliet,
Jule, Julie, Jolyon)*

Junius [Latin]
'Born in June'.

Jurgen See **George**

Just See **Justin**

Justin [Latin]
'The just one'. One of
upright principles and
morals.
(Justus, Just, Iestin)

Justinian See **Justin**

Justino See **Justin**

Justis [French]
'Justice'. A strict upholder
of the moral laws.

Justus See **Justin**

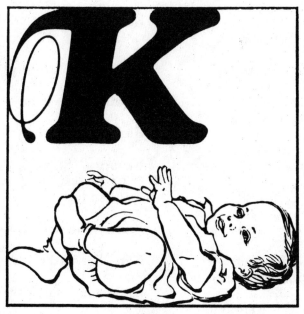

Girls

Kabira [Arabic]
'Powerful'.

Kagami [Japanese]
'Mirror'.

Kairos [Greek]
'Goddess born last to
Jupiter'.

Kala [Hindi]
'Black; time'.

Kalamit [Hebrew]
'Flower'.

Kaleena See **Kalinda**

Kali [Sanskrit]
'Energy'.

Kalila [Arabic]
'Beloved'.
(Kally, Kaylee, Kylila)

Kalinda [Sanskrit]
'Sun'.

Kalindi See **Kalinda**

Kally See **Kalila**

Kalonice [Greek]
'Beauty's victory'.

Kalyca [Greek]
'Rosebud'.

Kama [Sanskrit]
'Love'. The Hindu god of
love, like Cupid.

Kameko [Japanese]
'Child of the tortoise'.

Kamila See **Kamilah**

Kamilah [Arabic]
'The perfect one'.

Kamra [Arabic]
'Moon'.

Kanaka See **Canace**

Kanake See **Canace**

Kanya [Thai]
'Young lady'.

Kara See **Cara**

Karen See **Katherine**

Karena See **Katherine**

Karima [Arabic]
'Generous'.

Karin See **Katherine**

Karina See **Carina**

Karita See **Carita**

Kasmira [Slavic]
'Commands peace'.
(Casmira)

Kassandra See **Cassandra**

Kate See **Catherine**

Katherina See **Katherine**

Katherine [Greek]
'Pure maiden'. Another
spelling of Catherine.
*(Katharine, Katharina,
Katherina, Katheryn,
Kathryn, Katrin, Katrina,
Katryn, Kathleen,
Kathlene, Kitty, Katie,
Kathie, Kay, Kate, Kara,
Karen, Karena, Karin,
Karyn* and all var. of
Catherine*)*

Kathie See **Katherine**

Kathleen See **Katherine**

Kathryn See **Katherine**

Katie See **Katherine**

Katrin See **Katherine**

Katrina See **Catherine** or **Katherine**

Katryn See **Katherine**

Katy See **Catherine**

Kay See **Katherine**

Kayla [Hebrew]
'Crown'.

Kaylee See **Kalila**

Keely [Gaelic]
'The beautiful one'.

Kelci See **Kelsey**

Kelda [Norse]
'Bubbling spring'.
(Kelly)

Kelila [Hebrew]
'Crown; laurel'.

Kellina See **Kelly**

Kelly [Irish Gaelic]
'Warrior maid'.

Kelsey [Scandinavian]
'From the ship island'.

Kelsi See **Kelsey**

Kelula See **Kelila**

Kendra [Old English]
'Knowledgeable'.

Kenna See **Kendra**

Keren [Hebrew]
'Horn of antimoney'.

Kerrianne See **Kerry**

Kerridwen See **Ceiridwen**

Kerry [Gaelic]
'Dark one'.
(Kerri)

Kesia [African]
'Favourite'.

Kesley See **Kelsey**

Ketti See **Katherine**

Ketura [Hebrew]
'Incense'.

Kevin [Gaelic]
'Gentle and lovable'.
(Kelvina)

Kevina See **Kevin**

Kevyn See **Kevin**

Khalida [Arabic]
  'Immortal, everlasting'.

Khalipha [Arabic]
  'Successor'.

Kiah [African]
  'Season's beginning'.

Kial See **Kyle**

Kim [Origin not known]
  'Noble chief'.

Kimberley [English]
  'From the royal meadow'.

Kimberlyn See **Kimberley**

Kimbra See **Kimberley**

Kina [Greek]
  'Christian'.

Kineta [Greek]
  'Active and elusive'.

Kinnnereth [Hebrew]
  'From the Sea of Galilee'.

Kiona [N. American
  Indian]
  'Brown hills'.

Kira [Persian]
  'Sun'.

Kirbee See **Kirby**

Kirbie See **Kirby**

Kirby [Old English]
  'From the church town'.

Kirima [Eskimo]
  'A hill'.

Kirsten See **Kirstin**

Kirstie See **Kirstin**

Kirstin [Norse]
  'The annointed one'.
  (Kirstina, Kirstie, Kirsty)

Kirstina See **Kirstin**

Kirstyn See **Kirstin**

Kit See **Catherine**

Kitty See **Catherine**

Kohana [Japanese]
  'Little flower'.

Kolina [Greek]
  'Pure'.

Kora [Greek]
  'Young girl, maiden'.

Korella See **Kora**

Koren [Greek]
'Beautiful maiden'.

Koressa See **Kora**

Kristen See **Christine**

Krystyna See **Christine**

Kurva [Japanese]
'Mulberry tree'.

Kyla [Gaelic]
'Comely'.
(Kilah, Kylah, Kylie)

Kylie See **Kyla**

Kylynn See **Kyle**

Kyna [Gaelic]
'Great wisdom'.

Kyrenia See **Cyrena**

Kadmiel [Hebrew]
'God is the ancient one'.

Kadri [Arabic]
'My destiny'.

Kahaleel See **Kalil**

Kalil [Arabic]
'Good friend'.

Kamal [Arabic]
'Perfect'.

Kane [Celtic]
'Little, warlike one' or
'Radiant brightness'.

Kaniel [Arabic]
'Spear'.

Kano [Japanese]
'God of waters'.

Kareem [Arabic]
'Noble'.

Karim See **Kareem**

Karl See **Charles**

Karlan See **Charles**

Karlens See **Charles**

Karney See **Kearney**

Karr See **Carr**

Karsten [Slavonic]
'Christian'.

Kaspar See **Gaspar**

Kavan See **Cavan**

Kay [Celtic]
'Rejoiced in'. Also dim.
for any name beginning
with K.

Kayne See **Kane**

Kean [Irish]
'Fast'.

Keane [Anglo-Saxon]
'Bold and handsome'. A
sharp witted man.

Kearney See **Carney**

Kedar [Arabic]
'Powerful'.

Keefe [Celtic]
'Handsome, noble and
admirable'.

Keegan [Celtic]
'Little fiery one'.

Keelan [Celtic]
'Little slender one'.

Keelby See **Kelby**

Keeley [Celtic]
'Little, handsome one'.

Keen See **Keenan**

Keenan [Celtic]
'Little ancient one'.

Keir [Teutonic]
'Ever king'.

Keith [Celtic]
'A place' or 'From the
forest' (Welsh).

Kelbee See **Kelby**

Kelby [Old German]
'From the farm by the
spring'.

Kell [Norse]
'From the well'.

Kellen See **Kelly**

Keller [Gaelic]
'Little companion'.

Kelly [Gaelic]
'The warrior'.
(Kelley)

Kelsey [Norse/Teutonic]
'Dweller on the island'
(Norse) or 'From the
water' (Teutonic).

Kelton [Celtic]
'Celtic town'.

Kelvin [Gaelic]
'From the narrow stream'.
(Kelvan, Kelven)

Kelwin See **Kelvin**

Kembell See **Kimball**

Kemp [Anglo-Saxon]
'The warrior champion'.

Ken See **Kendall** or
Kenneth

Kendall [Celtic]
'Chief of the valley'.
(Kendal, Kendell, Ken)

Kendrick [Gaelic/
Anglo-Saxon]
'Son of Henry' (Gaelic) or
'Royal ruler' (Anglo-
Saxon)

Kenelm [Anglo-Saxon]
'Brave helmet'. A
courageous protector.

Kenley [Anglo-Saxon]
'Owner of a royal
meadow'.

Kenn [Celtic]
'Clear as bright water'.

Kennan See **Kenn**

Kennard [Anglo-Saxon]
'Bold and vigorous'.

Kennedy [Gaelic]
'The helmeted chief'.

Kennet See **Kenneth**

Kenneth [Celtic]
'The handsome' or
'Royal oath'.
*(Keneth, Kennet, Ken,
Kenny, Kent)*

Kennith See **Kenneth**

Kenny See **Kenneth**

Kenon See **Kenn**

Kenrick [Anglo-Saxon]
'Bold ruler'.

Kent [Celtic]
'Bright and white'. Also
dim. of Kenneth.

Kent See **Kenneth**

Kenton [Anglo-Saxon]
'From the royal estate'.

Kenward [Anglo-Saxon]
'Bold guardian'.

Kenway [Anglo-Saxon]
'Bold or royal warrior'.

Kenyon [Celtic]
'White haired'.

Kermit [Celtic]
'A free man'.
(Dermot, Derry, Kerry)

Kern [Gaelic]
'Little dark one'.

Kerr See **Carr** or **Kirby**

Kerry [Gaelic]
'Son of the dark one'.

Kerry See **Kermit**

Kerwin [Gaelic]
'Small black haired one'.

Kester [Anglo-Saxon]
'From the army camp'.

Also used as dim. of
Christopher.

Kester [Latin]
'Of the Roman camp'.

Kevan See **Kevin**

Kevin [Gaelic]
'Gentle, kind and lovable'.
(Kevan, Keven, Kev)

Kevon See **Kevin**

Key [Gaelic]
'Son of the fiery one'.

Khalid [Arabic]
'Immortal'.

Khalil [Arabic]
'Friend'.

Khalipha [Arabic]
'Successor'.

Khayam [Arabic]
'Tent maker'.

Kiel See **Kyle**

Kienan See **Keenan**

Kieran [Gaelic]
'Small and dark skinned'.
(Kieron, Kerrin, Kerry)

Kiernan See **Kieran**

Kilby [Teutonic]
'Farm by the spring'.

Killian [Gaelic]
'Little warlike one'.

Killie See **Killian**

Kim See **Kimball**

Kimball [Celtic]
'Royally brave' or
'Warrior chief'.
*(Kimble, Kimbell,
Kemble, Kim)*

Kincaid [Celtic]
'Battle chief'.

King [Anglo-Saxon]
'The sovereign'. The
ruler of his people.

Kingdom [Old English]
'King's hill'.

Kingsley [Anglo-Saxon]
'From the king's meadow'.

Kingston [Anglo-Saxon]
'From the king's farm'.

Kingswell [Anglo-Saxon]
'From the king's well'.

Kinnard [Gaelic]
'From the high

mountain'.
(Kinnaird)

Kinnell [Gaelic]
'Dweller on the top of the cliff'.

Kinsey [Anglo-Saxon]
'Royal victor'.

Kinsley See **Kingsley**

Kipp [Anglo-Saxon]
'Dweller on the pointed hill'.

Kippar See **Kipp**

Kippie See **Kipp**

Kirby [Teutonic]
'From the church village'.
(Kerby, Kerr)

Kirin [Latin]
'Spearman'.

Kirk [Norse]
'Dweller at the church'.

Kirkley [Anglo-Saxon]
'From the church meadow'.

Kirkwood [Anglo-Saxon]
'From the church wood'.

Kirwin See **Kerwin**

Kit See **Christopher**

Kitron [Hebrew]
'Crown'.

Knight [Anglo-Saxon]
'Mounted soldier'.

Knox [Anglo-Saxon]
'From the hills'.

Knut See **Canute**

Knute See **Canute**

Konrad See **Conrad**

Krisha See **Krishna**

Krishna [Hindu]
'Delightful'.

Kristian See **Christian**

Kristin See **Christian**

Kurt See **Conrad/Curtis**

Kwasi [African]
'Born on Sunday'.

Kyle [Gaelic]
'From the strait'.

Kynan See **Conan**

Kyne [Anglo-Saxon]
'The royal one'.

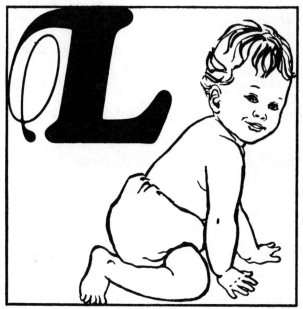

Girls

La Roux [French]
'The red haired one'.
(Larousse, Roux)

Labhaoise See **Louise**

Labiba [Arabic]
'Wise'.

Lacee See **Larissa**

Lacey See **Larissa**

Lacinia See **Lucy**

Lada [Russian]
'Mythological goddess of beauty'.

Ladonna [French]
'The lady'.

Laila See **Layla**

Laina See **Lane**

Lainey See **Elaine**

Lala [Slavic]
'The tulip flower'.

Lalage [Greek]
'Gentle laughter'.

Laleh [Persian]
'Tulip'.

Lalita [Sanskrit]
'Without guile'.

Lalota [Sanskrit]
'Pleasing'.

Lamya [Arabic]
'Dark lips'.

Lana See **Alana**

Lane [Middle English]
'From the narrow road'.

Lanelle [Old French]
'From the little lane'.

Lani [Hawaiian]
'The sky'.

Lara [Latin]
'Famous'.

Laraine See **Lorraine**

Lareena See **Larine**

Larentia [Latin]
'Foster mother'.
(*Laurentia*)

Larianna See **Larine**

Larina See **Lorraine**

Larine [Latin]
'Girl of the sea'.
(*Lareena, Larena,*
Larianna)

Larine See **Lorraine**

Laris See **Larissa**

Larissa [Greek]
'Cheerful maiden'. One
who is as happy as a lark.
(*Lacey*)

Lark [English]
'Singing bird'.

Lasca [Latin]
'Weary one'.

Lassie [Scots]
'Little girl'.

Latona See **Latonia**

Latonia [Latin]
'Belonging to Latona'. Was
the mother of Diana.
(*Latona, Latoya*)

Latoya See **Latonia**

Laura [Latin]
'Laurel wreath'. The
victor's crown of laurels.
*(Laurel, Lauren, Laureen,
Laurena, Laurene,
Lauretta, Laurette, Lora,
Loren, Lorena, Loretta,
Lorette, Lorita, Lorna,
Laure, Lorenza, Loralie,
Lorelie, Lorinda, Lorine,
Lori, Loree, Lorie, Lorrie,
Laurie)*

Laure See **Laura**

Laureen See **Laura**

Laurel See **Laura**

Lauren See **Laura**

Laurena See **Laura**

Laurentia See **Larentia**

Lauretta See **Laura**

Laurette See **Laura**

Laveda [Latin]
'One who is purified'.
(Lavetta, Lavette)

Lavelle [Latin]
'Cleansing'.

Lavena [Celtic]
'Joy'.

Lavender [English]
'Sweet smelling flower'.
(Lavvie)

Laverna See **Laverne**

Laverne [French]
'Spring like' or 'Alder
tree'.
*(Laverna, Verna, Verne,
Vern)*

Lavetta See **Laveda**

Lavette See **Laveda**

Lavina See **Lavinia**

Lavinia [Latin]
'Lady of Rome'.
(Lavina, Vina, Vinia)

Lavvie See **Lavender**

Layla See **Leila**

Layla [Arabic]
'Night'.

Layne See **Lane**

Leah [Hebrew]
'The weary one'.
(Lea, Lee, Leigh)

Leala [French]
'The true one'. One who is true to home, family and friends.

Leandra [Latin]
'Like a lioness'.

Leane See **Liana**

Leanna See **Lee**

Leatrice [Combination Leah/Beatrice]
'Tired but joyful'.
(*Leatrix*)

Leatrix See **Leatrice**

Lechsinska [Polish]
'Woodland spirit'.

Leda [Greek]
'Mother of beauty'. The mother of Helen of Troy.

Leda See **Alida, Letha** or **Letitia**

Lee [English]
'From the fields'. Also a var. of Leah.

Lee See **Leila**

Leeann See **Lee**

Leela See **Leila**

Leigh [Old English]
'From the meadow'.

Leila [Arabic]
'Black as the night'.
(*Leilia, Lela, Lilia, Leilah, Lilah, Leela, Lee*)

Leila See **Lilian**

Leilani [Hawaiian]
'Heavenly blossom'. The tropical flower of the Islands.
(*Lullani, Lillani*)

Leilia See **Leila**

Lela See **Leila** or **Lilian**

Lelia See **Lilian**

Lemma [Ethiopian]
'Developed'.

Lemuela [Hebrew]
'Dedicated to God'. A daughter dedicated to the service of God.
(*Lemuella*)

Lena [Latin]
'Enchanting one'. Also a dim. of Caroline, Madeleine, Helena.
(*Lina*)

Lena See **Helen**

Lene See **Lenis**

Lenette See **Lena**

Lenis [Latin]
'Smooth and white as the lily'.
(*Lene, Lenta, Lenita, Leneta, Lenos*)

Lenita See **Lenis**

Lennie See **Leona**

Lenora See **Helen**

Lenore See **Eleanor**

Lenos See **Lenis**

Lenta See **Lenis**

Leocadia [Spanish from Greek]
'Lionlike'.

Leoda [Teutonic]
'Woman of the people'.
(*Leola, Leota*)

Leodora See **Leandra**

Leola See **Leoda**

Leoline See **Leandra**

Leoma [Anglo-Saxon]
'Bright light'. One who

casts radiance around her.

Leona [Latin]
'The lioness'.
(*Leola, Leonie, Leone, Leoni, Lennie, Lenny*)

Leona See **Helen**

Leonarda [French]
'Like a lion'.
(*Leonarde, Leonardina, Leonardine*)

Leonarde See **Leonarda**

Leonardina See **Leonarda**

Leonardine See **Leonarda**

Leone See **Leona**

Leonelle See **Leandra**

Leonelle See **Leona**

Leonie See **Leona**

Leonora See **Eleanor**

Leontina See **Leontine**

Leontine [Latin]
'Like the lion'.
(*Leontina, Leontyne*)

Leopolda See **Leopoldina**

Leopoldina [Teutonic]
'The people's champion'.
Fem. of Leopold.
(Leopoldine, Leopolda)

Leopoldine See
Leopoldina

Leor [Hebrew]
'I have light'.

Leora See **Helen**

Leora [Greek]
'Light'.

Leota See **Leoda**

Les See **Lesley**

Leshem [Hebrew]
'Precious stone'.

Leshia See **Letitia**

Lesley [Celtic]
'Keeper of the grey fort'.
(Leslie, Lesli, Lesly, Les)

Leta See **Letha** or **Letitia**

Letha [Greek]
'Sweet oblivion'. Lethe the
river of forgetfulness.
*(Lethia, Lethitha, Leithia,
Leda, Leta)*

Lethia See **Letha**

Lethitha See **Letha**

Letisha See **Letitia**

Letitia [Latin]
'Joyous gladness'.
*(Laetitia, Leticia, Letizia,
Lettice, Lettie, Leta, Leda,
Tish)*

Lettice See **Letitia**

Lettie See **Letitia**

Levana [Latin]
'The sun of the dawn'. The
Goddess of childbirth.
(Levania)

Levania See **Levana**

Levina [English]
'A bright flash'. One who
passes like a comet.

Lewanna [Hebrew]
'As pure as the white
moon'.
(Luanna)

Lexie See **Alexandra**

Lexine See **Alexandra**

Leya [Spanish]
'Loyalty to the law'. A
strict upholder of morals
and principles.

Leyla [Turkish]
'Night'.

Lian [Chinese]
'The graceful willow'.

Liana [French]
'The climbing vine'.
(*Leane, Leana, Leanna,
Lianna, Lianne*)

Libby See **Elizabeth**

Liberata [Latin]
'Freed'.

Libusa [Russian]
'Beloved'.

Lida [Slavic]
'Beloved of the people'.

Ligia [Greek]
'Silver voice'.

Lila See **Leila**

Lilac [Persian]
'Dark mauve flower'.

Lilais See **Lilian**

Lilian [Latin]
'A lily'. One who is pure in
thought, word and deed.
(*Lillian, Liliana, Lilliana,
Liliane, Lilliane, Lilyan,
Lillyan, Lily, Lili, Lilli,*

*Lilly, Lilias, Lilais, Lillis,
Lela, Lelah, Lelia, Leila,
Lila, Lilah, Lilia, Lilla*)

Lilias See **Lilian**

Lilith [Arabic]
'Woman of the night'.
According to Eastern
belief, Lilith was the first
wife of Adam and the first
woman in the world; Eve
was his second wife.

Lily See **Lilian**

Lilyan See **Lillian**

Lina See **Caroline**

Lind See **Linda**

Linda [Spanish]
'Pretty one'. Also dim. of
Belinda, Rosalinda, etc.
(*Lind, Linde, Lindie,
Lindy, Lynda, Lynd*)

Linda See **Belinda**

Lindie See **Belinda** or
Linda

Lindsay [Old English]
'From the linden tree
island'.
(*Lindsey*)

Line See **Caroline**

Linetta See **Linnet**

Linnea [Norse]
'The lime blossom'.

Linnet [French]
'Sweet bird'.
*(Linnette, Linette,
Linetta, Linnetta, Lynette,
Lynnette)*

Liorah [Hebrew]
'I have light'.

Lisa See **Elizabeth**

Lisandra
Fem. variation of
Alexander.

Lisbeth See **Elizabeth**

Lisha [Arabic]
'The darkness before
midnight'.

Lishe See **Lisha**

Lissie See **Alida**

Lita See **Alida**

Liusade See **Louise**

Livi See **Olga**

Livia See **Olga**

Liyna [Arabic]
'Tender'.

Liza See **Elizabeth**

Lizabeta See **Elizabeth**

Lizzy See **Elizabeth**

Llawela [Welsh]
'Like a ruler'.
(Llawella)

Lodema [English]
'Leader or guide'.

Lodie See **Melody**

Lois See **Louise**

Lola [Spanish]
'Strong woman'.
(Loleta, Lolita, Lollie)

Lola See **Dolores**

Loleta See **Lola**

Lolita See **Dolores**

Lollie See **Lola**

Lomasi [North American
Indian]
'Pretty flower'.

Lona [Anglo-Spanish]
'Solitary watcher'.

Lora See **Helen** or **Laura**

Loralie See **Laura**

Lorelei [Teutonic]
'Siren of the river'. The
Rhine maiden who lured
unwary mariners to their
deaths.
(Lorelie, Lorelia, Lurleen)

Lorelia See **Lorelei**

Lorelle [Latin]
'Little'.

Lorelle [Latin, Old
German]
'Little'.

Loren See **Laura**

Lorena See **Laura**

Lorenza See **Laura**

Loretta See **Laura**

Lori See **Laura**

Lorilyn See **Lorelei**

Lorinda See **Laura**

Lorine See **Laura**

Loris See **Chloris**

Lorita See **Laura**

Lorna See **Laura**

Lorne See **Laura**

Lorraine [Teutonic/
French]
'Renowned in battle'
(Teutonic); 'The Queen'
(French).
*(Loraine, Laraine,
Larraine, Larayne, Larine,
Larina)*

Lotus [Greek]
'Flower of the sacred Nile'.

Louella See **Luella**

Louisa See **Louise**

Louise [Teutonic]
'Famous battle maid'. One
who leads victorious
armies into battle.
*(Louisa, Luise, Lois,
Loise, Louisitte,
Labhaoise, Liusade,
Loyce, Eloise, Eloisa,
Heloise, Aloisa, Aloisia,
Aloysia, Alison, Allison)*

Louisitte See **Louise**

Loutitia See **Letitia**

Love [English]
'Tender affection'.

Loyce See **Louise**

Luana [Teutonic]
'Graceful army maiden'.
(*Luane, Louanna,
Louanne, Luwana,
Luwanna, Luwanne*)

Luane See **Luana**

Luba [Russian]
'Love'.

Lubmila See **Luba**

Lubna [Arabic]
'Flexible'.

Lucette See **Lucy**

Lucia See **Lucy**

Luciana See **Lucy**

Lucianna [Combination
Lucy/Anne]

Lucida See **Lucy**

Lucile See **Lucy**

Lucinda See **Lucy**

Lucita See **Lucy**

Lucrece See **Lucretia**

Lucretia [Latin]
'A rich reward'.
(*Lucrezia, Lucrece,
Lucrecia*)

Lucy [Latin]
'Light'. One who brings
the lamp of learning to the
ignorant.
(*Luciana, Lucida,
Lucinda, Lucile, Lucille,
Lucette, Lucia, Luisadh,
Luighseach*)

Ludella [Anglo-Saxon]
'Pixie maid'.

Ludmilla [Slavic]
'Beloved of the people'.
(*Ludmila*)

Luella [Anglo-Saxon]
'The appeaser'.
(*Louella, Loella, Luelle*)

Luelle See **Luella**

Luighseach See **Lucy**

Luisadh See **Lucy**

Lulita See **Lola**

Lulu [Arabic]
'Pearl'.

Luna See **Lunetta**

Lunetta [Latin]
'Little Moon'.
(Luna, Luneta)

Lupe [Spanish]
'She wolf'. A fierce
guardian of the home.

Lura See **Lurline**

Lurleen See **Lorelei**

Lurlette See **Lurline**

Lurlina See **Lurline**

Lurline [Teutonic]
'Siren'. A version of
Lorelie.
*(Lurlina, Lura, Lurleen,
Lurlene, Lurlette)*

Luvena [Latin]
'Little beloved one'.

Lycoris [Greek]
'Twilight'.

Lydia [Greek]
'Cultured one'.
(Lidia, Lydie, Lidie)

Lydie See **Lydia**

Lynette [English]
'Idol'.
*(Lyn, Lynn, Lynne,
Linnet)*

Lynn [Celtic]
'A waterfall'. Also dim. of
Carolyn, Evelyn, etc.
(Lynne)

Lynne See **Jocelyn**

Lynnea See **Linnea**

Lyonelle [Old French]
'Young lion'.

Lyra See **Lyris**

Lyris [Greek]
'She who plays the harp'.
(Lyra)

Lysandra [Greek]
'The Liberator'. The
prototype of Women's Lib!

Laban [Hebrew]
'White'.

Labhras See **Lawrence**

Labhruinn See **Lawrence**

Labid [Arabic]
'Intelligent'.

Lach [Celtic]
'Dweller by the water'.
(Lache)

Lachlan [Celtic]
'The warlike'.

Lacy [Latin]
'From the Roman manor
house'.

Ladd [Anglo-Saxon]
'Attendant; page'.
(Laddie)

Laddie See **Ladd**

Ladislas [Slavic]
'A glory of power'.

Laibrook [Anglo-Saxon]
'Path by the brook'.

Laidley [Anglo-Saxon]
'From the water meadow'.

Laird [Celtic]
'The land owner'. The lord
of the manor.

Lakshman [Hindi]
'Younger brother of Ram'.

Lamar [Teutonic]
'Famous throughout the
land'.

Lambert [Teutonic]
'Rich in land'. An owner of
vast estates.

Lamech [Hebrew]
'Strong young man'.

Lamond See **Lamont**

Lamont [Norse]
'A lawyer'.
*(Lamond, Lammond,
Lammont)*

Lance See **Lancelot**

Lancelot [French]
'Spear attendant'.
(Launcelot, Launce,

Lancey, Lance)

Lancey See **Lancelot**

Lander [Anglo-Saxon]
'Owner of a grassy plain'.
*(Launder, Landor,
Landers)*

Landers See **Lander**

Landon [Anglo-Saxon]
'Dweller on the long hill'.
(Langdon, Langston)

Landor See **Lander**

Landric [Old German]
'Land ruler'.

Lane [Anglo-Saxon]
'From the narrow road'.

Lanfrance [Italian from
Teutonic]
'Free country'.

Lang [Teutonic]
'Tall or long limbed man'.

Langdon See **Landon**

Langford [Anglo-Saxon]
'Dweller by the long ford'.

Langley [Anglo-Saxon]
'Dweller by the long
meadow'.

Langsdon See **Langston**

Langston [Anglo-Saxon]
'The farm belonging to the
tall man'.

Langston See **Landon**

Langworth [Anglo-Saxon]
'From the long enclosure'.

Lann [Celtic]
'Sword'.

Laris [Latin]
'Cheerful'.

Larrance See **Lawrence**

Larry See **Lawrence**

Lars See **Lawrence**

Larson [Norse]
'Son of Lars'.

Latham [Norse]
'From the barns'.

Lathrop [Anglo-Saxon]
'From the barn farmstead'.

Latimer [Anglo-Saxon]
'The interpreter; the
language teacher'.

Laughton See **Lawton**

Launce See **Lancelot**

Lauren See **Lawrence**

Laurent See **Lawrence**

Lauric See **Lawrence**

Lauritz See **Lawrence**

Lawford [Anglo-Saxon]
'Dweller at the ford by the hill'.

Lawler [Gaelic]
'The mumbler'.

Lawley [Anglo-Saxon]
'From the meadow on the hill'.

Lawrence [Latin]
'Crowned with laurels'.
The victor's crown of bay leaves.
(Laurence, Larrance, Lawrance, Lorenz, Laurent, Lars, Larry, Lauren, Lauric, Lawry, Loren, Lorne, Lorin, Lon, Lonnie, Lorenzo, Lori, Lorrie, Lorry, Lauritz, Labhras, Labhruinn)

Lawson [Anglo-Saxon]
'Son of Lawrence'.

Lawton [Anglo-Saxon]
'From the town on the hill'.

Lazar See **Eleazar**

Lazaro See **Lazarus**

Lazarus See **Eleazar**

Lazhar [Arabic]
'Best appearance'.

Leal [Anglo-Saxon]
'Loyal, true and faithful'.

Leander [Greek]
'The lion man'.

Leandro See **Leander**

Lech [Polish]
'Woodland spirit'.

Ledyard [Teutonic]
'Nation's guardian'.

Lee [Anglo-Saxon/Gaelic]
'From the meadow' (Anglo-Saxon) or 'Poetic' (Gaelic).
(Leigh)

Lee See **Ashley**

Leger [Teutonic]
'People's spear'.

Leggett [French]

'Envoy or ambassador'.
(Leggitt, Liggett)

Leicester See **Lester**

Leif [Norse]
'The beloved one'.

Leigh See **Lee**

Leighton [Anglo-Saxon]
'Dweller at the farm by the meadow'.
(Layton)

Leith [Celtic]
'Broad, wide river'.

Leland [Anglo-Saxon]
'Dweller by the meadow land'.
(Leyland, Lealand)

Lem See **Lemuel**

Lemmie See **Lemuel**

Lemuel [Hebrew]
'Consecrated to God'.
(Lem, Lemmie)

Lenard See **Leonard**

Lennie See **Leonard**

Lennon [Gaelic]
'Little cloak'.

Lennox [Celtic]
'Grove of elm trees'.

Leo [Latin]
'Lion'.

Leo See **Leopold**

Leon [French]
'Lion-like'.

Leonard [Latin]
'Lion brave'. One with all the courage and tenacity of the king of beasts.
(Leoner, Lennard, Lenard, Leonhard, Len, Lennie, Lenny)

Leonardo See **Leonard**

Leoner See **Leonard**

Leonid See **Leonard**

Leonidas [Greek]
'Son of the lion'.

Leonidas See **Leonard**

Leopold [Teutonic]
'Brave for the people'. One who fights for his countrymen.
(Leo, Lepp)

Lepp See **Leopold**

Leroi See **Leroy**

Leroy [French]
'The king'.
(Lee, Roy)

Leslie [Celtic]
'From the grey fort'.
(Lesley, Les)

Lester [Anglo-Saxon]
'From the army camp'.
(Leicester)

Leverett [French]
'The young hare'.

Leverton [Anglo-Saxon]
'From the rush farm'.

Levi [Hebrew]
'United'.

Levin See **Levi**

Lewis [Teutonic]
'Famous battle warrior'.
(Louis, Ludwig, Lewes,
Ludovic, Ludovick,
Lugaidh, Luthais, Lou,
Lew, Ludo)

Liam See **William**

Lincoln [Celtic]
'From the place by the
pool'.

Lind [Anglo-Saxon]
'From the lime tree'.
(Linden, Lyndon)

Lind See **Lindsey**

Lindberg [Teutonic]
'Lime tree hill'.

Lindell [Anglo-Saxon]
'Dweller by the lime tree in
the valley'.

Linden See **Lind**

Lindley [Anglo-Saxon]
'By the lime tree in the
meadow'.

Lindon See **Lind**

Lindsey [Anglo-Saxon]
'Pool island'.
(Lindsay, Linsay, Linsey)

Linford [Anglo-Saxon]
'From the lime tree ford'.

Link [Anglo-Saxon]
'From the bank or edge'.

Linley [Anglo-Saxon]
'From the flax field'.

Linn See **Lynn**

Linton [Anglo-Saxon]
'From the flax farm'.

Linus [Greek]
'Flax coloured hair'.

Lion See **Lionel**

Lionel [French]
'The young lion'.
(Lion)

Lionello See **Lionel**

Lisle See **Lyle**

Litton [Anglo-Saxon]
'Farm on the hillside'.

Livingston [Old English]
'From Leif's town'.

Lleufer [Welsh]
'Splendid'.

Llewellyn [Welsh]
'Lion like' or 'Like a ruler'.

Lloyd [Welsh]
'Grey-haired'.
(Floyd)

Locke [Anglo-Saxon]
'Dweller in the
stronghold'.

Lockwood See **Locke**

Logan [Celtic]
'Little hollow'.

Loman [Celtic]
'Enlightened'.

Lombard [Latin]
'Long bearded one'.

Lon [Gaelic]
'Strong, fierce'. Also dim.
of Lawrence.

Lon See **Lawrence**

London [Middle English]
'Fortress of the moon'.

Lonnard See **Leonard**

Lonnie See **Lawrence**

Lonny See **Zebulon**

Loren See **Lawrence**

Lorenze See **Lawrence**

Lorenzo See **Lawrence**

Lori See **Lawrence**

Lorimer [Latin]
'Harness maker'.

Loring [Teutonic]
'Man from Lorraine'.

Lorrie See **Lawrence**

Lothaire See **Luther**

Lothar See **Luther**

Lothario See **Luther**

Lou See **Lewis**

Louis See **Lewis**

Lovel See **Lowell**

Lowe See **Lowell**

Lowell [Anglo-Saxon]
'The beloved one'.
(Lovel, Lovell)

Loyal See **Leal**

Lubin [Old English]
'Dear friend'.

Lucais See **Lucius**

Lucas See **Lucius**

Luce See **Lucius**

Lucian See **Lucius**

Lucio See **Lucius**

Lucius [Latin]
'Light'.
*(Lucas, Luke, Lucian,
Luck, Luc, Lukas, Lucais,
Luce, Lukey)*

Luck See **Lucius**

Ludlow [Anglo-Saxon]
'From the hill of the
prince'.

Ludo See **Lewis**

Ludolf [Old Germans]
'Famous wolf'.

Ludovic See **Lewis**

Ludwig See **Aloysius** or
Lewis

Luigi See **Lewis**

Luis See **Lewis**

Luke See **Lucius**

Lukey See **Lucius**

Lundy [French]
'Born on Monday'.

Lunn [Gaelic]
'From the grove'.

Lunt [Norse]
'Strong and fierce'.

Lute See **Luther**

Luthais See **Lewis**

Luther [Teutonic]
'Famous warrior'.
(Lothar, Lothaire,

Lothario, Lute)

Lyall See **Lyle**

Lycidas [Greek]
'Wolf son'.

Lyle [French]
'From the island'.
(Lyall, Lyell, Lisle, Liall)

Lyman [Anglo-Saxon]
'Man from the meadow'.
(Leyman)

Lyndon See **Lind**

Lynfa [Welsh]
'From the lake'.

Lynn [Welsh]
'From the pool or
waterfall'.
(Lyn, Lin, Linn)

Lysander [Greek]
'The liberator'.
(Sandy)

Girls

Mab [Gaelic]
'Mirthful joy'.
(Mave, Meave, Mavis)

Mabel [Latin]
'Amiable and loving'. An
endearing companion.
*(Mable, Maybelle, Maible,
Moibeal)*

Mada See **Madeline**

Maddy See **Madeline**

Madel See **Madeline**

Madelia See **Madeline**

Madeline [Greek]
'Tower of strength'. A
woman of great physical
and moral courage, on
whom many could lean in
difficult times.

*(Madeleine, Madelaine,
Madaline, Madaleine,
Madalaine, Madalena,
Maddalena, Maddalene,
Madelon, Madlin, Madel,
Madelia, Madella,
Madelle, Magdala,
Magdaa, Magdalen,
Magdalene, Magdalyn,
Magdalane, Malena,
Marleen, Marlene,
Marline, Marlena, Malina,
Mada, Madelle, Maddy,
Maighdlin, Mala)*

Madella See **Madeline**

Madelle See **Madeline**

Madelon See **Madeline**

Madge See **Margaret**

Madhur [Hindi]
'Sweet'.

Madison [Teutonic]
'Maud's son'.

Madlin See **Madeline**

Madora See **Medea**

Madra [Spanish]
'The matriarch'.

Mae See **May**

Maeve [Irish]
The warrior queen of
Connaught
(Mave, Meave)

Magdaa See **Madeline**

Magdala See **Madeline**

Magdalen See **Madeline**

Magdalene See
Madeleine

Magdalyn See **Madeline**

Magdi [Arabic]
'My glory'.

Magena [North American
Indian]
'The coming moon'.

Maggie See **Magnilda** or
Margaret

Magnilda [Teutonic]
'Great battle maid'.
*(Magnilde, Magnhilda,
Magnhilde, Mag, Maggie,
Nilda, Nillie)*

Magnilde See **Magnilda**

Magnolia [Latin]
'Magnolia flower'.
*(Mag, Maggie, Nola,
Nolie)*

Mahala [Hebrew]
'Tenderness'.
(Mahalah, Mahalia)

Mahalia See **Mahala**

Maia See **May**

Maida [Anglo-Saxon]
'The maiden'.
*(Maidie, Mady, Maidel,
Mayda, Mayde, Maydena)*

Maidel See **Maida**

Maidie See **Maida**

Maigrghread See
Margaret

Maisie See **Margaret**

Majesta [Latin]
'Majestic One'.

Mala See **Madeline**

Malan See **Melanie**

Malena See **Madeline**

Malise [Gaelic]
'Servant of God'.

Malva [Greek]
'Soft and tender'.
(Melva, Melba)

Malva See **Malvina** or
Mauve

Malvie See **Malvina**

Malvina [Gaelic]
'Polished chieftain'.
*(Malva, Melva, Melvina,
Malvie, Melvine)*

Mamie See **Mary**

Manette See **Mary**

Manon See **Mary**

Manuela [Spanish]
'God with us'.
(Manuella)

Mara See **Damara** or **Mary**

Maraam [Arabic]
'Aspiration'.

Maralla See **Mareria**

Marcelia See **Marcella**

Marcella [Latin]
'Belonging to Mars'.
*(Marcie, Marcia, Marcy,
Marcelle, Marcelline,
Marcelline, Marcile,
Marcille, Marcela,
Marcelia, Marchella,
Marchelle, Marchelline,
Marchita, Marquita,
Marsha, Marilda)*

Marcelle See **Marcella**

Marcelline See **Marcella**

Marchelle See **Marcella**

Marchelline See **Marcella**

Marchita See **Marcella**

Marcia See **Marcella**

Marcie See **Marcella**

Marcile See **Marcella**

Marelda [Teutonic]
'Famous battle maiden'.

Mareria [Latin]
'Of the sea'.

Maretta See **Mary**

Marfot See **Margaret**

Margalo See **Margaret**

Margaret [Latin]
'A pearl'.
(Margareta, Margaretta,
Margarita, Margery,
Margory, Marjery,
Marjorie, Margorie,
Margerie, Margharita,
Marget, Margette,

Margetta, Margalo,
Marguerite, Margerita,
Margueritta, Marguerita,
Marfot, Margarethe,
Margethe, Margaretha,
Maigrghread, Margo,
Margao, Marge, Maggie,
Meta, Meg, Maisie, Grete,
Greta, Grethe, Gretchen,
Peggy, Rita, Daisy)

Margareta See **Margaret**

Margaretta See **Margaret**

Marge See **Margaret**

Margerita See **Margaret**

Margery See **Margaret**

Marget See **Margaret**

Margo See **Margaret**

Maria See **Mary**

Mariam See **Marian**

Marian [Hebrew]
'Bitter and graceful'.
(Marion, Marianne,
Mariana, Marianna,
Maryanne, Mariam,
Mariom)

Mariana See **Marian**

Maribell See **Marybelle**

Marie See **Mary**

Mariel See **Mary**

Marietta See **Mary**

Marigold [English]
'Golden flower girl'.
(Marygold)

Marilda See **Marcella**

Marilla See **Amaryllis** or
Mary

Marilyn See **Mary**

Marina [Latin]
'Lady of the sea'.
(Marnie)

Marion See **Marian**

Mariposa [Spanish]
'Butterfly'.

Maris [Latin]
'Of the sea'.
(Marisa, Marris)

Maris See **Damara**

Marisa See **Maris**

Marla See **Mary**

Marleen See **Madeline**

Marlena See **Madeline**

Marlene See **Madeleine**

Marnie See **Marina**

Marquita See **Marcella**

Marsha See **Marcella**

Marta See **Martha**

Martella See **Martha**

Martha [Arabic]
'The mistress'.
*(Marta, Marthe, Martie,
Marty, Mattie, Matty,
Martella)*

Martie See **Martha**

Martina [Latin]
'Warlike one'. Fem. of
Martin.
(Martine, Marta, Tina)

Martine See **Martina**

Martita See **Martha**

Martynne See **Martha**

Marva See **Marvel**

Marvel [Latin]

'A wondrous miracle'.
*(Marva, Marvella,
Marvela, Marvelle)*

Marvella See **Marvel**

Mary [Hebrew]
'Bitterness'. Although
Hebrew in origin has
become one of the most
consistently popular
names for girls, since the
Christian era.
*(Mara, Maria, Marie,
Maretta, Marette, Marilyn,
Marylyn, Marylin, Marilla,
Marla, Marya, Miriam,
Mamie, Manette, Manon,
Maryse, Maire, Maureen,
Mearr, Moya, Mairi,
Mariel, Molly, May,
Marietta, Polly, Mitzi,
Mimi, Mariette)*

Marya See **Mary**

Maryam [Arabic]
'Purity'.

Marybelle
'A combination of Mary &
Belle'.

Maryellen
'A combination of Mary &
Ellen'.

Maryjo

'A combination of Mary &
Joanne'.

Marylou [Combination
Mary/Louise]

Maryse See **Mary**

Masa [Japanese]
'Straightforward, upright'.

Massa [Arabic]
'Uplifting'.

Massima [Italian, Latin]
'Greatest'.

Mathilda [Teutonic]
'Brave little maid'. One as
courageous as a lion.
*(Matilda, Matilde,
Mathilde, Maud, Maude,
Mattie, Tilda, Tilly,
Matelda, Maitilde)*

Matilde See **Mathilda**

Mattea [Hebrew]
'Gift of God'. Fem. of
Matthew.
*(Matthea, Matthia,
Mathea, Mathia)*

Mattie See **Mathilda** or
Martha

Maud See **Mathilda**

Mauralia See **Maurilla**

Maureen See **Mary**

Maurilla [Latin]
'Sympathetic woman'.
(*Maurilia, Mauralia*)

Mauve [Latin]
'Lilac coloured bird'.
(*Malva*)

Mave See **Mab**

Mavis [French]
'Song thrush'.

Mavis See **Mab**

Maxie See **Maxine**

Maxima See **Maxine**

Maxine [French]
'The greatest'. Fem. of
Maximilian.
(*Maxima, Maxene, Maxie*)

May [Latin]
'Born in May'. Also dim. of
Mary.
(*Maia*)

May See **Mary**

Maybelle See **Mabel**

Mayda See **Maida**

Mayde See **Maida**

Maydena See **Maida**

Mead [Greek]
'Honey wine'.
(*Meade*)

Meagan See **Megan**

Meaghan See **Megan**

Meara [Gaelic]
'Mirth'.

Mearr See **Mary**

Meave See **Mab**

Meda See **Halimeda**

Medea [Greek]
'The middle child' or
'Enchantress'.
(*Media, Madora, Medora*)

Medora [Literary]
Poetic character of Lord
Byron.

Medwenna [Welsh]
'Maiden, princess'.
(*Modwen, Modwenna*)

Megan [Celtic]
'The strong'. Popular
name for Welsh girls.
(*Meghan*)

Megara [Greek]
First wife of Hercules.

Meghann See **Megan**

Mehetabie See **Mehitabel**

Mehitabel [Hebrew]
'Favoured of God'. One of
the Chosen.
*(Mehetabel, Mehetabie,
Mehetabelle, Mehitable,
Mehitabelle, Metabel,
Hetty, Hitty)*

Melania See **Melanie**

Melanie [Greek]
'Clad in darkness'. Lady of
the night.
*(Melania, Malan, Melan,
Mel, Mellie, Melly,
Melany)*

Melantha [Greek]
'Dark flower'.
(Melanthe)

Melba See **Malva**

Melda See **Imelda**

Melina [Latin]
'Yellow canary'. Also der.
of Madeline.

Melina See **Carmel**

Melinda [Greek]
'Mild and gentle'. A quiet
home loving girl.
(Malinda)

Melior [Latin]
'Better'.

Melisanda See **Millicent**

Melisande See **Millicent**

Melisandra See **Melissa**

Melissa [Greek]
'Honey bee'.
(Melisa, Lisa, Mel)

Melita [Greek]
'Little honey flower'.
(Elita, Malita, Melitta)

Mell See **Amelia**

Melle [Celtic, French]
'Princess'.

Mellie See **Amelia**

Melloney See **Melanie**

Melly See **Melanie**

Melodia See **Melody**

Melody [Greek]
'Like a song'.
(Melodie, Melodia, Lodie)

Melva See **Malva**

Melvina See **Malvina**

Melvine See **Malvina**

Meraud [Greek]
'Emerald'.

Mercedes [Spanish]
'Compassionate,
merciful'. One who
forgives, not condemns.
(Mercy, Merci)

Mercia [Anglo-Saxon]
'Lady of Mercia'. One from
the old Saxon kingdom in
the centre of England.

Mercy See **Mercedes**

Mercy [Middle English]
'Compassion, mercy'.

Merdyce See **Mertice**

Meredith [Celtic]
'Protector from the sea'. A
popular name in Wales for
boys and girls.
*(Meridith, Meredyth,
Meridyth, Merideth,
Meredeth, Meredydd,
Merrie, Merry)*

Meredydd See **Meredyth**

Meriel See **Muriel**

Meris [Latin]
'Of the sea'.

Meritta See **Merritt**

Merla See **Merle**

Merle [Latin]
'The blackbird'.
*(Merl, Merlina, Merline,
Meryl, Myrlene, Merola,
Merla)*

Merlina See **Merle**

Merlina See **Merlyn**

Merline See **Merle**

Merlyn [Celtic, Spanish]
'Sea hill'.

Merna See **Myrna**

Merola See **Merle**

Merrie [Anglo-Saxon]
'Mirthful, joyous'. Also
dim. of Meredith.
(Meri, Merri, Merry)

Merrilees [Old English]
'St. Mary's field'.
(Merrilie)

Merrilie See **Merrilees**

Merritt [Anglo-Saxon]
'Worthy; of merit'.
*(Meritt, Merrit, Meritta,
Merritta)*

Merry See **Meredyth**

Mertice [Anglo-Saxon]
'Famous and pleasant'.
One who has not been
spoiled by adulation.
(Merdyce, Mertyce)

Mertice See **Myrtle**

Meryl See **Merle**

Messina [Latin]
'The middle child'.

Meta [Latin]
'Ambition achieved'.

Meta See **Margaret**

Metabel See **Mehitabel**

Metea [Greek]
'Gentle'.

Metis [Greek]
'Wisdom and skill'.
(Metys)

Mevena [Celtic, French]
'Agile'.

Mia [Latin]
'Mine'.

Michaela [Hebrew]
'Likeness to God'. Fem. of
Michael.
*(Michaelina, Michaeline,
Micheline, Michelline,
Micaela, Mikaela, Michel,
Michelle, Michella,
Michaella)*

Michaelina See **Michaela**

Michaeline See **Michaela**

Michal [Hebrew]
'God is perfect.'

Michel See **Michaela**

Michella See **Michaela**

Michi [Japanese]
'The way'.

Michiko [Japanese]
'Three thousand'.

Midori [Japanese]
'Green'.

Mignon [French]
'Little, dainty darling'. A
kitten-like creature of
charm and grace.
(Mignonette)

Mignonette See **Mignon**

Miki [Japanese]
'Stem'.

Mildred [Anglo-Saxon]
'Gentle counsellor'. The
diplomat power behind the
throne.
*(Mildrid, Milli, Millie,
Milly)*

Milicia See **Amelia**

Mill See **Amelia**

Millicent [Teutonic]
'Strong and industrious'.
The hard working
chatelaine.
*(Melicent, Melisande,
Mellicent, Melisende,
Melisanda, Melisenda,
Milicent, Milissent,
Milisent, Milli, Millie,
Milly)*

Millie See **Amelia** or
Mildred

Mimi See **Mary**

Mimosa [Latin]
'Imitative'.

Mina See **Adamina**, **Minta**
or **Wilhelmina**

Minda See **Minta**

Minda [Indian]
'Knowledge'.

Mindy See **Minta**

Minerva [Latin]
'Wise, purposeful one'.
The Goddess of Wisdom.

Minetta See **Minette**

Minette [French]
'Little kitten'.
(Minetta)

Minette See **Henrietta**

Minna [Old German]
'Tender affection'.

Minnie See **Minta**

Minta [Teutonic]
'Remembered with love'.
*(Mina, Minda, Mindy,
Minetta, Minnie)*

Minta [Greek]
'The mint plant'. Also dim.
of Araminta.
(Minthe, Mintha)

Minthe See **Minta**

Mira [Latin]
'Wonderful one'.

(Mirella, Mirilla, Myra, Myrilla, Mireille)

Mirabel [Latin]
'Admired for her beauty'.
(Mirabella, Mirabelle)

Mirabella See **Mirabel**

Miranda [Latin]
'Greatly admired'.
(Randa)

Mireilla See **Mira**

Mirella See **Mira**

Miriam See **Mary**

Mirle See **Myrtle**

Mirta [Greek, Spanish]
'Crown of beauty'.

Mirtala See **Mirta**

Misty [Old English]
'Covered with mist'.

Mitra [Persian]
'Name of angel'.

Mitzi See **Mary**

Miya [Japanese]
'Temple'.

Modesta See **Modesty**

Modeste See **Modesty**

Modestia See **Modesty**

Modestine See **Modesty**

Modesty [Latin]
'Shy, modest'. The retiring and bashful maiden.
(Modesta, Modeste, Modestia, Modestine, Desta)

Modwen See **Medwenna**

Moibeal See **Mabel**

Moina [Celtic]
'Soft'.

Moina See **Myrna**

Moira See **Morag**

Molly See **Mary**

Mona See **Monica**

Monca See **Monica**

Monica [Latin]
'Advice giver'.
(Monique, Mona, Monca)

Monika See **Monica**

Morag [Celtic]
  'Great'.
  (Moira, Moyra)

Morette See **Amorette**

Morgana [Welsh]
  'From the sea shore'.
  (Morgan)

Morganica See **Morgan**

Morganne See **Morgan**

Morgen See **Morgana**

Morna See **Myrna**

Mosella See **Moselle**

Moselle [Hebrew]
  'Taken from the water'.
  Fem. of Moses.
  *(Mosella, Mozel, Mozelle,
  Mozella)*

Mosera [Hebrew]
  'Bound to men'.

Motaza [Arabic]
  'Proud'.

Moya See **Mary**

Moyna See **Monica**

Moyra See **Morag**

Muire See **Muriel**

Muriel [Celtic]
  'Sea bright'.
  (Meriel, Muire)

Murielle See **Muriel**

Musetta [French]
  'Child of the Muses'.
  (Musette)

Musette See **Musetta**

Musidora [Greek]
  'Gift of the Muses'.

Mwynen [Welsh]
  'Gentle'.

Myfanwy [Welsh]
  'My rare one'.
  (Myvanwy)

Myrlene See **Merle**

Myrna [Gaelic]
  'Beloved'.
  *(Merna, Mirna, Moina,
  Morna, Moyna)*

Myrta See **Mirta**

Myrta See **Myrtle**

Myrtis See **Myrtle**

Myrtle [Greek]
'Victorious crown'. The
hero's laurel wreath.

*(Myrta, Myrtia, Myrtis,
Mirle, Mertle, Mertice)*

Boys

Mabon [Welsh]
'Youth'.

Mac [Celtic]
Used in many Scots and
Irish names and meaning
Son of. Also used in the
form 'Mc'. For instance
Macadam (Son of Adam),
McDonald (Son of
Donald) and so on.

Macarius [Latin]
'Blessed'.

Macy [French]
'From Matthew's estate'.

Madaan [Arabic]
'Striving'.

Maddock [Welsh]
'Beneficent'.
*(Madoc, Madock, Madog,
Maddox)*

Maddox See **Maddock**

Madison [Anglo-Saxon]
'Mighty in battle'.
(Maddison)

Madjid [Arabic]
'Glorious'.

Madog See **Maddock**

Maelgwyn [Welsh]
'Metal chief'.

Magee [Gaelic]
'Son of the fiery one'.

Magloire [French]
'My glory'.

Magnus [Latin]
'The great one'. One who
excels all others.

Maher [Arabic]
'Clever, skilful'.
[Hebrew]
'Excellent, industrious'.

Mahfuz [Arabic]
'Guardian'.

Maitland [Anglo-Saxon]
'Dweller in the meadow
land'.

Majnoon [Persian]
Legendary hero like
Romeo (story of Majnoon

and Leila).

Major [Latin]
'Greater'. Anything you
can do, he can do better!

Malachi [Hebrew]
'Angel'.

Malcolm [Celtic]
'The dove' or 'Follower of
St. Columba'.

Malik [Muslim]
'Master'.

Malin [Anglo-Saxon]
'Little warrior'.

Malise [Gaelic]
'Servant of Jesus'.

Malkawn [Hebrew]
'Their king'.

Mallory [Anglo-Saxon/
Latin]
'Army counsellor' (Anglo-
Saxon) or 'Luckless'
(Celtic).

Maloney [Gaelic]
'Believer in the Sabbath'.

Malory [Old French]
'Unfortunate'.
(Mallory)

Malvin [Celtic]
'Polished chief'.
(Melvin, Mal, Mel)

Mamoun [Arabic]
'Trustworthy'.

Manassa [Arabic]
'Causes to forget'.

Manasseh [Hebrew]
'Making one forget'.

Mandel [Teutonic]
'Almond'.

Mander [Old French]
'Stable lad'.

Manfred [Anglo-Saxon]
'Peaceful hero'.
(Manfried)

Manfried See **Manfred**

Manleich See **Manley**

Manley [Anglo-Saxon]
'The hero's meadow'.
(Manleich)

Manning [Anglo-Saxon]
'Hero's son'.

Manny See **Emmanuel**

Mano See **Emmanuel**

Manolo See **Emmanuel**

Mansfield [Anglo-Saxon]
'Hero's field'.

Mansoor [Arabic]
'Victorious'.

Manton [Anglo-Saxon]
'Hero's farm'.

Manuel See **Emmanuel**

Manville [French]
'From the great estate'.
(Manvil)

Marcel [Latin]
'Little follower of Mars'. A
warlike person.
(Marcellus, Marcello)

Marcello See **Marcel**

Marcellus See **Marcel**

Marco See **Mark**

Marcus See **Mark**

Marden [Anglo-Saxon]
'From the pool in the
valley'.

Marino [Italian from Latin]
'Sea'.

Mario See **Marius**

Marion [French]
'Bitter'. A French form of
Mary, often given as a
boy's name in compliment
to the Virgin.

Marius [Latin]
'The martial one'.
(Mario)

Marjan [Arabic]
'Small pearls'.

Mark [Latin]
'Follower of Mars; the
warrior'.
(Marcus, Marco, Marc)

Marl See **Merlin**

Marland [Anglo-Saxon]
'Dweller in the lake land'.

Marley [Anglo-Saxon]
'From the lake in the
meadow'.
(Marly)

Marlin See **Merlin**

Marlon See **Merlin**

Marlow [Anglo-Saxon]
'From the lake on the hill'.
(Marlowe)

Marmaduke [Celtic]
'Sea leader'.
(Duke)

Marmion [French]
'Very small one'.

Marsden [Anglo-Saxon]
'From the marshy valley'.
(Marsdon)

Marsh [Anglo-Saxon]
'From the marsh'.

Marshall [Anglo-Saxon]
'The steward'. The man
who looked after the estate
of a nobleman.

Marston [Anglo-Saxon]
'From the farm by the
lake'.

Martainn See **Martin**

Marten See **Martin**

Martie See **Martin**

Martin [Latin]
'Warlike person'. A
follower of Mars.
*(Marten, Marton, Mart,
Martie, Marty)*

Martino See **Martin**

Marvin [Anglo-Saxon]
'Famous friend'.
(Mervin, Merwin,

Merwyn)

Marwin See **Marvin**

Marwood [Anglo-Saxon]
'From the lake in the
forest'.

Maskil [Hebrew]
'Enlightened, educated'.

Maslin [French]
'Small Thomas'.
(Maslen, Maslon)

Maslon See **Maslin**

Mason [Latin]
'Worker in stone'. One
who built castles,
churches, houses, etc.
from stone.

Massey See **Thomas**

Mata See **Matthew**

Math [Welsh]
'Treasure'.

Mather [Anglo-Saxon]
'Powerful army'.

Mathias See **Matthew**

Matmon [Hebrew]
'Treasure'.

Matt See **Matthew**

Matthew [Hebrew]
'Gift of God'. One of the 12
Apostles.
*(Mathew, Mathias,
Mattias, Mata, Matthias,
Mat, Matt, Mattie, Matty)*

Mattias See **Matthew**

Mattie See **Matthew**

Maurey See **Maurice**

Maurice [Latin]
'Moorish looking; dark
complexioned'.
*(Morris, Morrell, Morel,
Morice, Maurey, Morry,
Morrie, Maury, Mo)*

Mauricio See **Maurice**

Maurizio See **Maurice**

Maxey See **Maximilian**

Maxi See **Maxwell**

Maxim See **Maximilian**

Maximilian [Latin]
'The greatest; the most
excellent'. One without
equal.
*(Max, Maxey, Maxie,
Maxim, Maxy,*

Maximilien)

Maximilien See
Maximilian

Maxwell [Anglo-Saxon]
'Large spring'.
(Max, Maxie, Maxi)

Mayer [Latin]
'Greater'. The major
character.
(Myer)

Mayfield [Anglo-Saxon]
'From the field of the
warrior'.

Mayhew [French]
'Gift of God'. Another form
of Matthew.

Maynard [Teutonic]
'Powerfully strong; brave'.
(Menard)

Mayo [Gaelic]
'From the plain of the yew
trees'.

Mead [Anglo-Saxon]
'From the meadow'.

Medwin [Teutonic]
'Strong and powerful
friend'.

Mehrdad [Persian]
'Gift of the sun'.

Meilyr [Welsh]
'Man of iron'.

Mekuria [Ethiopian]
'Pride'.

Melbourne [Anglo-Saxon]
'From the mill stream'.
*(Melburn, Melburne,
Milbourn, Milbourne,
Milburne, Milburn)*

Melburn See **Melbourne**

Melchior [Persian]
'King of light'.

Meldon [Anglo-Saxon]
'From the mill on the hill'.

Melmoth [Celtic]
'Servant of Math'.

Melville [French]
'From the estate of the
industrious'.
(Melvil, Mel)

Melvin See **Malvin**

Menachin [Hebrew]
'Comforter'.
(Menahem)

Menahem See **Menachin**

Menard See **Maynard**

Mendel [Semitic]
'Wisdom'.

Mercer [Anglo-Saxon]
'Merchant'.

Meredith [Welsh]
'Guardian from the sea'.
*(Meredydd, Meridith,
Merideth, Meredyth,
Meridyth, Merry)*

Meredydd See **Meredith**

Merl See **Merlin**

Merle [Latin]
'The blackbird; the black
haired one'.

Merlin [Anglo-Saxon]
'The falcon'. The
legendary wizard of King
Arthur's court.
*(Marlin, Marlen, Marlon,
Marl, Merl)*

Meron [Hebrew]
'Army'.

Merrick See **Emery**

Merrill [French]
'Little famous one'.
(Merritt)

Merrill See **Myron**

Merritt See **Merrill**

Merry See **Meredith**

Merton [Anglo-Saxon]
'From the farm by the sea'.

Mervin See **Marvin**

Merwin See **Marvin**

Meryll [French from Old German]
'King'.

Methuselah [Hebrew]
'Man of the javelin'.

Meven [Celtic, French]
'Agile'.

Meyer [Teutonic]
'Steward'.

Micah See **Michael**

Michael [Hebrew]
'Like unto the Lord'.
(Micah, Mitchell, Michel, Mischa, Mitch, Mich, Mike, Mickie, Micky)

Mickie See **Michael**

Midyan [Arabic]
'Rule'.

Mihriban [Turkish]
'Tender, affectionate'.

Mike See **Michael**

Milan [Slavic]
'Beloved'.

Milbourn See **Melbourne**

Milburn [Old English]
'Mill stream'.

Milburne See **Melbourne**

Miles [Greek/Latin]
'The millstone' (Greek) or 'The soldier' (Latin).

Milford [Anglo-Saxon]
'From the mill ford'.
(Millford)

Millard [French]
'Strong and victorious'.

Miller [Anglo-Saxon]
'Grain grinder'.

Milo [Latin]
'The miller'.

Milt See **Milton**

Milton [Anglo-Saxon]
'From the mill town'.

Milward [Anglo-Saxon]
'The mill keeper'.

Miner [French/Latin]
'A miner' (French); 'Young
person' (Latin).
(Minor)

Miroslav [Slavonic]
'Peace, glory'.

Mischa See **Michael**

Mitch See **Michael**

Mitchell See **Michael**

Mithell See **Michael**

Modred [Anglo-Saxon]
'Brave counsellor'. One
who advised honestly
without fear of reprisal.

Moe See **Moses**

Moelwyn [Welsh]
'Fair headed'.

Moise See **Moses**

Mokbil [Arabic]
'The approaching one'.

Mokhtar [Arabic]
'Chosen'.

Monroe [Celtic]

'From the red swamp'.
(Munro, Monro, Munroe)

Montague [French]
'From the pointed
mountain'.
(Monte, Monty, Montagu)

Monte See **Montague**

Montega [Osage Indian]
'New arrows'.

Montgomery [French]
'The mountain hunter'.
(Monte, Monty)

Moore [French]
'Dark complexioned;
Moor'.
(More)

Mordecai [Hebrew]
'Belonging to Marduk'.

Moreland [Anglo-Saxon]
'From the moors'.

Morfin See **Morven**

Morgan [Welsh]
'White sea'. The foam
flecked waves.
(Morgen)

Moriah [Hebrew]
'Man chosen by Jehovah'.

Moritz See **Maurice**

Morley [Anglo-Saxon]
'From the moor meadow'.

Morrell See **Maurice**

Morrell [Latin]
'Dark'.

Morris See **Maurice**

Morrison [Anglo-Saxon]
'Maurice's son'.
(Morison)

Morse [Anglo-Saxon]
'Maurice's son'.

Mort See **Mordecai**

Morten See **Morton**

Mortimer [French]
'From the quiet water'.
*(Mortemer, Mortermer,
Morthermer)*

Morton [Anglo-Saxon]
'From the farm on the
moor'.

Morven [Gaelic]
'Blond giant'.
(Morfin)

Mose See **Moses**

Moses [Hebrew]
'Saved from the water'.
The great prophet of
Israel.
*(Moise, Mose, Mosie,
Moe, Moss)*

Mosie See **Moses**

Moss See **Moses**

Moustapha [Arabic]
'Chosen'.

Mubarak [Arabic]
'Blessed'.

Muhammad [Arabic]
'Praised'.

Muir [Celtic]
'From the moor'.

Mungo [Gaelic]
'Lovable'.

Munir [Arabic]
'Illuminating, light'.

Munroe See **Monroe**

Murdoch [Celtic]
'Prosperous from the sea'.
(Murdock, Murtagh)

Murphy [Gaelic]
'Sea warrior'.

Murray [Celtic]
'The mariner; sea fighter'.

Murtagh See **Murdoch**

Mustapha See **Moustapha**

Myer See **Mayer**

Myles See **Miles**

Myles See **Miles**

Mylo See **Milo**

Myron [Greek]
'The fragrant oil'.
(Merrill)

Girls

Naamah [Hebrew]
'Pleasant, beautiful'.

Naashom [Hebrew]
'Enchantress'.
(Nashom, Nashoma)

Naava [Hebrew]
'Beautiful'.

Nabeela [Arabic]
'Noble'.

Nabila See **Nabeela**

Nabrissa [French, Greek]
'Peace'.

Nada See **Nadine**

Nadeen See **Nadine**

Nadia See **Nadine**

Nadine [French]
'Hope'.
(Nada, Nadia)

Nadira [Arabic]
'Rare, precious'.

Nafisa [Arabic]
'Precious'.

Naida [Latin]
'The water nymph'. From
the streams of Arcadia.
(Naiada)

Nairne [Gaelic]
'From the river'.

Nalani [Hawaiian]
'Calmness of the heavens'.

Nama See **Namah**

Namah [Hebrew]
'Beautiful, pleasant'.

Namana See **Naamah**

Nan See **Anne**

Nana See **Anne**

Nancy See **Anne**

Nandelle [German]
'Adventuring life'.

Nanetta See **Anne**

Nanette See **Anne**

Nani [Hawaiian]
'Beautiful'.

Nanice See **Ann**

Nanine See **Anne**

Nanon See **Anne**

Naomi [Hebrew]
'The pleasant one'.
*(Naoma, Noami, Nomi,
Nomie)*

Napea [Latin]
'Girl of the valley'.
(Napaea, Napia)

Nara [English]
'Nearest and dearest'. Also
dim. of Narda.

Nara See **Narda**

Narda [Latin]
'Fragrant perfume'. The
lingering essence.
(Nara)

Narmada [Hindi]
'Gives pleasure'.

Nashoma See **Naashom**

Nasiba [Arabic]
'Love, poetry'.

Nasima [Arabic]
'Gentle breeze'.

Nastasya See **Natalie**

Nasya [Hebrew]
'Miracle of God'.

Natala See **Natalie**

Natale See **Natalie**

Natalie [Latin]
'Born at Christmas tide'.
*(Natalia, Natala, Natale,
Natasha, Nathalie, Natica,
Natika, Natacha,
Natividad, Nastasya,
Nattie, Netta, Nettie,
Netty, Noel, Noelle,
Novella)*

Natalina See **Natalie**

Natasha See **Natalie**

Natene See **Nathania**

Nathania [Hebrew]
'Gift of God'.
*(Natene, Nathene,
Nathane)*

Natica See **Natalie**

Natividad See **Natalie**

Nattie See **Natalie**

Neala [Gaelic]
'The champion'. Fem. of
Neil.

Nebula [Latin]
'A cloud of mist'.

Neda [Slav]
'Born on Sunday'.
(Nedda)

Nedi See **Neda**

Nela See **Cornelia** or **Nila**

Nelda [Anglo-Saxon]
'Born under the elder tree'.

Nelie See **Cornelia**

Nell See **Helen**

Nellwyn [Greek]
'Bright friend and
companion'.

Neola [Greek]
'The young one'.

Neoma [Greek]
'The new moon'.

Nerice See **Nerima**

Nerima [Greek]
   'From the sea'.
   (Nerissa, Nerine, Nerita,
   Nerice)

Nerine See **Nerima**

Nerissa See **Nerima**

Nerissa [Greek]
   'Of the sea'.

Nerita See **Nerima** or
   Nerissa

Nerys [Welsh]
   'Lordly one'.

Nessa See **Agnes**

Nessie See **Agnes**

Nesta See **Agnes**

Netania [Hebrew]
   'Gift of God'.

Netie See **Henrietta**

Netta See **Antonia,**
   Henrietta, Natalia, etc.

Nettie See **Antonia**

Neva [Spanish]
   'As white as the moon'.
   (Nevada)

Nevada See **Neva**

Neysa See **Agnes**

Nicholina See **Nicole**

Nicola See **Nicole**

Nicole [Greek]
   'The people's victory'.
   (Nicola, Nichola,
   Nicholina, Nicol,
   Nicolina, Nicoline, Nikola,
   Nikki, Nickie, Nicky)

Nicoline See **Nicole**

Nikki See **Nicole**

Nikoletta See **Nicole**

Nila [Latin]
   'From the Nile'.
   (Nela)

Nilda See **Magnilda**

Nillie See **Magnilda**

Nina [Spanish]
   'The daughter'.
   (Nineta, Ninetta, Ninette)

Nina See **Anne**

Nineta See **Nina**

Ninette See **Anne** or **Nina**

Ninon See **Anne**

Nirah [Hebrew]
'Light'.

Nissa [Scandinavian]
'Friendly elf'. A fairy who
can be seen only by lovers.

Nissie See **Nixie**

Nita See **Anne**, **Jane** or
Bonita

Nixie [Teutonic]
'Water sprite'.
(Nissie, Nissy)

Nizana [Hebrew]
'Flower bud'.

Noami See **Naomi**

Noel See **Natalie**

Noelle See **Natalia**

Nokomis [American
Indian]
'The grandmother'. From
the legend of Hiawatha.

Nola [Gaelic]
'Famous one'. See also
Olivia.

Nola See **Magnolia** or
Olive

Noleta [Latin]
'Unwilling'.
(Nolita)

Nolie See **Magnolia**

Nolita See **Noleta**

Nollie See **Olive**

Nomi See **Naomi**

Nona [Latin]
'Ninth born'.

Nonnie See **Anona**

Nora See **Honora**,
Eleanor, **Helen**

Norah See **Helen**

Norberta [Teutonic]
'Bright heroine'.
*(Norberte, Norbertha,
Norberthe)*

Norberte See **Norberta**

Nordica [Teutonic]
'Girl from the North'.
(Nordika)

Noreen See **Honora** or
Norma

Norma [Latin]
'A pattern, or rule'. The

template of the perfect girl.
(Normi, Normie, Noreen)

Normi See **Norma**

Norna [Norse]
'Destiny'. The goddess of
Fate.

Nova See **Novia**

Novella See **Natalie**

Novia [Latin]
'The newcomer'.
(Nova)

Nuala [Gaelic]

'Fair shouldered one'.

Numidia [Latin]
'The traveller'.

Nunciata [Italian]
'She has good news'.
(Annunciata)

Nydia [Latin]
'A refuge'.

Nyssa [Greek]
'Starting point'.

Nyx [Greek]
'White haired'.

Naaman [Hebrew]
'Pleasant one'.

Nabil [Arabic]
'Noble'.

Nadim [Arabic]
'Repentant'.

Nadir [Arabic]
'Rare, precious'.

Nadiv [Hebrew]
'Noble'.

Nahum [Hebrew]
'Comfort'.

Nairn [Celtic]
'Dweller by the alder tree'.

Najibullah [Arabic]
'God-given intelligence'.

Naldo See **Reginald**

Namir [Hebrew]
'Leopard'.

Napoleon [Greek]
'Lion of the woodland dell'.

Nash [Old French]
'Cliff'.

Nashif [Arabic]
'Hard'.

Nasim [Persian]
'Breeze'.

Nat See **Nathan**

Natal See **Noel**

Nathan [Hebrew]
'Gift of God'.
(Nathaniel, Nat, Nataniel, Nate, Nattie)

Nathaniel See **Nathan**

Neacail See **Nicholas**

Neal [Gaelic]
'The champion'.
(Niall, Neil, Neill, Neall, Neale, Neel, Niels, Niles, Nils)

Neal See **Cornelius**

Ned See **Edward**,
Edmund or **Edgar**

Neddy See **Edward**

Nefen See **Nevin**

Nehemiah [Hebrew]
'Consolation of the Lord'.

Nelson [Celtic]
'Son of Neal'.

Nemo [Greek]
'From the glen'.

Nero [Latin]
'Dark complexioned, black haired'.

Neron See **Nero**

Nestor [Greek]
'Ancient wisdom'.

Neville [Latin]
'From the new town'.
(Nevil, Nevile, Nev)

Nevin [Anglo-Saxon/ Gaelic]
'The nephew' (Anglo-Saxon) or 'Worshipper of Saints' (Gaelic).
(Nevins, Niven, Nivens)

Nevins See **Nevin**

Newbold [Old English]
'From the new building'.

Newel See **Noel**

Newell [Anglo-Saxon]
'From the new hall'.
(Newall)

Newland [Anglo-Saxon]
'From the new lands'.
(Newlands)

Newlands See **Newland**

Newlin [Celtic]
'Dweller by the new pool'. *(Newlyn)*

Newman [Anglo-Saxon]
'The newcomer; the new arrival'.

Newton [Anglo-Saxon]
'From the new estate'.

Niall See **Neal**

Nic See **Dominic**

Nicander [Greek]
'Man of victory'.

Niccolo See **Nicholas**

Nichol See **Nicholas**

Nicholas [Greek]
'Victorious people's army'.
The leader of the people.
(Nicolas, Nichol, Nicholl,
Niles, Nicol, Neacail,
Nick, Nickie, Nicky, Nik,
Nikki, Cole, Claus, Klaus,
Colin, Colley)

Nickie See **Nicholas**

Nicky See **Dominic**

Nico [Greek]
'Victory'.

Nicodemus [Greek]
'Conqueror for the people'.
(Nick, Nickie, Nicky, Nik,
Nikki, Nikky)

Nicolai See **Nicholas**

Nigel [Latin]
'Black haired one'.

Nikos See **Nicholas**

Niles See **Nicholas** or **Neal**

Nils See **Neal**

Nils See **Nelson**

Nilson See **Nelson**

Nimrod [Hebrew]
'Valiant'.

Ninian See **Vivien**

Niran [Thai]
'Eternal'.

Niven See **Nevin**

Nivens See **Nevin**

Nixon [Anglo-Saxon]
'Nicholas's son'.
(Nickson)

Noach See **Noah**

Noah [Hebrew]
'Rest, comfort and peace'.

Noam [Hebrew]
'Sweetness, friendship'.

Nobel See **Noble**

Noble [Latin]
'Noble and famous'.
(Nobel, Nolan)

Noda [Hebrew]
'Famous'.

Noel [French]
'Born at Christmas'. A
suitable name for a boy
born on Christmas Day.
(Nowell, Newel, Newell,
Natal, Natale)

Nolan See **Noble**

Noland See **Nolan**

Noll See **Oliver**

Nollie See **Oliver**

Norbert [Teutonic]
'Brilliant sea hero'. The courageous commander of ships.

Norbie See **Norbert**

Norm See **Norman**

Norman [French]
'Man from the north; a Northman'. The venturesome and bold Viking from Scandinavia. *(Normand, Norris, Normie, Norm)*

Normand See **Norman**

Normie See **Norman**

Norris See **Norman**

North See **Northrop**

Northcliffe [Anglo-Saxon]
'Man from the north cliff'. *(Northcliff)*

Northrop [Anglo-Saxon]
'From the northern farm'. *(Northrup, Nortrop, Nortrup)*

Northrup See **Northrop**

Norton [Anglo-Saxon]
'From the north farm'.

Nortrop See **Northrop**

Nortrup See **Northrop**

Norval [Old French]
'Northern valley'.

Norvel See **Norville**

Norvie See **Norville**

Norville [French]
'From the north town'. *(Norvil, Norvel, Norvie)*

Norvin [Anglo-Saxon]
'Friend from the north'. *(Norwyn, Norwin, Norvyn)*

Norward [Anglo-Saxon]
'Guardian from the north'.

Norwell [Anglo-Saxon]
'From the north well'.

Norwood [Anglo-Saxon]
'From the north forest'.

Norwyn See **Norvin**

Nowell See **Noel**

Nuncio [Italian from Latin] 'Messenger'.

Nunzio See **Nuncio**

Nye See **Aneurin**

Girls

Obelia [Greek]
'A pointed pillar'.

Octavia [Latin]
'The eighth child'.
*(Octavie, Ottavia, Ottavie,
Tavia, Tavi, Tavie, Tavy)*

Octavie See **Octavia**

Oda [Teutonic]
'Rich'.

Odele See **Odelia**

Odelette [French]
'A small lyric'.
(Odelet)

Odelia [Teutonic]
'Prosperous one'.
*(Odelie, Odella, Odelinda,
Odilla, Odilia, Otha,
Othilla, Ottilie)*

Odelie See **Odelia**

Odeline See **Odile**

Odella See **Odelia**

Odessa [Greek]
'A long journey'.

Odette [French]
'Home lover'. One who
makes a house a home.

Odila See **Odile**

Odile [French, German]
'Rich'.

Odilla See **Odelia**

Ofrah [Hebrew]
'Young hind; lively
maiden'.

Ola [Scandinavia]
'Descendant'. The
daughter of a chief.

Olave [Teutonic]
'Ancestor's relic'.

Olenka See **Olga**

Oleta See **Olethea**

Olethea [Latin]
'Truth'.
(Alethea, Oleta)

Olga [Teutonic]
'Holy'. One who has
been anointed in the
service of God.
*(Olva, Olivia, Olive, Elga,
Livi, Livie, Livia, Livvi,
Ollie)*

Olga See **Elga**

Olien [Russian]
'Deer'.

Olimpie See **Olympia**

Olinda [Latin]
'Fragrant herb'.

Olive [Latin]
'Symbol of peace'. The
olive branch. Also der. of
Olga.
*(Olivia, Livia, Nollie,
Nola, Olivette, Olva)*

Olive See **Olga**

Olivette See **Olive**

Olivia See **Olga**

Ollie See **Olga**

Olva See **Olga**

Olwyn [Welsh]
'White clover'.
(Olwen)

Olympe See **Olympia**

Olympia [Greek]
'Heavenly one'.
*(Olympe, Olympie,
Olimpie, Pia)*

Ona See **Una**

Onawa [American Indian]
'Maiden who is wide
awake'.

Ondina See **Ondine**

Ondine [Latin]
'Wave'.
(Undine)

Oneida [North American
Indian]
'Expected'.
(Onida)

Oona, Oonagh See **Una**

Opal [Sanskrit]
'Precious jewel'.
(Opalina, Opaline)

Opalina See **Opal**

Opaline See **Opal**

Ophelia [Greek]
'Wise and immortal'.
(Ofelia, Ofilia, Phelia)

Ora [Latin]
'Golden one'.
*(Orabel, Orabella,
Orabelle)*

Ora See **Aurelia**

Orabel See **Ora**

Orabella See **Ora**

Oralee [Hebrew]
'My light'.

Orali See **Oralee**

Oralia See **Aurelia**

Orane [French]
'Rising'.

Ordelia [Teutonic]
'Elf's spear'.

Orea [Greek]
'Of the mountain'. The
original maid of the
mountains.

Orel See **Bambi**

Orela [Latin]
'Divine pronouncement'.
The oracle.

Orenda [American Indian]
'Magic power'.

Oria See **Oriana**

Oriana [Latin]
'Golden one'.

Oriane See **Oriana**

Oriel See **Aurelia**

Orla [Irish]
'Golden lady'.

Orlanda See **Rolanda**

Orlena [French]
'Gold'.

Orna [Gaelic]
'Pale coloured'.

Orpah [Hebrew]
'A fawn'. From the Song of
Solomon.

Orquidea [Spanish]
'Orchid'.

Orsa See **Ursula**

Orsola See **Ursula**

Orva [Teutonic]
'Spear friend'.

Osanna [Latin]
'Filled with mercy'.

Osnat [Hebrew]
'Favourite of the deity'.

Otha See **Odelia**

Othilla See **Odelia**

Ottavia See **Octavia**

Ottavie See **Octavia**

Ottilie See **Odelia**

Owena [Welsh]
'Well-born'.

Ozora [Hebrew]
'Strength of the Lord'.

Oakes [Anglo-Saxon]
'Dweller by the oak tree'.

Oakley [Anglo-Saxon]
'From the oak tree
meadow'.
(Oakly, Okely, Okeley)

Oates See **Otis**

Obadiah [Hebrew]
'Servant of the Lord'. The
obedient one.

Obadias See **Obadiah**

Oberon See **Auberon**

Obert [Teutonic]
'Wealthy and brilliant'.

Octave See **Octavius**

Octavian See **Octavius**

Octavius [Latin]
'The eighth born'.
*(Octave, Octavian,
Octavus, Tavey)*

Octavus See **Octavius**

Odell [Teutonic]
'Wealthy one'.
(Odin, Odo)

Odie See **Odelle**

Odin See **Odell**

Odo See **Odell**

Odolf [Teutonic]
'The wealthy wolf'.

Ogdan See **Ogden**

Ogden [Anglo-Saxon]
'From the oak valley'.

Ogilvie [Celtic]
'From the high peak'.

Oglesby [Anglo-Saxon]
'Awe inspiring'.

Okely See **Oakley**

Olaf [Scandinavian]
'Ancestral relic' or
'Peaceful reminder'.
(Olav, Olen, Amhlaoibh)

Olav See **Olaf**

Ole [Scandinavian]
'Squire'.

Olen See **Olaf**

Olin See **Olaf**

Oliver [Latin]
'Symbol of peace'. The
olive branch.
*(Oliver, Ollie, Noll, Nollie,
Nolly)*

Olivero See **Oliver**

Oliviero See **Oliver**

Ollie See **Oliver**

Olney [Anglo-Saxon]
'Olla's island'.

Olvan See **Oliver**

Oman [Scandinavian]
'High protector'.

Omar [Arabic]
'The first son' or 'Most
high follower of the
Prophet'.

Onilwyn [Welsh]
'Ash grove'.

Onslow [Anglo-Saxon]
'Hill of the zealous one'.

Oram [Anglo-Saxon]
'From the enclosure by the
riverbank'.

Oran [Gaelic]
'Pale skinned man'.
*(Oren, Orin, Orran,
Orren, Orrin)*

Orban [French from Latin]
'Globe'.

Ordway [Anglo-Saxon]
'The spear fighter'.

Oren See **Oran**

Orestes [Greek]
'The mountain climber'.

Orford [Anglo-Saxon]
'Dweller at the cattle ford'.

Orin See **Oran**

Orion [Greek]
'The son of light'.

Orlan [Anglo-Saxon]
'From the pointed land'.

Orlando See **Roland**

Orman See **Ormond**

Ormen See **Ormond**

Ormin See **Ormond**

Ormond [Teutonic]
'Spearman' or 'Shipman'.
*(Orman, Ormand, Ormen,
Ormin)*

Ornette [Hebrew]
'Light, cedar tree'.

Oro [Spanish]
'Golden haired one'.

Orrick [Anglo-Saxon]
'Dweller by the ancient
oak tree'.

Orrin See **Oran**

Orson [Latin/Anglo-
Saxon]
'Little bear' (Latin) or 'Son
of the spearman'.

Orton [Anglo-Saxon]
'From the shore-
farmstead'.

Orval [Anglo-Saxon]
'Spear mighty'.

Orville [French]
'From the golden town'.
(Orvil)

Orvin [Anglo-Saxon]
'Spear friend'.

Osbert [Anglo-Saxon]
'Divinely bright warrior'.

*(Bert, Bertie, Berty, Oz,
Ozzie)*

Osborn [Anglo-Saxon]
'Divine warrior'.
*(Osborne, Osburn,
Osburne, Osbourn,
Osbourne)*

Osburn See **Osborn**

Oscar [Anglo-Saxon]
'Divine spearman'. 'A
fighter for God'.
*(Oskar, Oz, Ozzie, Os,
Ossie)*

Osgood [Scandinavian]
'The divine Goth'.

Osmar [Anglo-Saxon]
'Divinely glorious'.

Osmond [Anglo-Saxon]
'Divine protector'.

Osred [Anglo-Saxon]
'Divine counsellor'.

Oswald [Anglo-Saxon]
'Divinely powerful'.

Oswin [Old English]
'Friend of God'.

Othman [Teutonic]
'The prosperous one'.

Otho See **Otto**

Otis [Greek]
'Keen of sight and
hearing'.

Ottavio [Italian from Latin]
'Eighth'.

Otto [Teutonic]
'Wealthy, prosperous
man'.
(Otho)

Ottokar [German]
'Happy warrior'.

Otway [Teutonic]
'Fortunate in battle'.

Owen [Celtic]
'The young, well born
warrior'.
(Owain, Evan)

Oxford [Anglo-Saxon]
'From the ford where oxen
crossed'.

Oxton [Anglo-Saxon]

Ozzie See **Osbert**

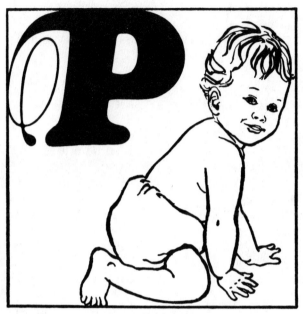

Girls

Paciane [French from
Latin]
'Peace'.

Paige [Anglo-Saxon]
'Young child'.
(Page)

Pallas [Greek]
'Wisdom and knowledge'.
Another name for the
Goddess of Wisdom.

Palma [Latin]
'Palm tree'.
(Palmer, Palmira)

Palmira See **Palma**

Paloma [Spanish]
'The dove'. A gentle,
tender girl.
(Palometa, Palomita)

Palometa See **Paloma**

Pam See **Pamela**

Pamela [Greek]
'All sweetness and honey'.
A loving person of great
kindness.
*(Pamella, Pamelina,
Pammie, Pammy, Pam)*

Pamelina See **Pamela**

Pammie See **Pamela**

Pamphila [Greek]
'All loving'. One who loves
all humanity.

Pandora [Greek]
'Talented, gifted one'.

Pansy [Greek]
'Fragrant, flowerlike'.

Panthea [Greek]
'Of all the Gods'.
(Panthia)

Paola [Italian]
'Little'.

Parasha See **Paschasia**

Parnella [French]
'Little rook'.
*(Parnelle, Pernella,
Pernelle)*

Parnelle See **Parnella**

Parthenia [Greek]
'Sweet virgin'.

Parvaneh [Persian]
'Butterfly'.

Paschasia [Latin]
'Born at Easter'.

Patience [Latin]
'Patient one'. A popular
'virtue' name.
(Pattie, Patty, Patienza)

Patienza See **Patience**

Patrice See **Patricia**

Patricia [Latin]
'Well born maiden'. A girl
born to the noblest of
families.
*(Patrice, Patrizia, Pat,
Patti, Patty, Patsy)*

Patsy See **Patricia**

Pattie See **Patience**

Paula [Latin]
'Little'. Fem. of Paul.
*(Paule, Paulette, Paulina,
Pauline, Paulita, Pauletta,
Pauli, Paulie, Paola)*

Paule See **Paula**

Paulena See **Paula**

Pauletta See **Paula**

Paulette See **Paula**

Pauli See **Paula**

Pauline See **Paula**

Paulita See **Paula**

Pavla See **Paula**

Peace [Latin]
'Tranquillity, calm'.

Pearl [Latin]
'Precious jewel'. One of
unmatched beauty. Also
der. of Margaret.
*(Pearle, Perle, Perl, Perlie,
Perline, Perlina, Pearlie)*

Peggy See **Margaret**

Pelagia [Greek]
'Mermaid'.

Penelope [Greek]
'The weaver'. The patient
wife of Ulysses who
stitched while he roamed.
(Pen, Penny)

Penny See **Penelope**

Penthea [Greek]
'Fifth child'.
(Penta, Penthia)

Penthia See **Penthea**

Peony [Latin]
'The gift of healing'.

Pepita See **Josephine**

Perdita [Latin]
'The lost one'.

Perfecta [Spanish]
'The most perfect being'.

Perlie See **Pearl**

Perlina See **Pearl**

Perline See **Pearl**

Pernella See **Parnella**

Pernelle See **Parnella**

Peronel [Latin]
'A rock'.
(Peronelle)

Perrine See **Petrina**

Persephone [Greek]
'Goddess of the
underworld'.

Persis [Latin]
'Woman from Persia'.

Peta [Greek]
'A Rock'.

Petica [Latin]
'Noble one'.

Petra See **Petrina**

Petrina [Greek]
'Steadfast as a rock'. Fem.
of Peter.
*(Petra, Petronia, Petula,
Petronella, Petronelle,
Petronilla, Petronille,
Pierette, Pierrette,
Perrine)*

Petronella See **Petrina**

Petronelle See **Petrina**

Petronia See **Petrina**

Petronilla See **Petrina**

Petronille See **Petrina**

Petula [Latin]
'Seeker'.

Petula See **Petrina**

Petunia [Indian]
'Reddish flower'.

Phaidra See **Phedra**

Phedra [Greek]
'Bright one'. The daughter
of Minos of Crete.
(Phaidra, Phedre)

Phelia See **Ophelia**

Phemie See **Euphemia**

Philadelphia [Greek]
'Brotherly love'.

Philana [Greek]
'Friend of humanity'.
(Filana)

Philantha [Greek]
'Lover of flowers'. Child of
the blossoms.
(Philanthe, Filantha)

Philanthe See **Philantha**

Philberta [Teutonic]
'Very brilliant'.
*(Philberthe, Philbertha,
Filberta, Filberte,
Filbertha, Filberthe)*

Philberthe See **Philberta**

Philippa [Greek]
'Lover of horses'. Fem. of
Philip.
*(Phillippa, Phillipa, Pippa,
Phillie, Filippa, Filipa)*

Phillida [Greek]
'Loving woman'.

Phillie See **Philippa**

Philmen See **Filma**

Philomela [Greek]
'Lover of song'.

Philomena [Greek]
'Lover of the moon'. The
nightingale.

Phoebe [Greek]
'Bright, shining sun'.
Fem. of Phoebus (Apollo).
(Phebe)

Phoenix [Greek]
'The eagle'. The legendary
bird who renewed its
youth in its own ashes.
(Fenix)

Pholma See **Filma**

Photina [Greek]
'Light'.

Phyllida See **Phyllis**

Phyllis [Greek]
'A green bough'.
*(Phyllida, Phillida, Phillis,
Philis, Phylis, Fillida,
Filida, Filis, Fillis)*

Pia [Latin]
'Pious'.

Pia See **Olympia**

Pierette See **Petrina**

Pietra See **Petrina**

Pilar [Spanish]
'A foundation or pillar'.

Piper [English]
'Player of the pipes'.

Pippa See **Philippa**

Placida [Latin]
'Peaceful one'.
(Placidia)

Placidia See **Placida**

Platona [Greek]
'Broad shouldered'. Fem.
of Plato. A woman of
wisdom.

Polly See **Mary**

Pomona [Latin]
'Fruitful and fertile'.

Poppaea See **Poppy**

Poppy [Latin]
'Red flower'.
(Poppaea)

Portia [Latin]
'An offering to God'.
(Porcia)

Poupée [French]
'Doll'.

Prabha [Hindi]
'Light'.

Preeti [Hindi]
'Love'.

Prima [Latin]
'First born'.

Primavera [Spanish]
'Child of the spring'.

Primrose [Latin]
'The first flower'. The
harbinger of spring.
*(Primula, Primmie, Rose,
Rosa)*

Primula See **Primrose**

Prisca See **Priscilla**

Priscilla [Latin]
'Of ancient lineage'. The
descendant of princes.
*(Prisilla, Pris, Prissie,
Cilla)*

Prospera [Latin]
'Favourable'.

Prudence [Latin]
'Cautious foresight'.
*(Prudentia, Prud, Prue,
Prudie, Prudy)*

Prudentia See **Prudence**

Prudie See **Prudence**

Prunella [French]
'Plum coloured'.
(Prunelle)

Prunelle See **Prunella**

Psyche [Greek]
'Of the soul or mind'. The
true inner being.

Purity [Middle English]
'Purity'.

Pyrena [Greek]
'Fiery one'. The warmth of
the home.
(Pyrenia)

Pyrenia See **Pyrena**

Pythia [Greek]
'A prophet'. The oracle.
(Pythea)

Pablo See **Paul**

Pace See **Pascal**

Paco [Italian]
'To pack'.

Padarn [Welsh]
'Fatherly'.

Paddy See **Patrick**

Padgett [French]
'The young attendant; a
page'.
(Padget, Paget, Page)

Padraic See **Patrick**

Page See **Padgett**

Paige See **Padgett**

Paine [Latin]
'The country rustic; a
pagan'.
(Payne)

Paley See **Paul**

Palladin [North American
Indian]
'Fighter'.

Palm See **Palmer**

Palmer [Latin]
'The palm bearing pilgrim'.

Pancras [Greek]
'All strength'.

Paolo See **Paul**

Pari [French]
'Fatherly'.

Park [Anglo-Saxon]
'From the park'.
(Parke)

Parker [Anglo-Saxon]
'The park keeper'. One
who guarded the park
lands.

Parkin [Anglo-Saxon]
'Little Peter'.
(Perkin, Peterkin)

Parlan See **Bartholomew**

Parnell See **Peter**

Parr [Anglo-Saxon]
'Dweller by the cattle pen'.

Parrish [Anglo-Saxon]
'From the church parish'.
(Parish)

Parry [Celtic/French]
'Harry's son (Ap Harry)'
(Celtic) or 'Protector'
(French).

Pascal [Italian]
'Easter born'. The new
born pascal lamb.

Pasquale See **Pascal**

Pat See **Patrick**

Patin See **Patton**

Patricio See **Patrick**

Patrick [Latin]
'The noble patrician'. One
of noble birth and from a
noble line.
*(Patric, Padraic, Peyton,
Padraig, Padruig, Patrice,
Paddy, Pat, Patsy, Rick)*

Patrizio See **Patrick**

Patrizius See **Patrick**

Patsy See **Patrick**

Patton [Anglo-Saxon]
'From the warrior's farm'.

Paul [Latin]
'Little'.
*(Pablo, Paolo, Paley,
Paulie, Pauley)*

Pauley See **Paul**

Pavel See **Paul**

Paxton [Anglo-Saxon]
'From the warrior's estate'.

Payne See **Paine**

Payton [Anglo-Saxon]
'Dweller on the warrior's
farm'.

Peadar See **Peter**

Pearce See **Peter**

Pedro See **Peter**

Pell [Anglo-Saxon]
'Scarf'.

Pelton [Anglo-Saxon]
'From the farm by the
pool'.

Pembroke [Celtic]
'From the headland'.

Penley [Anglo-Saxon]
'From the enclosed
meadow'.

Penn [Anglo-Saxon]
'Enclosure'.

Penrod [Teutonic]
'Famous commander'.

Penrose [Celtic]
'Mountain promontory'.

Penwyn [Welsh]
'Fair headed'.

Pepin [Teutonic]
'The petitioner' or 'The
persevered'.
(Peppin, Pepi, Peppi)

Peppi See **Pepin**

Percival [French]
'Valley piercer'.
*(Parsefal, Parsifal,
Perceval, Percy, Perc,
Perce, Purcell)*

Peregrine [Latin]
'The wanderer'.
(Perry)

Pericles [Greek]
'Far famed'.

Perkin See **Parkin**

Pernell See **Peter**

Perrin See **Peter**

Perry [Anglo-Saxon]
'From the pear tree'. Also
dim. of Peregrine.

Perry See **Peregrine**

Perseus [Greek]
'Destroyer'.

Perth [Celtic]
'Thorn bush thicket'.

Pete See **Peter**

Peter [Latin]
'The stone; the rock'. The
first Pope.
*(Parnell, Pearce, Pedro,
Pernell, Perrin, Petrie,
Pierce, Pierre, Piers,
Pietro, Pete, Peadar,
Pierrot, Pierro, Piero)*

Peterkin See **Parkin**

Petrie See **Peter**

Peverall [French]
'The piper'.
*(Peverell, Peverill,
Peveral, Peverel, Peveril)*

Peverell See **Peverall**

Peverill See **Peverall**

Peyton See **Patrick** or
Payton

Pharamond [German]
'Journey protection'.

Phelan [Gaelic]
'Brave as the wolf'.

Phelips See **Phillips**

Phelps [Anglo-Saxon]
'Son of Philip'.

Phelps See **Philip**

Philbert [Teutonic]
'Brilliant'.

Philemon [Greek]
'Kiss'.

Philip [Greek]
'Lover of horses'.
(Philipp, Phillip, Phillipp,
Filip, Fillip, Phelps, Pilib,
Filib, Phil, Phillie, Philly)

Phillie See **Philip**

Phillips [Anglo-Saxon]
'Philip's son'.
(Phelips, Phellips,
Phellipps, Philips,
Phillipps, Felips, Fellips)

Philo [Greek]
'Friendly love'.

Phineas [Greek]
'Mouth of brass'.

Pickford [Anglo-Saxon]
'From the ford at the peak'.

Pickworth [Anglo-Saxon]
'From the estate of the
hewer'.

Pierce See **Peter**

Piero See **Peter**

Pierre See **Peter**

Pierro See **Peter**

Pierrot See **Peter**

Piers See **Peter**

Pietro See **Peter**

Pilib See **Philip**

Pippin [Dutch from
Teutonic]
'Father'.

Pitney [Anglo-Saxon]
'Preserving one's island'.

Pitt [Anglo-Saxon]
'From the hollow'.

Placide See **Placido**

Placido [Spanish]
'Serene'.

Plato [Greek]
'The broad shouldered one'. The great philosopher.

Platt [French]
'From the plateau'.

Pollard [Old German]
'Cropped hair'.

Pollock [Anglo-Saxon]
'Little Paul'.

Pollux [Greek]
'Crown'.

Pomeroy [French]
'From the apple orchard'.

Porter [French]
'Gatekeeper'.

Powell [Celtic]
'Alert' or 'Son of Howell'.

Pravat [Thai]
'History'.

Prentice [Anglo-Saxon]
'A learner or apprentice'.

Prentiss See **Prentice**

Prescott [Anglo-Saxon]
'From the priest's house'.
(Prescot)

Preston [Anglo-Saxon]
'From the priest's farm'.

Prewitt [French]
'Little valiant warrior'.
(Prewit, Prewett, Prewet, Pruitt)

Price [Celtic]
'Son of a loving man'.

Primo [Latin]
'The first born son'.

Prince [Latin]
'Chief'.

Prior [Latin]
'The Father Superior, the Head of the Monastery'.
(Pryor)

Probus [Latin]
'Honest'.

Proctor [Latin]
'The administrator'.

Prosper [Latin]
'Fortunate'.

Purcell See **Percival**

Purvis [English]
'To provide food'.

Putnam [Anglo-Saxon]
'From the pit dweller's
estate'.

Pwyll [Welsh]
'Prudence'.

Girls

Qadira [Arabic]
'Powerful'.

Qiturah [Arabic]
'Fragrance'.

Queena [Teutonic]
'The queen'. The supreme
woman.
(Queenie)

Queenie See **Queena**

Quenberga [Latin]
'Queen pledge'.

Quenby [Scandinavian]
'Womanly; perfect wife'.

Quendrida [Latin]
'Queen threatener'.

Querida [Spanish]
'Beloved one'. *(Cherida)*

Questa [French]
'Searcher'.

Quinta [Latin]
'The fifth child'.
(Quintilla, Quintella, Quintina)

Quintana See **Quinta**

Quintella See **Quinta**

Quintessa [Latin]
'Essence'.

Quintilla See **Quinta**

Quintina See **Quinta**

Qabil [Arabic]
'Able'.

Qadim [Arabic]
'Ancient'.

Qadir [Arabic]
'Powerful'.

Quemby See **Quimby**

Quenby See **Quimby**

Quennel [French]
'Dweller by the little oak'.

Quent See **Quentin**

Quentin [Latin]
'The fifth born'.
*(Quinton, Quintin,
Quent)*

Quigley [Gaelic]
'Distaff'.

Quillan [Gaelic]
'Cub'.

Quillon [Latin]
'Sword'.

Quimby [Norse]
'From the woman's
estate'.
*(Quinby, Quemby,
Quenby)*

Quinby See **Quimby**

Quincy [French/Latin]
'From the fifth son's
estate'.

Quinlan [Gaelic]
'The well formed one'. One
with the body of an
Adonis.

Quinn [Gaelic]
'Wise and intelligent'.

Quinton See **Quentin**

Quintus See **Quentin**

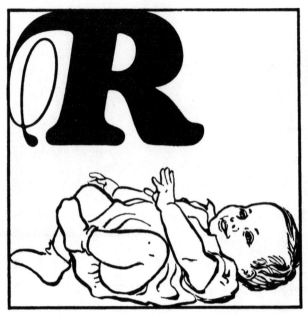

Girls

Rabi [Arabic]
'The harvest'.

Rachel [Hebrew]
'Innocent as a lamb'. One who suffers in silence. *(Rachele, Rachelle, Raquel, Rahel, Raoghnailt, Rochelle, Rae, Ray, Shelley)*

Rachelle See **Rachel**

Rachida [Arabic]
'Wise'.

Radella [Anglo-Saxon]
'Elf-like adviser'. A fairy-like creature whose advice is weighty.

Radinka [Slavic]
'Alive and joyful'.

Radmilla [Slavic]
'Worker for the people'.

Rae [Middle English]
'A doe deer'. Also dim. of
Rachel.

Rae See **Rachel**

Rahima [Arabic]
'Merciful'.

Raina See **Regina**

Raissa [French]
'The believer'.
(Raisse)

Raisse See **Raissa**

Rama See **Ramona**

Ramona [Teutonic]
'Wise protector'. Fem. of
Raymond.
*(Ramonda, Raymonde,
Raymonda, Mona, Rama)*

Ramonda See **Ramona**

Ramonde See **Ramona**

Rana [Sanskrit]
'Of royal birth; a queen'.
(Ranee, Rani)

Randa See **Miranda**

Ranee See **Rana**

Rania See **Rana**

Ranique See **Rana**

Raoghnailt See **Rachel**

Raphaela [Hebrew]
'Blessed healer'. One
having the God-given
healing touch.
*(Rafaela, Rafaella,
Raphaella)*

Raquel See **Rachel**

Rasha [Arabic]
'Young gazelle'.

Rashida [African]
'Righteous'.

Rasia See **Rose**

Ray See **Rachel**

Raymonda
Fem. of Raymond.

Rayna See **Regina**

Rayna See **Rana**

Reba See **Rebecca**

Rebecca [Hebrew]
'The captivator'.
*(Rebeka, Rebekah,
Rebekka, Rebeca, Reba,
Riva, Riba, Beckie, Becky,
Bekky)*

Rechaba [Hebrew]
'Horse woman'.

Reena See **Rena**

Regan See **Regina**

Regina [Latin]
'A queen; born to rule'.
*(Regan, Regine, Raina,
Reine, Raine, Rayna,
Reina, Rioghnach, Rina,
Gina)*

Regine See **Regina**

Reiko [Japanese]
'Gratitude'.

Reine See **Regina**

Reini See **Irene**

Rena [Hebrew]
'Song'.

Rena See **Irene**

Renata [Latin]
'Born again'. The spirit of
reincarnation.

*(Rene, Renee, Rennie,
Renate)*

Renata See **Irene**

Rene See **Irene, Renata**

Renita [Latin]
'A rebel'.

Rennie See **Renata**

Reseda [Latin]
'Mignonette flower'.

Retha See **Areta**

Reva [Latin]
'Strength regained'.

Rexana [Latin]
'Regally graceful'. One
whose bearing is regal.
(Rexanna)

Rhea [Greek]
'Mother' or 'Poppy'. The
mother of the Grecian
Gods.
(Rea)

Rhedyn [Welsh]
'Fern'.

Rheta [Greek]
'An orator'.

Rhiannon [Welsh]
'Nymph'.

Rhianwen [Welsh]
'Blessed maiden'.

Rhoda [Greek]
'Garland of roses; girl from
Rhodes'.
(Rhodia)

Rhoda See **Rose**

Rhodanthe [Greek]
'The rose of roses'.

Rhodia See **Rhoda** or **Rose**

Rhona See **Rona**

Rhonda [Welsh]
'Grand'.

Rhonwen [Welsh]
'White lance'.

Ria [Spanish]
'The river'.

Riba See **Rebecca**

Rica See **Roderica** or
Ulrica

Ricadonna [Italian]
'Ruling lady'. One who
rules in her own right or
on behalf of her son.

Ricarda [Teutonic]
'Powerful ruler'. Fem. of
Richard.
*(Richarda, Richarde,
Rickie, Ricky, Dickie,
Dicky)*

Richarde See **Ricarda**

Rilla [Teutonic]
'A stream or brook'.
(Rille, Rillette)

Rille See **Rilla**

Rillette See **Rilla**

Rina See **Regina**

Rinah [Hebrew]
'Song; joy'.

Rioghnach See **Regina**

Risa [Latin]
'Laughter'.

Rita See **Margaret**

Riva [French]
'Riverbank'.

Roanna [Latin]
'Sweet and gracious'.
(*Rohanna, Rohanne*)

Roberta [Anglo-Saxon]
'Of shining fame'. Fem. of
Robert.
(*Robina, Roberta,
Robinia, Robinette,
Robertha, Roberthe,
Ruberta, Ruperta,
Bobette, Bobina, Bobbie,
Bobby, Bertie*)

Robin [Old English]
'Bright or shining with
fame'.
(*Robina, Robyn*)

Robina See **Robin**

Robinette See **Roberta**

Robinia See **Roberta**

Rochalla See **Rochelle**

Rochelle [French]
'From the small rock'.
(*Rochalla, Rochalle,
Rochella, Rochette*)

Rochette See **Rochelle**

Roddie See **Roderica**

Roderica [Teutonic]
'Famous ruler'. Fem. of
Roderick.
(*Rodericka, Rica, Roddie,
Roddy, Rickie*)

Rodina See **Rhoda**

Rohana [Hindu]
'Sandalwood; sweet
incense'.
(*Rohanna, Rohane*)

Rohane See **Rohana**

Rohanne See **Roanna**

Rohesia See **Rose**

Rois See **Rose**

Rola See **Rolanda**

Rolanda [Teutonic]
'From the famed land'.
Fem. of Roland.
(*Rolande, Orlanda,
Orlande, Ro, Rola*)

Rolande See **Rolanda**

Roma See **Romola**

Romella See **Romola**

Romelle See **Romola**

Romilda [Teutonic]
'Glorious warrior maiden'.
(*Romilde, Romhilda,
Romhilde*)

Romilde See **Romilda**

Romola [Latin]
'Lady of Rome'.
(Roma, Romella, Romelle,
Romula)

Romula See **Romola**

Rona [Scandinavian]
'Mighty power'.

Ronalda [Teutonic]
'All powerful'. Fem. of
Ronald.
(Ronalde, Ronnie, Ronny)

Ronalda See **Rona**

Ronalde See **Ronalda**

Ronnie See **Ronalda** or
Veronica

Ros See **Rosalind**

Rosa See **Primrose** or
Rose

Rosabel [Latin]
'Beautiful rose'.
(Rosabella, Rosabelle)

Rosabella See **Rosabel**

Rosalee See **Rose**

Rosaleen See **Rose**

Rosalia See **Rose**

Rosalie See **Rose**

Rosalind [Latin]
'Fair and beautiful rose'.
(Rosalinda, Rosaline,
Rosalynd, Rosaline,
Roseline, Roselyn,
Rosalyn, Roslyn, Ros,
Roz, Rozalind, Rozaline,
Rozeline)

Rosalinda See **Rosalind**

Rosaline See **Rosalind**

Rosamond [French]
'Rose of the world'.
(Rosemond, Rosemund,
Rosamund, Rosamunda,
Rosamonda, Rosmunda,
Rosemonde, Rozamond)

Rosamunda See
Rosamond

Rosanna [English]
'Graceful rose'.
(Rosanne)

Rosanne See **Rosanna**

Rose [Greek]
'The rose'. The most
beautiful of flowers'.
*(Rosa, Rosie, Rosalie,
Rosalia, Rosella, Rohesia,
Roselle, Rosetta, Rosette,
Rosina, Rasia, Rosia,
Rozello, Rhoda, Rhodia,
Rosalee, Rosaleen,
Rosena, Rosene, Rosel,
Rozalina, Rosella, Rosy,
Rois)*

Rose See **Primrose**

Rosel See **Rose**

Rosella See **Rose**

Roselle See **Rose**

Rosemary [Latin]
'Dew of the sea'.
(Rosemarie)

Rosemond See
Rosamond

Rosemund See
Rosamond

Rosena See **Rose**

Rosene See **Rose**

Rosetta See **Rose**

Rosette See **Rose**

Rosia See **Rose**

Rosie See **Rose**

Rosina See **Rose**

Rosslyn [Welsh]
'Moorland lake'.

Rosy See **Rose**

Roux See **La Roux**

Rowena [Anglo-Saxon]
'Friend with white hair'.
(Rowenna)

Roxana [Persian]
'Brilliant dawn'.
*(Roxane, Roxanna,
Roxanne, Roxine, Roxina,
Rox, Roxie, Roxy)*

Roxane See **Roxana**

Roxie See **Roxana**

Roxina See **Roxana**

Roxine See **Roxana**

Royale [French]
'Regal being'. Fem. of Roy.

Rozalina See **Rose**

Rozella See **Rose**

Ruberta See **Roberta**

Rubetta See **Ruby**

Rubette See **Ruby**

Rubia See **Ruby**

Rubina See **Ruby**

Ruby [Latin]
'Precious red jewel'.
*(Rubetta, Rubette, Rubia,
Rubina, Rubie)*

Rudella See **Rudelle**

Rudelle [Teutonic]
'Famous person'.
(Rudella)

Ruella [Combination Ruth/
Ella]

Rufina [Latin]
'Red-haired one'.

Rugina [Latin]
'Girl with bright red hair'.

Rula [Latin]
'A sovereign'. One who
rules by right.

Ruperta See **Roberta**

Ruri [Japanese]
'Emerald'.

Ruth [Hebrew]
'Compassionate and
beautiful'.
(Ruthie)

Ruthie See **Ruth**

Rutilia [Latin]
'Fiery red'.

Rab See **Robert**

Rabbie See **Robert**

Race See **Horace**

Rachid [Arabic]
  'Wise'.

Rad [Anglo-Saxon]
  'Counsellor; adviser'. Also
  dim. of Radcliffe.

Radbert [Teutonic]
  'Brilliant counsellor'.

Radborne [Anglo-Saxon]
  'From the red stream'.
  *(Radbourne, Redbourne,
  Radbourn, Redbourn)*

Radcliffe [Anglo-Saxon]
  'From the red cliff'.
  *(Radcliff, Redcliff,
  Redcliffe)*

Radford [Anglo-Saxon]
  'From the red ford'.
  *(Redford, Radvers,
  Redvers)*

Radi [Arabic]
  'Content'.

Radley [Anglo-Saxon]
  'From the red meadow'.
  (Radleigh)

Radmund See **Redmond**

Radnor [Anglo-Saxon]
  'From the red shore'.

Radolf [Anglo-Saxon]
  'Wolf counsellor'. Wolf is
  used in the sense 'brave
  man'.

Radvers See **Radford**

Rafael See **Raphael**

Rafe See **Raphael**

Raff See **Ralph**

Rafferty [Gaelic]
  'Prosperous and rich'.

Raghib [Arabic]
  'Willing'.

Raghnall See **Reginald**

Raheem [Arabic]
  'Kind'.

Rainart [German]
'Strong judgement'.

Rainier See **Raynor**

Raleigh [Anglo-Saxon]
'Dweller in the meadow of
the roe deer'.
*(Ralegh, Rawley,
Rawleigh)*

Ralph [Anglo-Saxon]
'Counsel wolf'.
*(Ralf, Raff, Rolf, Rolph,
Raoul)*

Ralston [Anglo-Saxon]
'Dweller on Ralph's farm'.

Rambert [Teutonic]
'Brilliant and mighty'.

Ramiro [Spanish]
'Great judge'.

Ramon See **Raymond**

Ramón See **Raymond**

Ramsden [Anglo-Saxon]
'Ram's valley'.

Ramsey [Anglo-Saxon]
'From Ram's island' or
'From the raven's island'.

Rance [African]
'Borrowed all'.

Rand See **Randal**

Randal [Old English]
'Shield wolf'.
*(Randall, Rand,
Randolph, Randolf,
Ranulf)*

Randolph See **Randal**

Ranger [French]
'Keeper of the forest'. The
gamekeeper who looked
after the trees and the
wildlife.

Rankin [Anglo-Saxon]
'Little shield'.

Ransell See **Rance**

Ransford [Anglo-Saxon]
'From the raven's ford'.

Ransley [Anglo-Saxon]
'From the raven's
meadow'.

Ransom [Anglo-Saxon]
'Shield warrior's son'.

Ranulf See **Randal**

Raoul See **Ralph**

Raphael [Hebrew]
'Healed by God'.
*(Rafael, Rafaello,
Raffaello, Raff)*

Ras See **Erasmus**

Rashid [Arabic]
'Director, pious'.

Rasmus See **Erasmus**

Raul See **Ralph**

Ravi [Hindu]
'Sun'.

Rawley See **Raleigh**

Rawlins [French]
'Son of the wolf
counsellor'.

Rawson [Anglo-Saxon]
'Son of the little wolf'.

Ray [French]
'The sovereign'. Also dim.
of Raymond.

Rayburn [Old English]
'From the deer brook'.

Raymond [Teutonic]
'Wise protection'.
*(Raymon, Raimond,
Reamonn, Raymund,
Ray)*

Raymund See **Raymond**

Raynold See **Reginald**

Raynor [Scandinavian]
'Mighty army'.
(Rainer, Rainier)

Reade [Anglo-Saxon]
'The red headed one'.
(Read, Reed, Reede).

Reading [Anglo-Saxon]
'Son of the red haired one'.
(Redding)

Redbourne See
Radbourne

Redcliff See **Radcliffe**

Redford See **Radford**

Redley See **Radley**

Redman [Anglo-Saxon]
'Counsellor; advice giver'.

Redmond [Anglo-Saxon]
'Counsellor, protector,
advisor'.
(Radmund, Redmund)

Redpath See **Ridpath**

Redvers See **Radford**

Redwald [Anglo-Saxon]
'Mighty counsellor'.

Reece [Celtic]
'The ardent one'. One who
loves living.
(Rhett)

Reed See **Reade**

Reeve [Anglo-Saxon]
'The steward'. One who
looked after a great lord's
affairs.

Regan [Gaelic]
'Royalty, a king'.
(Reagan, Reagen, Regen)

Reggie See **Reginald**

Reginald [Teutonic]
'Mighty and powerful
ruler'.
*(Raghnall, Raynold,
Reinhold, Reynold,
Ronald, Reg, Reggie,
Reggy, Ron, Ronnie,
Ronny, Naldo)*

Rehard See **Reynard**

Reinhold See **Reginald**

Remington [Anglo-Saxon]
'From the farm where the
blackbirds sing'.

Remus [Latin]
'Fast rower'. A speedy
oarsman.

Renaldo See **Reginald**

Renato See **Reginald**

Renaud See **Reynard**

Renault See **Reginald**

Rene See **Reginald**

Renfred [Anglo-Saxon]
'Mighty and peaceful'. A
peaceful warrior who
could fight when
necessary.

Renfrew [Celtic]
'From the still river'.

Rennard See **Reynard**

Renny [Gaelic]
'Little mighty and
powerful'. Also der. of
Rene.

Renshaw [Anglo-Saxon]
'From the forest of the
ravens'.

Renton [Anglo-Saxon]
'From the farm of the roe
buck'.

Renwick [Teutonic]
'Raven's nest'.

Reuben [Hebrew]
'Behold a son'.
(Ruben, Rube, Rubey, Ruby)

Rex [Latin]
'The king'. The all powerful monarch.
(Rey, Roy)

Rexford [Anglo-Saxon]
'From the king's ford'.

Rey See **Rex**

Reynard [Teutonic]
'Mighty courage' or 'The fox'.
(Rehard, Rennard, Raynard, Reinhard, Renaud)

Reynold See **Reginald**

Reza [Arabic]
'Resigned to life, accepting'.

Rhain [Welsh]
'Lance'.

Rhett See **Reece**

Rhodes [Greek]
'The place of roses'.

Rhun [Welsh]
'Grand'.

Rhydwyn [Welsh]
'Dweller by the white ford'.

Rhys [Celtic]
'Hero'.
(Reece, Rees)

Ricardo See **Richard**

Rich See **Richard**

Richard [Teutonic]
'Wealthy, powerful one'.
(Ricard, Richerd, Rickert, Riocard, Rick, Rickie, Ricky, Rich, Ritch, Ritchie, Dick, Dickie, Dicky, Dickon, Diccon)

Richie See **Alaric**

Richman See **Richmond**

Richmond [Anglo-Saxon]
'Powerful protector'.
(Richman)

Rick See **Alaric**

Ricker [Teutonic]
'Powerful army'.

Rickert See **Richard**

Rickie See **Alaric**

Rickward [Anglo-Saxon]
'Powerful guardian'.
(Rickwood)

Rickwood See **Rickward**

Ricky See **Richard**

Ricy See **Alaric**

Riddock [Gaelic]
'From the barren field'.

Rider [Anglo-Saxon]
'Knight; horse-rider'.
(Ryder)

Ridge [Anglo-Saxon]
'From the ridge'.

Ridgeway [Anglo-Saxon]
'From the ridge road'.

Ridgley [Anglo-Saxon]
'From the ridge meadow'.

Ridley See **Radley**

Ridpath [Anglo-Saxon]
'From the red path'.
(Redpath)

Rigby [Anglo-Saxon]
'Valley of the ruler'.

Rigg [Anglo-Saxon]
'From the ridge'.

Riley [Gaelic]
'Valiant and warlike'.
(Reilly, Ryley)

Rinaldo See **Reginald**

Ring [Anglo-Saxon]
'A ring'.

Riocard See **Richard**

Riordan [Gaelic]
'Royal bard'
(Reardon, Rearden)

Ripley [Anglo-Saxon]
'From the valley of the echo'.

Risley [Anglo-Saxon]
'From the brushwood meadow'.

Riston [Anglo-Saxon]
'From the brushwood farm'.

Ritchie See **Richard**

Ritter [Teutonic]
'A knight'.

Roald [Teutonic]
'Famous ruler'.

Roan [Anglo-Saxon]
'From the rowan tree'.
(Rowan)

Roarke [Gaelic]
'Famous ruler'.
(Rorke, Rourke, Ruark)

Robby See **Robert**

Robert [Teutonic]
'Bright, shining fame'. A
man of brilliant reputation.
*(Roberto, Robin, Rupert,
Ruprecht, Rob, Robbie,
Robby, Rab, Rabbie,
Rabby, Bob, Bobbie,
Bobby)*

Roberto See **Robert**

Robinson [Anglo-Saxon]
'Son of Robert'.

Rochester [Anglo-Saxon]
'Camp on the rocks'.

Rock [Anglo-Saxon]
'From the rock'.
(Roc, Rocky)

Rockley [Anglo-Saxon]
'From the rocky meadow'.
(Rockly)

Rockly See **Rockley**

Rockwell [Anglo-Saxon]
'From the rocky well'.

Rocky See **Rock**

Rod See **Roderick**

Rodd See **Roderick**

Roddie See **Roderick**

Roden [Anglo-Saxon]
'From the valley of the
reeds'.

Roderick [Teutonic]
'Famous, wealthy ruler'.
*(Rodrick, Rodric, Roderic,
Broderic, Broderick,
Brodrick, Rod, Roddie,
Roddy, Rick, Rickie,
Ricky, Rory)*

Roderigo See **Roderick**

Rodge See **Roger**

Rodger See **Roger**

Rodhlann See **Roland**

Rodi See **Rodney**

Rodman [Teutonic]
'Famous hero'.
(Rodmond, Rodmund)

Rodney [Teutonic]
'Famous and renowned'.
*(Rod, Roddie, Roddy,
Rodi)*

Rodolph See **Rudolph**

Girls

Saba [Greek]
'Woman of Sheba'.

Sabella [Latin]
'The wise'.
(Sabelle)

Sabelle See **Sabella**

Sabina [Latin]
'Woman of Sabine'.
(Sabine, Savina, Bina,
Saidhbhain, Binnie)

Sabine See **Sabina**

Sabira [Arabic]
'Patient'.

Sabra [Hebrew]
'The restful one'.

Sabrina [Latin]
'A princess'.
(Brina, Sabrine)

Sabrine See **Sabrina**

Sacha [Greek]
'Helpmate'.
(Sasha)

Sacharissa [Greek]
'Sweet'.

Sadella See **Sarah**

Sadhth See **Sophia**

Sadie See **Sarah**

Sadira [Persian]
'The lotus eater'.

Saffron [English]
From the plant.

Safia [Arabic]
'Pure'.

Sahlah [Arabic]
'Smooth'.

Saidhbhain See **Sabina**

Salaidh See **Sarah**

Salema [Hebrew]
'Girl of peace'.
(Selemas, Selima)

Salina [Greek]
'From the salty place'.

Sallie See **Sarah**

Sally See **Sarah**

Saloma See **Salome**

Salome [Hebrew]
'Peace'. 'Shalom' the
traditional Hebrew
greeting — Peace.
(Saloma, Salomi)

Salomi See **Salome**

Salvia [Latin]
'Sage herb'.
(Salvina)

Salvina See **Salvia**

Samala [Hebrew]
'Asked of God'.

Samantha [Aramaic]
'A listener'.

Samara [Hebrew]
'Watchful, cautious;
guarded by God'.

Samella See **Samuela**

Samelle See **Samuela**

Samuela [Hebrew]
'His name is God'. Fem. of
Samuel.
*(Samella, Samelle,
Samuella, Samuelle)*

Samuelle See **Samuela**

Sancha See **Sancia**

Sancia [Latin]
'Sacred'.
(Sancha, Sanchia)

Sandra See **Alexandra**

Sandy See **Alexandra**

Sapphira [Greek]
'Eyes of sapphire colour'.

Sarah [Hebrew]
'Princess'. One of royal
status.
*(Sara, Sari, Sarene,
Sarine, Sarette, Sadella,
Sadie, Sorcha, Salaidh,
Sadye, Sal, Sallie, Sally,
Sharie, Sarita, Sorcha,
Salaidh, Morag, Zara,
Zarah, Zaria)*

Saree [Arabic]
'Most noble'.

Sarene See **Sarah**

Sarette See **Sarah**

Sari See **Sarah**

Sarita See **Sarah**

Sasha See **Alexandra**

Sashenka See **Alexandra**

Savanna [Spanish]
'An open plain'.

Savina See **Sabina**

Saxona [Teutonic]
'A sword bearer'.

Scarlett [Middle English]
'Scarlet coloured'.
(Scarlet, Scarletta)

Scarletta See **Scarlett**

Scholastica [Latin]
'Scholar'.

Sebestianan See
Sebastiane

Sebastiane [Latin]
'Revered one'.
*(Sebastianan,
Sebastianne, Sebastianna,
Sebastienna, Sebastienne)*

Sebastianna See
Sebastiane

Sebila [Latin]
'Wise old woman'.

Secunda [Latin]
'Second born'.

Seema [Hebrew]
'Treasure'.

Seirian [Welsh]
'Sparkling'.

Seiriol [Welsh]
'Bright'.
(Siriol)

Sela See **Selena**

Selda See **Griselda**

Selena [Greek]
'The Moon'.
*(Selina, Selene, Selinda,
Salene, Sela, Selie, Sena,
Selia, Celene, Celina,
Celinda, Celie, Lena)*

Selene See **Selena**

Selia See **Selena**

Selie See **Selena**

Selima [Hebrew]
'Peaceful'.

Selinda See **Selena**

Selma [Celtic]
'The fair'. Also der. of
Anselma.

Selma See **Anselma**

Semele [Latin]
'The single one'.
(Semelia)

Semelia See **Semele**

Semira [Hebrew]
'Height of the heavens'.

Sena See **Selena**

Senalda [Spanish]
'A sign'.

Seonaid See **Jane**

Septima [Latin]
'Seventh born'.

Sera See **Seraphina**

Seraphina [Hebrew]
'The ardent believer'. One
with a burning faith'.
*(Serafina, Seraphine,
Serafine, Sera)*

Seraphine See **Seraphina**

Serena [Latin]
'Bright tranquil one'.

Serica [Latin]
'Silken'.

Serilda [Teutonic]
'Armoured battle maid'.
(Serilde, Serhilda,

Serhilde)

Serilde See **Serilda**

Shahdi [Persian]
'Happiness'.

Shaina [Hebrew]
'Beautiful'.

Shaira [Arabic]
'Thankful'.

Shakira See **Shaira**

Shani [African]
'Marvellous'.

Shanley [Gaelic]
'Child of the old hero'.

Shannah See **Shannon**

Shannon [Gaelic]
'Small, wise'.

Shari See **Sharon**

Sharleen See **Charlotte/
Caroline**

Sharon [Hebrew]
'A princess of exotic
beauty'.
*(Sherry, Shari, Sharri,
Sharry)*

Sharry See **Sharon**

Shayna See **Shaina**

Shayne See **Shaina**

Shea [Gaelic]
'From the fairy fort'.

Shea See **Shelah**

Sheba See **Saba**

Sheela See **Sheena**

Sheena [Gaelic]
'Dim-sighted'.
(Sheela, Sheelah, Sheilah)

Sheila [Celtic]
'Musical'. Var. of Cecilia.
*(Sheela, Sheelah, Sheilah,
Selia)*

Shelagh See **Sheila**

Shelah [Hebrew]
'Asked for'.
*(Shela, Shaya, Sheya,
Shea)*

Shelby [Old English]
'From the ledge estate'.

Shelley [English]
'From the edge of the
meadow'.

Shelly See **Rachel**

Shena See **Jane**

Shereen [Arabic]
'Sweet'.

Sheri See **Shirley**

Sherrie See **Cherie**

Sherry See **Charlotte,
Sharon** or **Cherie**

Sheryl See **Charlotte,
Shirley** or **Cherie**

Sheya See **Shelah**

Shifra [Hebrew]
'Beautiful'.

Shina [Japanese]
'Good virtue'.

Shiri [Hebrew]
'My song'.

Shirleen See **Shirley**

Shirley [Anglo-Saxon]
'From the white meadow'.
*(Shirlee, Shirlie, Shirleen,
Shirlene, Sheryl, Sherry,
Sheri)*

Shoshana [Hebrew]
'Rose'.

Shula [Arabic]
'Flame, brightness'.

Shulamith [Hebrew]
'Peace'.

Sibella See **Sybil**

Sibie See **Sybil**

Sibilla See **Sybil**

Sibyl See **Sybil**

Sidney/Sidonia See
Sydney

Sidonie See **Sydney**

Sidra [Latin]
'Glittering lady of the
stars'.
(Sidria)

Sidria See **Sidra**

Sierna [Greek]
'A sweetly singing
mermaid'.

Sigfreda [Teutonic]
'Victorious and peaceful'.
(Sigfrieda, Sigfriede)

Sigfriede See **Sigfreda**

Signa [Latin]
'Signed on the heart'.

Sigrath See **Sigrid**

Sigrid [Norse]
'Victorious counsellor'.
(Sigrath, Sigrud, Sigurd)

Sigrud See **Sigrid**

Sigurd See **Sigrid**

Sile See **Julia**

Sileas See **Cecilia** or **Julia**

Silva See **Sylvia**

Silvana [Latin]
'Wood dweller'.

Silvana See **Sylvia**

Silvie See **Sylvia**

Simona See **Simone**

Simone [Hebrew]
'Heard by the Lord'. Fem.
of Simon/Simeon.
*(Simona, Simonette,
Simonetta)*

Simonetta See **Simone**

Simonette See **Simone**

Sine See **Jane**

Sinead [Welsh] See **Jane**

Siobhan [Irish] See **Jane**
or **Judith**

Sirena [Greek]
'Sweet singing mermaid'.
Originally from the sirens
who lured men to their
deaths. Used sometimes
during World War II for
babies born during an air
raid.
(Sirene, Sireen)

Sirene See **Sirena**

Sisle See **Cecilia**

Sissie See **Cecilia**

Skye See **Skylar**

Skylar [Dutch]
'Sheltering'.
(Skye)

Solana [Spanish]
'Sunshine'.

Solange [Latin]
'Good shepherdess'.

Solita [Latin]
'Solitary one'.

Solvig [Teutonic]
'Victorious battle maid'.

Sonia See **Sophia**

Sonja See **Sophia**

Sophia [Greek]
'Wisdom'.
*(Sophie, Sophy, Sofia,
Sonia, Sonja, Sonya,
Sofie, Sadhbh, Sadhbha,
Beathag)*

Sophie See **Sophia**

Sophronia [Greek]
'Sensible one'.

Sorcha [Gaelic]
'Bright one'.

Sorcha See **Sarah**

Sperata [Latin]
'Hoped for'.

Spring [English]
'Joyous season'.

Stacy/Stacia See
Anastasia/Eustacia

Starr [English]
'A star'.
(Star)

Stefa See **Stephanie**

Steffie See **Stephanie**

Stella See **Estelle**

Stelle See **Estelle**

Stephania See **Stephanie**

Stephanie [Greek]
'A crown; garland'. Fem.
of Stephen.
*(Stephania, Stephena,
Stevana, Stevania,
Stevena, Stevenia,
Stephenie, Stephenia,
Stephena, Stefa, Stepha,
Steffie, Stevie)*

Stephena See **Stephanie**

Stevie See **Stephanie**

Storm [Anglo-Saxon]
'A tempest'. One of
turbulent nature.

Sue See **Susan**

Suki See **Susan**

Sulia [Latin]
'Downy, youthful'.

Suliana See **Sulia**

Sumalee [Thai]
'Beautiful flower'.

Sumi [Japanese]
'Refined'.

Sunita [Hindi]
'Good conduct and deeds'.

Sunny [Anglo-Saxon]
'Bright and cheerful'. The
brightness of the sun after
the storm.

Susan [Hebrew]
'Graceful lily'.
*(Susana, Susanna,
Susanne, Susannah,
Suzanna, Suzanne,
Suzette, Susette, Suzetta,
Sue, Susi, Susie, Susy,
Suzie, Suzy, Suki, Sukey,
Suky, Zsa-Zsa)*

Susana See **Susan**

Susi See **Susan**

Suzetta See **Susan**

Suzette See **Susan**

Swetlana [German]
'A star'.

Sybil [Greek]
'Prophetess'. The female
soothsayer of ancient
Greece.
*(Cybil, Sibyl, Sibil, Sibel,
Sibell, Sybyl, Sibilla,
Sibella, Sybella, Sibille,*

*Sibylle, Sybille, Sib, Sibie,
Sibbie, Sibby)*

Syd See **Sydney**

Sydel [Hebrew]
'That enchantress'.
(Sydelle)

Sydney [French/Hebrew]
'From St. Denis' (French);
'The enticer' (Hebrew).
Fem. of Sidney.
*(Sidney, Sidonia, Sidonie,
Sid, Syd)*

Syl See **Sylvia**

Sylgwyn [Welsh]
'Born on Whitsunday'.

Sylvia [Latin]
'From the forest'.
*(Silvia, Silva, Sylva,
Silvana, Slyvana, Zilvia,
Zilva, Sil, Syl, Silvie)*

Syna [Greek]
'Together'.
(Syne)

Syne See **Syna**

Syntyche [Greek]
'With good fortune'.

Sabeel [Arabic]
'The way'.

Saber [French]
'A sword'.

Sabin [Latin]
'Man from the Sabines'.

Sadik [Arabic]
'Truthful'.

Safford [Anglo-Saxon]
'From the willow ford'.

Saladin [Arabic]
'Goodness of the faith'.

Salim [Arabic]
'Safe, healthy, peace'.

Salisbury [Old English]
'Fortified stronghold'.

Salomon [Hebrew]
'Peaceful'.

Salton [Anglo-Saxon]
'From the willow farm'.

Salvador [Latin]
'The saviour'.
(Salvadore, Salvator,

Salvatore)

Salvator See **Salvador**

Salvestro [Italian]
'Woody'.

Salvidor See **Salvador**

Sam See **Sampson**

Sammy See **Sampson**

Sampson [Hebrew]
'Sun's man'.
*(Samson, Simpson,
Simson, Sam, Sammy,
Sim)*

Samson See **Sampson**

Samuel [Hebrew]
'His name is God'.
(Sam, Sammie, Sammy)

Sanborn [Anglo-Saxon]
'From the sandy brook'.
(Samborn)

Sancho [Spanish]
'Sincere and truthful'.

Sander See **Alexander**

Sanders [Anglo-Saxon]
'Son of Alexander'.
(*Sanderson, Saunderson,
Saunders, Sandie, Sandy*)

Sanderson See **Sanders**

Sandie See **Alexander**

Sandy See **Lysander**

Sanford [Anglo-Saxon]
'From the sandy ford'.

Sansom See **Sampson**

Santo [Italian]
'Saint like'.

Santon [Anglo-Saxon]
'From the sandy farm'.

Sanzio [Italian]
'Holy'.

Sardis [Hebrew]
'Prince of Joy'.

Sarge See **Sargent**

Sargent [Latin]
'A military attendant'.
(*Sergeant, Sergent, Sarge,
Sargie*)

Sargie See **Sargent**

Sasha See **Alexander**

Saul [Hebrew]
'Called by God'.

Saunders See **Alexander**

Saunderson See **Sanders**

Saville [French]
'The willow estate'.
(*Savile*)

Sawyer [Anglo-Saxon]
'A sawer of wood'.

Saxe See **Saxon**

Saxon [Anglo-Saxon]
'People of the swords'.
(*Saxe*)

Sayer [Celtic]
'Carpenter'.
(*Sayre, Sayers, Sayres*)

Sayers See **Sayer**

Scanlon [Gaelic]
'A snarer of hearts'.

Schuyler [Dutch]
'A scholar; a wise man' or
'To shield'.

Scipio [Latin]
'Walking stick'.

Scott [Latin/Celtic]
'From Scotland' (Latin) or
'Tattoed warrior' (Celtic).
(Scot, Scottie, Scotty)

Scottie See **Scott**

Scoville [French]
'From the Scottish estate'.

Scully [Gaelic]
'Town crier'. The bringer
of news in the days before
mass media.

Seabert [Anglo-Saxon]
'Sea glorious'.
(Seabright, Sebert)

Seabright See **Seabert**

Seabrook [Anglo-Saxon]
'From a brook by the sea'.
(Sebrook)

Seamus See **Jacob** or
James

Sean See **John**

Searle [Teutonic]
'Armed warrior'.
(Searl)

Seaton [French]
'From Say's farm'.
(Seton, Seeton, Seetin)

Sebald [Old English]
'Bold in victory'.

Sebastian [Latin]
'Reverenced one'. An
august person.
(Sebastien, Seb)

Sebastiano See **Sebastian**

Sebert [Old English]
'Famous for victory'.

Sebert See **Seabert**

Secundus [Latin]
'Second'.

Sedgley [Anglo-Saxon]
'From the swordsman's
meadow'.
(Sedgeley)

Sedgwick [Anglo-Saxon]
'From the sword grass
place'.
(Sedgewick)

Seeley [Anglo-Saxon]
'Happy and blessed'.
(Seely, Sealey)

Seetin See **Seaton**

Seger [Anglo-Saxon]
'Sea warrior'.
(Seager, Segar)

Selby [Teutonic]
'From the manor farm'.

Selden [Anglo-Saxon]
'From the valley of the
willow tree'.

Selig [Teutonic]
'Blessed happy one'.

Selwyn [Teutonic]
'Friend at the manor
house'.
(Selwin)

Senior [French]
'Lord of the manor'.
(Seigneur)

Sennett [French]
'Old and wise'. The all
knowing seer.

Seosaidh See **Joseph**

Septimus [Latin]
'Seventh born son'.

Sergent See **Sargent**

Serge/Sergeant See
Sargeant

Sergio See **Sargent**

Serle [Teutonic]
'Bearer of arms and
weapons'.

Seth [Hebrew]
'The appointed by God'.

Seton [Anglo-Saxon]
'From the farm by the sea'.

Seumas [Gaelic] See
James

Severn [Anglo-Saxon]
'The boundary'.

Sewald See **Sewell**

Sewall See **Sewell**

Seward [Anglo-Saxon]
'The sea defender'.

Sewell [Anglo-Saxon]
'Sea powerful'.
(Sewald, Sewall, Siwald)

Sexton [Anglo-Saxon]
'Sacristan'. A church
official.

Sextus [Latin]
'Sixth born son'.

Seyed [Arabic]
'Master'.

Seymour [French/Anglo-
Saxon]
'From St. Maur' (French)
or 'From the sea moor'
(Anglo-Saxon).

Shadwell [Anglo-Saxon]
'From the well in the
arbour'.

Shafiq [Arabic]
'Kind, compassionate'.

Shalom [Hebrew]
'Peace'.

Shamus See **Jacob** or
James

Shanahan [Gaelic]
'The wise one'.

Shanan See **Shannon**

Shandy [Anglo-Saxon]
'Little boisterous one'.

Shane See **John**

Shanley [Gaelic]
'The venerable hero'.

Shannon [Gaelic]
'Old wise one'.

Shattuck [Anglo-Saxon]
'Little shad-fish'.

Shaw [Anglo-Saxon]
'From the grove'.

Shay See **Shea**

Shea [Gaelic]
'Stately, courteous, and
inventive person'. A man
of many parts.
(Shay)

Sheehan [Gaelic]
'Peaceful one'.

Sheffield [Anglo-Saxon]
'From the crooked field'.

Shelby [Anglo-Saxon]
'From the estate on the
cliff edge'.

Sheldon [Anglo-Saxon]
'From the hill ledge'.

Shelley [Anglo-Saxon]
'From the meadow on the
hill ledge'.

Shelton [Anglo-Saxon]
'From the farm on the hill
ledge'.

Shem [Hebrew]
'Renown'.

Shepard [Anglo-Saxon]
'The sheep tender; the
shepherd'.
*(Shepherd, Sheppard,
Shepperd, Shep, Shepp,
Sheppy)*

Shepley [Anglo-Saxon]
'From the sheep meadow'.

Shepp See **Shepard**

Sheppy See **Shepard**

Sherborne [Anglo-Saxon]
'From the clear stream'.
(*Sherbourn, Sherbourne,
Sherburne, Sherburn*)

Sherburn See **Sherborne**

Sheridan [Gaelic]
'Wild savage'.

Sherlock [Anglo-Saxon]
'White haired man'.

Sherman [Anglo-Saxon]
'Wool shearer; sheep
shearer'.

Sherwin [Anglo-Saxon]
'Loyal friend' or 'Swift
footed'.

Sherwood [Anglo-Saxon]
'Bright forest'.

Sherwynd See **Sherwin**

Shipley [Anglo-Saxon]
'From the sheep meadow'.

Shipton [Anglo-Saxon]
'From the sheep farm'.

Sholom See **Shalom**

Sholto [Gaelic]
'The wild duck'.

Sian See **John**

Sid See **Sidney**

Siddell [Anglo-Saxon]
'From a wide valley'.

Sidney [French]
'A follower of St. Denis' or
'Man from Sidon'.
(*Sid, Syd, Sydney*)

Sigfrid [Teutonic]
'Peace after victory'.
(*Sigfried, Siegfrid,
Siegfried*)

Sigismund See **Sigmund**

Sigmund [Teutonic]
'Victorious protector'.
(*Sigismund, Sigismond,
Sigmond*)

Sigurd [Scandinavian]
'Victorious guardian'.
(*Sigerd*)

Sigwald [Teutonic]
'Victorious ruler'.

Silas [Latin]
'From the forest'.
*(Silvan, Silvanus,
Silvester, Sylvan,
Sylvester, Si)*

Silvan See **Silas**

Silvano See **Silas**

Silvanus See **Silas**

Silvester See **Silas**

Sim See **Sampson**

Simeon See **Simon**

Simon [Hebrew]
'One who hears'.
*(Simeon, Siomonn, Sim,
Ximenes)*

Simpson See **Sampson**

Sinclair [French]
'From St. Clair' or 'Shining
light'.
(St. Clair)

Siward [Teutonic]
'Conquering guardian'.

Skeat See **Skeets**

Skeeter See **Skeets**

Skeets [Anglo-Saxon]
'The swift'.
(Skeat, Skeet, Skeeter)

Skelly [Gaelic]
'Historian'.

Skelton [Anglo-Saxon]
'From the farm on the hill
ledge'.

Skerry [Scandinavian]
'From the rocky island'.

Skip [Scandinavian]
'Owner of the ship'.
(Skipp, Skippy)

Skippy See **Skip**

Skipton [Anglo-Saxon]
'From the sheep farm'.

Slade [Anglo-Saxon]
'Valley dweller'.

Slaven See **Slevin**

Slavin See **Slevin**

Sleven See **Slevin**

Slevin [Gaelic]
'The mountain climber'.
(Slaven, Slavin, Sleven)

Sloan [Gaelic]
'Warrior'.
(Sloane)

Sly See **Silas**

Smedley [Anglo-Saxon]
'From the flat meadow'.
(Smedly)

Smith [Anglo-Saxon]
'The blacksmith'.

Snowden [Anglo-Saxon]
'From the snowy hill'. Man
from the snowcapped
mountains.

Socrates [Greek]
'Self-restrained'.

Sol [Latin]
'The sun'. Also dim. of
Solomon.

Solly See **Solomon**

Solomon [Hebrew]
'Wise and peaceful'. The
wisdom of Solomon.
(Solamon, Soloman,
Salomon, Sol, Sollie,
Solly)

Solon [Greek]
'Wise man'. Greek form of
Solomon.

Somerled [Teutonic]
'Summer wanderer'.

Somerset [Anglo-Saxon]
'From the summer place'.
The place where the
wanderers rested for the
summer.

Somerton [Anglo-Saxon]
'From the summer farm'.

Somerville [Anglo-Saxon]
'From the summer estate'.
(Sommerville)

Sonny See **Tyson**

Sophocles [Greek]
'Glory of wisdom'.

Sorrel [French]
'With brownish hair'.

Southwell [Anglo-Saxon]
'From the south well'.

Spalding [Anglo-Saxon]
'From the split meadow'.
(Spaulding)

Spangler [Teutonic]
'The tinsmith'.

Spark [Anglo-Saxon]
'Gay gallant'. The man
about town.

Speed [Anglo-Saxon]
'Success, prosperity'.

Spence See **Spencer**

Spencer [French]
'Shopkeeper; dispenser of
provisions'.
(Spenser, Spence)

Spiro [Greek]
'Breath of the gods'.

Sproule [Anglo-Saxon]
'Energetic, active person'.
(Sprowle)

Squire [Anglo-Saxon]
'Knight's shield bearer'.

St Clair See **Sinclair**

St John [English]
A contraction of Saint
John.

Stacey [Latin]
'Prosperous and stable'.
(Stacy)

Staffard See **Stafford**

Stafford [Anglo-Saxon]
'From the ford by the
landing place'.

Stamford [Anglo-Saxon]
'From the stony crossing'.
(Stanford)

Stan See **Stanislaus**

Stanbury [Anglo-Saxon]
'From a stone fortress'.
(Stanberry)

Stancliffe [Anglo-Saxon]
'From the rocky cliff'.
*(Stancliff, Standcliff,
Standcliffe)*

Standcliff See **Stancliffe**

Standish [Anglo-Saxon]
'From the stony park'.

Stanfield [Anglo-Saxon]
'From the stony field'.

Stanford See **Stamford**

Stanhope [Anglo-Saxon]
'From the stony hollow'.

Stanislas See **Stanislaus**

Stanislaus [Slavic]
'Stand of glory'.
*(Stanislas, Stanislav,
Aineislis, Stan)*

Stanislav See **Stanislaus**

Stanislaw See **Stanislaus**

Stanley [Slavic/Anglo-
Saxon]
'Pride of the camp' (Slavic)

or 'From the stony meadow' (Anglo-Saxon). *(Stanley, Stanleigh, Stanly, Stan)*

Stanton [Anglo-Saxon]
'From the rocky lake' or 'From the stony farm'.

Stanway [Anglo-Saxon]
'From the stony road'.

Stanwick [Anglo-Saxon]
'From the stony village'.

Stanwood [Anglo-Saxon]
'From the stony forest'.

Starling [Anglo-Saxon]
'The starling'.

Starr [Anglo-Saxon]
'A star'.

Stavros [Greek]
'Cross'.

Stedman [Anglo-Saxon]
'Farm owner'. One who owns the land he tills.

Stefan See **Stephen**

Stein [Teutonic]
'The stone'.

Stephanus See **Stephen**

Stephen [Greek]
'The crowned one'. A man who wears the victor's laurel wreath. *(Steven, Stephenson, Stevenson, Stefan, Steffen, Steve, Stevie)*

Stephenson See **Stephen**

Sterling [Teutonic/Celtic]
'Good, honest, worthy' (Teutonic) or 'From the yellow house' (Celtic). *(Stirling)*

Sterne [Anglo-Saxon]
'The austere one; an ascetic'. *(Stern, Stearne, Stearn)*

Steve See **Stephen**

Steven See **Stephen**

Stevie See **Stephen**

Stew See **Stewart**

Steward See **Stewart**

Stewart [Anglo-Saxon]
'The steward'. Name of the Royal House of Scotland. *(Steward, Stuart, Stew, Stu)*

Stillman [Anglo-Saxon]
'Quiet and gentle man'.
(Stilman)

Stinson [Anglo-Saxon]
'Son of stone'.

Stirling See **Sterling**

Stockley [Anglo-Saxon]
'From the cleared
meadow'.

Stockton [Anglo-Saxon]
'From the farm in the
clearing'.

Stockwell [Anglo-Saxon]
'From the well in the
clearing'.

Stoddard [Anglo-Saxon]
'The horse keeper'.

Stoke [Anglo-Saxon]
'A village'.

Storm [Anglo-Saxon]
'The tempest'.

Storr [Scandinavian]
'Great man'.

Stowe [Anglo-Saxon]
'From the place'.

Strahan [Gaelic]
'The poet'.

Stratford [Anglo-Saxon]
'The street crossing the
ford'.

Stroud [Anglo-Saxon]
'From the thicket'.

Struthers [Gaelic]
'From the rivulet'.
(Strothers)

Stuart See **Stewart**

Styles [Anglo-Saxon]
'From the dwelling by the
stile'.
(Stiles)

Suffield [Anglo-Saxon]
'From the south field'.

Sulien [Welsh]
'Sun-born'.

Sullie See **Sullivan**

Sullivan [Gaelic]
'Man with black eyes'.
(Sullie, Sully)

Sully [Anglo-Saxon]
'From the south meadow'.
Also dim. of Sullivan.

Sumner [Latin]
'One who summons'. The
church official who
summoned the
congregation to prayer.

Sutcliffe [Anglo-Saxon]
'From the south cliff'.
(Sutcliff)

Sutherland [Scandinavian]
'From a southern land'.

Sutton [Anglo-Saxon]
'From the south town'.

Sven [Scandinavian]
'Youth'.

Swain [Anglo-Saxon]
'Herdsman' or 'Knight's attendant'.
(Sweyn, Swayne)

Sweeney [Gaelic]
'Little hero'.

Swinton [Anglo-Saxon]
'From the pig farm'.

Swithin [Old English]
'Strong'.
(Swithun)

Swithun See **Swithin**

Sydney See **Sidney**

Sylvester See **Silas**

Symington [Anglo-Saxon]
'From Simon's farm'.

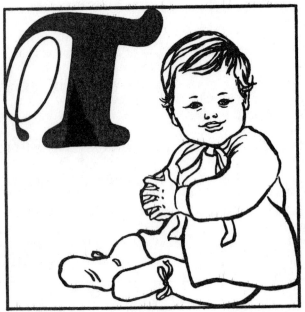

T

Girls

Tabbie See **Tabitha**

Tabina [Arabic]
'Muhammed's follower'.

Tabitha [Aramaic]
'The gazelle'. One of gentle
grace.
(Tabithe, Tabbie, Tabby)

Tabithe See **Tabitha**

Tacita See **Tacitah**

Tacitah [Latin]
'Silence'.
(Tacita)

Tacy [Latin]
'Peace'.

Tahani [Arabic]
'Congratulations'.

Tahira [Arabic]
'Pure'.

Takara [Japanese]
'Treasure'.

Talia [Greek]
'Blooming'.

Taliba [Arabic]
'Student'.

Talitha [Aramaic]
'The maiden'.

Tallie See **Tallulah**

Tallu See **Tallulah**

Tallulah [American-Indian]
'Laughing water'. One
who bubbles like a spring.
(*Tallula, Tallu, Tally,
Tallie*)

Tama [Japanese]
'Jewel'.

Tamar See **Tamara**

Tamara [Hebrew]
'Palm tree'.
(*Tamar, Tammie, Tammy*)

Tammy [Hebrew]
'Perfection'. Also dim. of
Tamara.

Tammy See **Tamara**

Tamsin See **Thomasina**

Tandi See **Tansy**

Tangerine [Anglo-Saxon]
'Girl from Tangiers'.

Tangwystl [Welsh]
'Peace pledge'.

Tani [Japanese]
'Valley'.

Tania [Russian]
'The fairy queen'. Also
dim. of Titania.
(*Tanya*)

Tania See **Titania**

Tansy [Latin]
'Tenacious'. A woman of
determination.

Tara [Gaelic]
'Towering rock'. The
home of the ancient kings
of Ireland.

Tarah See **Tara**

Tate [Old English]
'To be cheerful'.
(*Tatum*)

Tatiana [Latin]
'Silver-haired'.

Tatum See **Tate**

Tavia See **Octavia**

Tavie See **Octavia**

Taylor [Middle English]
'A tailor'.

Tecla See **Thecla**

Teddie See **Theodora**

Tegan [Welsh]
'Beautiful'.

Tegwen [Welsh]
'Beautiful-blessed'.

Tempest [French]
'Stormy one'.
(Tempesta, Tempeste)

Tempesta See **Tempest**

Teodora See **Theodora**

Teodore See **Theodora**

Terentia [Greek]
'Guardian'. Fem. of
Terence.
*(Terencia, Teri, Terri,
Terrie, Terry)*

Teresa [Greek]
'The harvester'.
*(Theresa, Therese,
Terese, Teressa, Teresita,
Toireasa, Terri, Terrie,
Terry, Tessa, Tessie,
Tessy, Tess, Tracie,
Tracy, Zita)*

Teresina See **Teresa**

Teresita See **Teresa**

Terra See **Tara**

Terri See **Terentia**

Terry See **Terentia/Teresa**

Tertia [Latin]
'Third child'.

Terza [Greek]
'Girl from the farm'.

Tess See **Teresa**

Tessa [Greek]
'Fourth child'. Also var. of
Teresa.

Tessa See **Teresa**

Tessy See **Teresa**

Tewdews [Welsh]
'Divinely given'.

Thaddea [Greek]
'Courageous being'. A girl
of great bravery and
endurance.
(*Thada, Thadda*)

Thalassa [Greek]
'From the sea'.

Thalia [Greek]
'Luxurious blossom'.

Thea [Greek]
'Goddess'. Also dim. of
Dorothea, Theadora,
Anthea, etc.

Thea See **Theodora**

Theadosia See **Theodora**

Theana See **Theano**

Theano [Greek]
'Divine name'.
(*Theana*)

Theaphania See
Theophila

Thecla [Greek]
'Divine follower'. A
disciple of St. Paul.
(*Tecla, Thekla*)

Theda See **Theodora**

Thelma [Greek]
'The nursling'.

Theo See **Theodora**

Theodora [Greek]
'Gift of God'. Another
version of Dorothy.
(*Theda, Theadora,
Theadosia, Theodosia,
Teodora, Teodore, Dora,
Fedora, Fedore, Feodora,
Feodore, Feadore,
Feadora, Teddie, Theo,
Thea* and all forms of
Dorothy)

Theodora See **Dorothy**

Theodosia See **Theodora**

Theofila See **Theophania**

Theofilia See **Theophania**

Theola [Greek]
'Sent from God'.
(*Theo, Lola*)

Theone [Greek]
'In the name of God'.
(*Theona*)

Theophania [Greek]
'Beloved of God'.
(*Theofilia, Theofila,
Theophilia*)

Theophanie See
  Theophila

Theophila [Greek]
  'Appearance of God'.
  *(Theaphania, Theafania,
  Theophanie, Theofanie,
  Tiffanie, Tiffy)*

Theophilia See
  Theophania

Theora [Greek]
  'Watcher for God'.

Thera [Greek]
  'Wild, untamed one'.

Therese See **Teresa**

Thetis [Greek]
  'Positive one'. One who
  knows her own mind.
  (Thetys)

Thia See **Anthea**

Thirza [Hebrew]
  'Pleasantness'.
  (Thyrza, Tirza)

Thomasa See **Thomasina**

Thomase See **Thomasina**

Thomasina [Hebrew]
  'The twin'. Fem. of
  Thomas.

*(Thomasine, Tomasine,
Thomase, Thomasa,
Tomase, Tomasa,
Tomasina, Tamsin)*

Thomasine See
  Thomasina

Thora [Norse]
  'Thunder'. From the God
  of Thunder — Thor.

Thorberta [Norse]
  'Brilliance of Thor'.
  *(Thorberte, Thorbertha,
  Thorberte)*

Thorberte See **Thorberta**

Thordia See **Thordis**

Thordie See **Thordis**

Thordis [Norse]
  'Spirit of Thor'. The sound
  of thunder.
  (Thordia, Thordie)

Thyra [Greek]
  'Shield bearer'.

Tia [Greek]
  'Princess'.

Tibelda [Teutonic]
  'Boldest person'.

Tiberia [Latin]

'From the Tiber'. The river
of ancient Rome.

Tierney [Gaelic]
'Grandchild of the lordly'.

Tiffanie See **Theophila**

Tiffany [Greek]
'Manifestation of God'.

Tiffy See **Theophila**

Tilda See **Mathilda**

Tilly See **Mathilda**

Tim See **Timothea**

Timandra [Greek]
'Honour'.

Timmy See **Timothea**

Timothea [Greek]
'Honouring God'.
(Tim, Timmie, Timmy)

Tina See **Christine,
Martina, Augusta** etc.

Tiphani See **Tiffany**

Tirza [Spanish]
'Cypress'.

Tish See **Letitia**

Tita [Latin]
'Honoured title'.

Titania [Greek]
'Giantess'. Also the name
of the queen of fairies.
(Tania, Tanya)

Tizane [Hungarian]
'A gypsy'. See also Gitana.

Tobe See **Tobey**

Tobey [Hebrew]
'God is good'.
(Toby, Tobe, Tobi)

Toinette See **Antonia**

Tomi [Japanese]
'Riches'.

Toni See **Antonia**

Tonia See **Antonia**

Topaz [Latin]
'The topaz gem'.

Tourmalina See
Tourmaline

Tourmaline [Srilangarese]
'A carnelian'.
(Tourmalina)

Tracie See **Teresa**

Tracy [Gaelic]
'Battler'. Also der. of
Teresa.
(Tracey)

Traviata [Italian]
'The frail one'.
Traditionally a courtesan.

Trescha See **Teresa**

Triantafilia [Greek]
'Rose'.

Trilby [Italian]
'A singer who trills'.

Trina [Greek]
'Girl of purity'.

Triphenia See **Tryphena**

Trista [Latin]
'Melancholia; sorrow'.

Trix See **Beatrice**

Trixie See **Beatrice**

Trudie See **Gertrude**

Trudy [Teutonic]
'Loved one'. Also dim. of
Gertrude.
(Trudi, Trudie, Trudey)

Tryphena [Latin]
'The delicate one'.
*(Triphena, Triphenia,
Tryphenia)*

Tuesday [Anglo-Saxon]
'Born on Tuesday'.

Tullia [Gaelic]
'Peaceful one'.

Turaya [Arabic]
'Star'.

Twyla [Middle English]
'Woven of double thread'.

Tymandra See **Timandra**

Tyne [Old English]
'River'.

Tab [Teutonic]
'The drummer'.
(Tabb, Tabby)

Tabby See **Tab**

Taber See **Tab**

Tabor See **Tab**

Tad See **Thaddeus**

Tadd [Celtic]
'Father'. Also dim. for
Thaddeus and Theodore.
(Tad)

Taddeo See **Thaddeus**

Taddy See **Thaddeus**

Tadeas See **Tadeo**

Tadeo [Spanish, Latin]
'Praise'.

Taffy [Celtic]
Welsh form of David.

Taggart [Gaelic]
'Son of the prelate'.

Taillefer See **Telford**

Talbert See **Talbot**

Talbot [French]
'The looter'. One who lived
by his spoils and pillages.

Talfryn [Welsh]
'Brow of the hill'.

Taliesin [Welsh]
'Radiant brow'.

Tamar [Hebrew]
'Palm tree'.

Tamas See **Thomas**

Tammany See **Thomas**

Tammy See **Thomas**

Tancred [Old German]
'Thoughtful adviser'.

Tangwyn [Welsh]
'Blessed peace'.

Tann See **Tanner**

Tanner [Anglo-Saxon]
'Leather worker'.

Tanton [Anglo-Saxon]
'From the quiet river farm'.

Tarleton [Anglo-Saxon]
'Thor's farm'.

Tarrant [Old Welsh]
'Thunder'.

Tate [Anglo-Saxon]
'Cheerful'.
(Tait, Teyte)

Tavey See **Octavius**

Tavis [Celtic]
'Son of David'. Also der.
(Scottish) of Thomas.
(Tavish, Tevis)

Tavish See **Tavis**

Taylor [Anglo-Saxon]
'The Tailor'.
(Tailor)

Teador See **Theodore**

Teague [Celtic]
'The poet'.

Tearlach See **Charles**

Tearle [Anglo-Saxon]
'Stern, severe one'.

Tecwyn [Welsh]
'Fair and white'.

Ted See **Theodore**

Teddie See **Theodore**

Teddy See **Edward**

Tedmond [Anglo-Saxon]
'King's protector'.

Tedric See **Theodoric**

Telfer See **Telford**

Telfor See **Telford**

Telford [French]
'Iron hewer'.
(Telfer, Telfor, Telfour, Taillefer)

Templeton [Anglo-Saxon]
'Town of the temple'.

Tennyson [Anglo-Saxon]
'Son of Dennis'.
(Tenison, Tennison)

Teodorico See **Theodoric**

Terence [Latin]
'Smooth, polished and tender'.
(Terrene, Torrance, Terry)

Terencio See **Terence**

Terrell See **Terrill**

Terrene See **Terence**

Terrill [Teutonic]
'Follower of Thor'.
(Terrell, Tirrell, Tyrrell,
Terell, Tirell, Tyrell,
Terrel, Tirrel, Tyrrel)

Terry See **Terence**

Tevis See **Tavis**

Thad See **Thaddeus**

Thaddeus [Hebrew/Greek]
'Praise to God' (Hebrew)
or 'Courageous and stout
hearted' (Greek).
(Tad, Thad, Taddy)

Thaine [Anglo-Saxon]
'Warrior attendant'. A
military attendant on a
king or ruler.
(Thane, Thayne)

Thatch See **Thatcher**

Thatcher [Anglo-Saxon]
'A thatcher of roofs'.
(Thatch)

Thaw [Anglo-Saxon]
'Ice breaker'. The perfect
party guest.

Thaxter See **Thatcher**

Thayer [Anglo-Saxon]
'The nation's army'.

Themistocles [Greek]
'Law and right'.

Theobald [Teutonic]
'Bold leader of the people'.
(Tybalt, Tibbald, Thibaud,
Thibaut, Tioboid)

Theodore [Greek]
'Gift of God'.
(Feodor, Feodore, Tudor,
Dore, Ted, Teddie, Teddy)

Theodoric [Teutonic]
'Ruler of the people'. The
elected leader.
(Theodorick, Derek,
Derrick, Tedric, Derk,
Dirk, Ted, Teddie, Teddy)

Theodosius [Greek]
'God given'.

Theon [Greek]
'Godly man'.

Theophilus [Greek]
'Divinely loved'.

Theron [Greek]
'The hunter'.

Thibaud See **Theobald**

Thibaud [French]
'People's prince'.

Thibaut See **Theobald**

Thomas [Hebrew]
'The twin'. The devoted
brother.
*(Tomas, Tammany, Tam,
Tammy, Thom, Tom,
Tommy, Massey)*

Thor [Scandinavian]
'God of Thunder'. The
ancient Norse God.
(Tor)

Thorald [Scandinavian]
'Thor's ruler'. One who
ruled in the name of the
thunder-god.
*(Torald, Thorold, Terrell,
Tyrell)*

Thorbert [Scandinavian]
'Brilliance of Thor'.
(Torbert)

Thorburn [Scandinavian]
'Thor's bear'.
(Torburn)

Thorfinn See **Torin**

Thorin See **Thor**

Thorley [Anglo-Saxon]
'From Thor's meadow'.
(Torley)

Thormund [Anglo-Saxon]
'Protected by Thor'.
*(Thormond, Thurmond,
Tormond, Tormund)*

Thorn See **Thornton**

Thorndyke [Anglo-Saxon]
'From the thorny ditch'.

Thorne [Anglo-Saxon]
'From the thorn tree'.

Thornley [Anglo-Saxon]
'From the thorny
meadow'.
*(Thornly, Thorneley,
Thornely)*

Thornton [Anglo-Saxon]
'From the thorny place'.

Thorold [Old English]
'Thor's strength'.

Thorpe [Anglo-Saxon]
'From the small village'.
(Thorp)

Thorstein See **Thurston**

Thurlow [Anglo-Saxon]
'From Thor's hill'.

Thurmond See
Thormund

Thurston [Anglo-Saxon]
'Thor's jewel'.
(Thorstein, Thurstan)

Tibbald See **Theobald**

Tibor [Slavonic]
'Holy place'.

Tierman [Gaelic]
'Lord and master'. The
overlord or lord of the
manor.
(Tierney)

Tierney See **Tierman**

Tiffany [French]
'The divine appearance of
God'.

Tilden [Anglo-Saxon]
'From the fertile valley'.

Tilford [Anglo-Saxon]
'From the good man's
farm'.

Tim See **Timothy**

Timmie See **Timothy**

Timon [Greek]
'Honour, reward, value'.

Timoteo See **Timothy**

Timotheus See **Timothy**

Timothy [Greek]
'Honouring God'.
*(Tim, Timmie, Timmy,
Tiomoid)*

Tioboid See **Theobald** or
Tobias

Tiomoid See **Timothy**

Tirell See **Terrill**

Tirrell See **Terrill**

Tito See **Titus**

Titus [Greek/Latin]
'Of the giants' (Greek)
or 'Saved' (Latin).
(Tito)

Tobiah See **Tobias**

Tobias [Hebrew]
'God is good'.
*(Tobe, Toby, Tioboid,
Tobit)*

Tobit See **Tobias**

Todd [Latin]
'The fox'.

Toft [Anglo-Saxon]
'A small farm'.

Toland [Anglo-Saxon]
'Owner of taxed land'.

Tolman [Old English]
'Tax collector'.

Tom See **Thomas**

Tomaso See **Thomas**

Tomkin [Anglo-Saxon]
'Small Thomas'.
(Tomlin)

Tomlin See **Tomkin**

Tommy See **Thomas**

Tony See **Anthony**

Torbert See **Thorbert**

Torburn See **Thorburn**

Torin [Gaelic]
'Chief'.
(Thorfinn)

Torley See **Thorley**

Tormey [Gaelic]
'Thunder spirit'.
(Tormy)

Tormond See **Thormund**

Tormund See **Thormund**

Torquil [Teutonic]
'Thor's pledge'.

Torr [Anglo-Saxon]
'From the tower'.

Torrance [Gaelic]
'From the little hills'. Also
der. of Terence.

Torrance See **Terence**

Tostig [Welsh]
'Sharp'.

Townley [Anglo-Saxon]
'From the town meadow'.
(Townly)

Townsend [Anglo-Saxon]
'From the end of the
town'.

Tracy [Latin]
'Bold and courageous'.

Trahern [Celtic]
'Iron strength'. One who
could bend an iron bar in
his bare hands.
*(Trehern, Trehearn,
Trehearne, Trahearn,
Trahearne)*

Travers [Latin]
'From the crossroads'.
(Travis)

Travis See **Travers**

Travus See **Travers**

Tredway [Anglo-Saxon]
'Mighty warrior'.

Trefor See **Trevor**

Trelawny [Cornish]
'From the church town'.
(Trelawney)

Tremayne [Celtic]
'From the house in the
rock'.
(Tremaine)

Trent [Latin]
'The torrent'.

Trevelyan [Celtic]
'From Elian's farm'. An old
Cornish name.

Trevor [Gaelic]
'Prudent, wise and
discreet'. One who can be
trusted to keep secrets.
(Trefor)

Trey [Middle English]
'The third'.

Trigg [Scandinavian]
'True and faithful'.

Tripp [Anglo-Saxon]
'The traveller'.

Tristan [Celtic]
'The noisy one'.
(Tristin, Tristen, Drostan)

Tristin See **Tristan**

Tristram [Celtic]
'The sorrowful one'. Do
not confuse with Tristan.

Trowbridge [Anglo-Saxon]
'From the tree bridge'.

Troy [French]
'From the land of the
people with curly hair'.

True [Anglo-Saxon]
'Faithful and loyal'.

Truesdale [Anglo-Saxon]
'The home of the beloved
one'.
(Trusdale)

Truman [Anglo-Saxon]
'A faithful follower'. A
loyal servant.
(Trueman, Trumane)

Trumane See **Truman**

Trumble [Anglo-Saxon]
'Bold and strong'.

Trusdale See **Truesdale**

Tucker [Anglo-Saxon]
'Cloth thickener'. A var. of
Fuller.

Tudor See **Theodore**

Tulio [Spanish]
'Lively'.

Tully [Gaelic]
'Obedient to the will of
God'.

Tupper [Anglo-Saxon]
'A sheep raiser'. One who
reared and tended sheep.

Turner [Latin]
'Lathe worker'.

Turpin [Scandinavian]
'Thunder like'. Finnish
form of Thor.

Tuxford [Scandinavian]
'From the ford of the
champion spear thrower'.

Twain [Anglo-Saxon]
'Divided in two'. A
co-heir.

Twitchell [Anglo-Saxon]
'From a narrow
passageway'.

Twyford [Anglo-Saxon]
'From the twin river'.

Tybalt See **Theobald**

Tye [Anglo-Saxon]
'From the enclosure'.

Tyler [Anglo-Saxon]
'Maker of tiles or bricks'.
(Tiler, Ty)

Tymon See **Timothy**

Tynam [Gaelic]
'Dark; grey'.

Tyrone [Greek]
'The sovereign'.

Tyrus See **Thor**

Tyson [Teutonic]
'Son of the German'.
(Sonny, Ty)

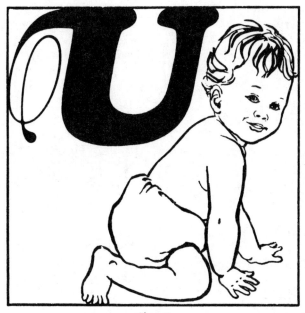

Girls

Uda [Teutonic]
'Prosperous'. A child of
fortune.
(Udella, Udelle)

Udella See **Uda**

Udelle See **Uda**

Ula [Celtic/Teutonic]
'Jewel of the sea' (Celtic);
'The inheritor' (Teutonic).
(Oola)

Ulima [Arabic]
'The learned'. A woman
wise in counsel.

Ulrica [Teutonic]
'Ruler of all'.
(Ulrika, Rica)

Ultima [Latin]
'The most distant'.

Ulva [Teutonic]
'The she-wolf'. A symbol
of bravery.

Umeko [Japanese]
'Plum-blossom child'.

Una [Latin]
'One'. The one and only
girl.
(Ona, Oona, Oonagh)

Undine [Latin]
'A wave'. The wave of
water.
(Ondine)

Undine See **Ondine**

Unity [Middle English]
'Unity'.

Urania [Greek]
'Heavenly'. The Muse of
Astronomy.

Urith [Old German]
'Deserving'.

Ursa See **Ursula**

Ursel See **Ursula**

Ursie See **Ursula**

Ursola See **Ursula**

Ursula [Latin]
'The she-bear'.
*(Ursa, Ursel, Ursie, Ursy,
Ursulette, Ursola, Ursule,
Ursuline, Orsa, Orsola)*

Ursule See **Ursula**

Ursulette See **Ursula**

Ursuline See **Ursula**

Uta [German]
'Rich'.

Utano [Japanese]
'Song field'.

Udale See **Udell**

Udall See **Udell**

Udell [Anglo-Saxon]
'From the yew tree valley'.
(Udale, Udall)

Udolf [Anglo-Saxon]
'Prosperous wolf'.

Uilleam See **William**

Uillioc See **Ulysses**

Uland [Teutonic]
'Noble land'.

Ulbrecht [German]
'Noble splendour'.

Ulfred [Anglo-Saxon]
'Peace of the wolf'.

Ulger [Anglo-Saxon]
'Courageous wolf
(spearman)'.

Ulick See **Ulysses**

Ullock [Anglo-Saxon]
'Sport of the wolf'.

Ulmar See **Ulmer**

Ulmer [Anglo-Saxon]
'Famous wolf'.
(Ulmar)

Ulric [Teutonic]
'Ruler of all'.
(Alric, Ulrich)

Ulysses [Greek]
'The angry one; the hater'.
(Ulises, Uillioc)

Umberto See **Humbert**

Unwin [Anglo-Saxon]
'The enemy'.

Upton [Anglo-Saxon]
'From the hill farm'.

Upwood [Anglo-Saxon]
'From the hill forest'.

Urban [Latin]
'From the city'. A
townsman.

Urbano See **Urban**

Uri [Hebrew]
'Light'.

Uriah [Hebrew]
  'The Lord is my light; the
  Lord's light'.
  (Urias, Uriel)

Urias See **Uriah**

Uriel See **Uriah**

Urien [Welsh]
  'Town-born'.

Urson See **Orson**

Uzziah [Hebrew]
  'Might of the Lord'.

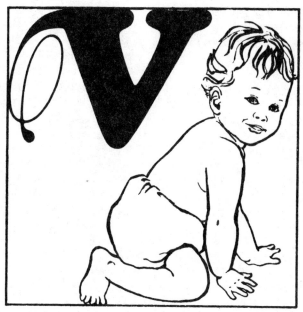

Girls

Vala [Teutonic]
'The chosen one'. Ideal name for the adopted daughter.

Valborga [Teutonic]
'Protecting ruler'. *(Walburga, Walborga, Valburga)*

Valburga See **Valborga**

Valda [Teutonic]
'Ruler'. *(Walda, Welda)*

Valeda See **Valentina**

Valencia See **Valentina**

Valentina [Latin]
'Strong and vigorous'.
(Valentine, Valencia,
Valentia, Valeda, Valida,
Val, Vallie)

Valentine See **Valentina**

Valera See **Valentina**

Valeria See **Valerie**

Valerie [French]
'Strong'.
(Valeria, Valery, Valory,
Valorie, Valorey, Valora,
Val, Vallie)

Valeska [Slavic]
'Glorious ruler'.
(Waleska)

Valida See **Velda**

Valma [Welsh]
'Mayflower'.
(Valmai)

Valmai See **Valma**

Valona See **Valonia**

Valonia [Latin]
'From the vale'.
(Valona)

Valora See **Valerie**

Valory See **Valerie**

Vancy See **Evangeline**

Vanessa [Greek]
'The butterfly'. A name
also derived by Jonathan
Swift from 'Esther van
Homrigh', one of his
correspondents.
(Van, Vanni, Vannie,
Vanny, Vanna, Vania,
Vanya)

Vangie See **Evangeline**

Vania See **Vanessa**

Vania [Hebrew]
'God's precious gift'.

Vanina See **Vania**

Vannie See **Vanessa**

Vanora See **Genevieve**

Varina [Slavic]
'Stranger'.

Vahsti [Persian]
'Beautiful one'.

Veda [Sanskrit]
'Wisdom and knowledge'.
(Vedis)

Vedetta See **Vedette**

Vedette [Italian]
'The sentinel'.
(Vedetta)

Vedis See **Veda**

Vega [Arabic]
'The great one'.

Velda [Teutonic]
'Very wise'.
(Valida)

Velda [Dutch]
'Field'.

Velika [Slavic]
'The falling one'.
(Velica)

Velma See **Wilhelmina**

Velvet [English]
'Soft as velvet'.

Venetia [Latin]
'Lady of Venice'.

Venita See **Venus**

Ventura [Spanish]
'Happiness and good
luck'.

Venus [Latin]
'Loveliness; beauty'. The
Goddess of Beauty and
Love.

*(Venita, Vinita, Vinny,
Vinnie)*

Vera [Latin]
'Truth'. One who is honest
and steadfast.
*(Vere, Verena, Verene,
Verina, Verine, Verla)*

Verbena [Latin]
'The sacred bough'.

Verda [Latin]
'Fresh youth'. The verdant
qualities of spring.

Verda See **Verna**

Vere See **Vera**

Verena See **Vera** or **Verna**

Verene See **Vera**

Verity [Latin]
'Truth'.

Verla See **Vera**

Verna [Latin]
'Spring like'.
*(Vernice, Vernita,
Verneta, Verda, Verena,
Vernis, Virna, Virina)*

Verna See **Laverne**

Verne See **Laverne**

Vernice See **Verna**

Vernis See **Verna**

Vernita See **Verna**

Verona [Latin]
'Lady of Verona'. Also
dim. of Veronica.

Verona See **Veronica**

Veronica [Latin]
'True image'. Also var. of
Bernice.
*(Verona, Vonnie, Vonny,
Ronnie, Ronny,* and all
var. of *Bernice)*

Veronica See **Bernice**

Veronique See **Veronica**

Vesna [Slavic]
'Spring'.

Vespera [Latin]
'The evening star'.

Vesta [Latin]
'Guardian of the sacred
flame'. A Vestal virgin.
'Melodious one'.

Veta See **Vita**

Vevila [Gaelic]
'Melodious one'.

Vicenta See **Vincentia**

Victoria [Latin]
'The victorious one'.
Attained popularity in
Britain following the long
reign of Queen Victoria.
*(Tory, Victorine, Vitoria,
Vittoria, Victorie, Vicki,
Vicky)*

Victorie See **Victoria**

Victorine See **Victoria**

Vida [Hebrew]
'Beloved one'. Fem. of
David.

Vidette [Hebrew]
'Beloved'.

Vidonia [Portuguese]
'Vine branch'.

Vigilia [Latin]
'The alert; vigilant'.

Vignette [French]
'The little vine'.

Villette [French]
'From the village'.

Vina [Spanish]
'From the vineyard'.

Vina See **Alvina** or **Lavinia**

Vincentia [Latin]
'The conqueror'. Fem. of
Vincent.
(Vincencia, Vicenta)

Vinia See **Lavinia**

Vinita See **Venus**

Vinnie See **Venus**

Viola See **Violet**

Violante See **Violet**

Violet [Latin]
'Modest flower'. Like the
shy, retiring violet.
*(Viola, Violetta, Violette,
Vi, Iolanthe, Yolanda,
Yolande, Yolanthe,
Violante)*

Violetta See **Violet**

Virdis [Latin]
'Fresh, blooming'.

Virgie See **Virginia**

Virgilia [Latin]
'The staff bearer'.

Virginia [Latin]
'The virgin; maidenly and
pure'.
*(Virginie, Virgi, Virgie,
Virgy, Ginger, Ginny,*

Ginnie, Jinny)

Virginie See **Virginia**

Viridis [Latin]
'The green bough'.

Virina See **Verna**

Vita [Latin]
'Life'. One who likes
living.
(Evita, Veta, Vitia)

Vitia See **Vita**

Vitoria See **Victoria**

Viveca [Latin,
Scandinavian]
'Living voice'.

Vivia See **Vivian**

Vivian [Latin]
'Alive'. Vivid and vibrant
with life.
*(Viviana, Vivien, Vivienne,
Vivienna, Vivyan, Vyvyan,
Viviane, Viviene, Viv, Vivi,
Vivia, Vivie)*

Viviana See **Vivian**

Volante [Latin]
'The flying one'. One who
steps so lightly that she
seems to fly.

Voleta [French]
'A floating veil'
(Voletta)

Von See **Yvonne**

Vonnie See **Veronica**

Vonny See **Veronica**

Vachel [French]
'Little cow'.

Vadim See **Vladimir**

Vail [Anglo-Saxon]
'From the valley'.
(Vale, Valle)

Val [Teutonic]
'Mighty power'. Also dim.
for any name beginning
with 'Val'.

Valarian [Latin]
'Healthy'.
(Valarius)

Valarius See **Valarian**

Valdemar [Teutonic]
'Famous ruler'.
(Valdimar, Valdemar)

Valente See **Valentine**

Valentin See **Valentine**

Valentine [Latin]
'Healthy, strong and
valorous'.
*(Valentin, Valentino,
Vailintin, Valente, Valiant)*

Valentino See **Valentine**

Valerian [Latin]
'Strong and powerful' or
'Belonging to Valentine'.

Valiant See **Valentine**

Valle See **Vail**

Vallis [French]
'The Welshman'.

Van [Dutch]
'From' or 'Of'. More
generally used as a prefix
to a surname, but
occasionally found on its
own as a forename.

Vance [Anglo-Saxon]
'From the grain barn'.

Varden [Anglo-Saxon]
'From a green hill'.
(Vardon, Verden, Verdon)

Vardon See **Varden**

Varian [Latin]
'Changeable'.

Varick [Teutonic]
'Protecting ruler'.

Vassily [Slavic]
'Unwavering protector'.

Vassily See **Basil**

Vaughan [Celtic]
'The small one'.
(Vaughn, Vawn)

Venn [Old English]
'Handsome'.

Vere [Latin]
'Faithful and true'. The
loyal one.

Vern See **Vernon**

Verne See **Vernon**

Verner See **Vernon**

Verney [French]
'From the alder grove'.

Vernon [Latin]
'Growing, flourishing'. As
the trees in spring.
(Verne, Verner, Vern)

Verrell [French]
'The honest one'.
(Verrall, Verrill, Verill)

Verrill See **Verrell**

Vick See **Victor**

Victor [Latin]
'The conqueror'.
(Vic, Vick, Victoir)

Vince See **Victor**

Vincent See **Victor**

Vinson [Anglo-Saxon]
'Son of Vincent'.

Virge See **Virgil**

Virgil [Latin]
'Staff bearer' or 'Strong and
flourishing'.
*(Vergil, Virge, Virgie,
Virgy)*

Vito [Latin]
'Alive; vital'.

Vittorio See **Victor**

Vivien [Latin]
'Lively one'.
(Vivian, Ninian)

Vladimir [Slavic]
'Royally famous'. A
renowned monarch.

Vladislav [Slavic]
'Glorious ruler'.

Volney [Teutonic]
'Of the people'.

Vychan [Welsh]
'Little'.

Vyvyan [Latin]
'Lively'.

Girls

Wahida [Arabic]
‘Unique’.

Walborga See **Valborga**

Walburga See **Valborga**

Walda See **Valda**

Waleska See **Valeska**

Walida [Arabic]
‘New-born girl’.

Wallace See **Wallis**

Wallis [Anglo-Saxon]
‘The Welshwoman; the
stranger’.
(Wallace, Wallie, Wally)

Wally See **Wallis**

Wanda [Teutonic]
'The wanderer'. The
restless roamer.
*(Wandie, Wandis, Wenda,
Wendy, Wendeline)*

Wandie See **Wanda**

Wandis See **Wanda**

Wanetta [Anglo-Saxon]
'The pale one'.
(Wanette)

Wanette See **Wanetta**

Warda [Teutonic]
'The guardian'.

Wasima [Arabic]
'Pretty'.

Welda See **Valda**

Welma See **Wilhelmina**

Wenda See **Wanda**

Wendeline See **Wanda**

Wendy See **Gwendoline**,
Wanda

Wesla [Old English]
'From west meadow'.

Whitney [Old English]
'From the white island'.

Wilf See **Wilfreda**

Wilfreda [Teutonic]
'The peacemaker'. Fem. of
Wilfred.
*(Wilfrieda, Wilfreida,
Freda, Wilf, Freddie)*

Wilhelmina [Teutonic]
'The protectress'. One
who guards resolutely
what is her own.
*(Wilma, Welma, Velma,
Willa, Willie, Willy,
Minnie, Minny, Billie,
Billy, Helma, Mina,
Guilla)*

Willa [Anglo-Saxon]
'Desirable'. Also dim. of
Wilhelmina.

Willa See **Billie**,
Wilhelmina

Willie See **Wilhelmina**

Willow [English]
Plant name.

Wilma See **Wilhelmina**

Wilona [Old English]
'Desired'.

Win See **Edwina**

Wina See **Edwina**

Winifred [Teutonic]
'Peaceful friend'. A restful
person to have around.
*(Winifrida, Winifreida,
Winifrieda, Winnie,
Winny)*

Winifrida See **Winifred**

Winna [African]
'Friend'.

Winnah See **Winna**

Winnie See **Edwina** or
Winifred

Winola [Teutonic]
'Gracious friend'.

Winona [American-Indian]
'First born daughter'.
*(Winonah, Wenona,
Wenonah)*

Winsome [English]
'Pleasant, attractive'.

Wren [Old English]
'Wren'.

Wynn See **Winifred**

Wynne [Celtic]
'Fair, white maiden'.
(Win, Wyne)

Wace [Anglo-Saxon]
'A vassal'.

Wade [Anglo-Saxon]
'Mover; wanderer'.

Wadley [Anglo-Saxon]
'From the wanderer's
meadow'.

Wadsworth [Anglo-Saxon]
'From the wanderer's
estate'.

Wagner [Teutonic]
'A waggoner'.

Wainwright [Anglo-Saxon]
'Waggon maker'.

Waite [Anglo-Saxon]
'A guard; a watchman'.

Wake [Anglo-Saxon]
'Alert and watchful'.

Wake See **Wakefield**

Wakefield [Anglo-Saxon]
'From the west field'.

Wakeley [Anglo-Saxon]
'From the wet meadow'.

Wakeman [Anglo-Saxon]
'Watchman'.

Walbert [Old English]
'Bright power'.

Walby [Anglo-Saxon]
'From the ancient walls'.

Walcott [Anglo-Saxon]
'Cottage dweller'.

Waldemar See **Valdemar**

Walden [Anglo-Saxon]
'Dweller in the valley in
the woods'.

Waldo [Teutonic]
'The ruler'.

Waldron [Teutonic]
'Strength of the raven'.

Walford [Old English]
'Welshman's ford'.

Walker [Anglo-Saxon]
'The walker'.

Wallace [Anglo-Saxon]
'The Welshman; the
stranger'. *(Wallis,
Walsh, Welch, Welsh,
Wallache, Wallie, Wally)*

Wallache See **Wallace**

Walmond [Teutonic]
'Mighty protector'.
(Walmund)

Walsh See **Wallace**

Walter [Teutonic]
'Mighty warrior'.
*(Walther, Walters, Wat,
Wally, Walt)*

Walton [Anglo-Saxon]
'From the forest town'.

Walworth [Anglo-Saxon]
'From the stranger's farm'.

Walwyn [Anglo-Saxon]
'Friendly stranger'.

Warand [Teutonic]
'Protecting'.

Warburton [Anglo-Saxon]
'From the castle town'.

Ward [Anglo-Saxon]
'Watchman; guardian'.

Wardell [Anglo-Saxon]
'From the hill watch'.

Warden [Anglo-Saxon]
'The guardian'.

Wardley [Anglo-Saxon]
'From the watchman's
meadow'.

Ware [Anglo-Saxon]
'Prudent one'. A very
astute person.

Warfield [Anglo-Saxon]
'From the field by the
weir'.

Warford [Anglo-Saxon]
'From the ford by the weir'.

Waring See **Warren**

Warley [Anglo-Saxon]
'From the meadow by the
weir'.

Warmund [Teutonic]
'Loyal protector'
(Warmond)

Warner [Teutonic]
'Protecting army'.
(Werner, Verner)

Warren [Teutonic]
'The gamekeeper'. One
who looked after the game
preserves.

Warton [Anglo-Saxon]
'From the farm by the
weir'.

Warwick [Anglo-Saxon]
'Strong fortress'.
(*Warrick*)

Washburn [Anglo-Saxon]
'From the river in spate'.

Washington [Anglo-Saxon]
'From the keen eyed one's
farm'.

Watford [Anglo-Saxon]
'From the hurdle by the
ford'.

Watkins [Anglo-Saxon]
'Son of Walter'.
(*Watson*)

Watson See **Watkins**

Waverley [Anglo-Saxon]
'The meadow by the aspen
trees'.
(*Waverly*)

Wayland [Anglo-Saxon]
'From the pathway near
the highway'.

Wayne [Teutonic]
'Waggon maker'.
(*Waine, Wain*)

Webb [Anglo-Saxon]
'A weaver'.
(*Webber, Weber, Webster*)

Webber See **Webb**

Webley [Anglo-Saxon]
'From the weaver's
meadow'.

Webster See **Webb**

Webster [Old English]
'Weaver'.

Weddell [Anglo-Saxon]
'From the wanderer's hill'.

Welborne [Anglo-Saxon]
'From the spring by the
brook'.
(*Welbourne*)

Welby [Anglo-Saxon]
'From the farm by the
spring'.

Welch See **Wallace**

Weldon [Anglo-Saxon]
'From the well on the hill'.

Welford [Anglo-Saxon]
'From the ford by the
spring'.

Wellington [Anglo-Saxon]
'From the rich man's
farm'.

Wells [Anglo-Saxon]
'From the spring'.

Welsh See **Wallace**

Welton [Anglo-Saxon]
'From the farm by the
spring'.

Wenceslaus [Slavic]
'Wreath of glory'.
(Wenceslas)

Wendall See **Wendell**

Wendell [Teutonic]
'The wanderer'.
(Wendel)

Wentworth [Anglo-Saxon]
'Estate belonging to the
white haired one'.

Werner See **Warner**

Wesley [Anglo-Saxon]
'From the west meadow'.
(Wesleigh, Westleigh)

Westbrook [Anglo-Saxon]
'From the west brook'.

Westby [Anglo-Saxon]
'From the homestead in
the west'.

Westcott [Anglo-Saxon]
'From the west cottage'.

Westleigh See **Wesley**

Weston [Anglo-Saxon]
'From the west farm'.

Wetherell [Anglo-Saxon]
'From the sheep hill'.
(Wetherill, Wetherall)

Wetherill See **Wetherell**

Wetherley [Anglo-Saxon]
'From the sheep
meadow'. *(Wetherly)*

Weylin [Celtic]
'Son of the wolf'.

Weylin See **Wayland**

Wharton [Anglo-Saxon]
'Farm in the hollow'.

Wheatley [Anglo-Saxon]
'From the wheat meadow'.

Wheeler [Anglo-Saxon]
'The wheel maker'.

Whistler [Anglo-Saxon]
'The whistler; the piper'.

Whitby [Anglo-Saxon]

'From the white farmstead'.

Whitcomb [Anglo-Saxon]
'From the white hollow'.
(Whitcombe)

Whitelaw [Anglo-Saxon]
'From the white hill'.

Whitfield [Anglo-Saxon]
'From the white field'.

Whitford [Anglo-Saxon]
'From the white ford'.

Whitley [Anglo-Saxon]
'From the white meadow'.

Whitlock [Anglo-Saxon]
'White haired one'.

Whitman [Anglo-Saxon]
'White haired man'.

Whitmore [Anglo-Saxon]
'From the white moor'.

Whitney [Anglo-Saxon]
'From the white island'.
(Whitny, Witney, Witny)

Whittaker [Anglo-Saxon]
'One who dwells in the white field'.
(Whitaker)

Wiatt See **Guy**

Wickham [Anglo-Saxon]
'From the enclosed field by the village'.
(Wykeham)

Wickley [Anglo-Saxon]
'From the village meadow'.

Wilbert See **Wilbur**

Wilbur [Teutonic]
'Resolute and brilliant'. A determined and clever person.

Wildon [Old English]
'From the wooden hill'.

Wiley See **William**

Wilford [Anglo-Saxon]
'From the willow ford'.

Wilfred [Teutonic]
'Firm peace maker'. Peace, but not at any price.
(Wilfrid, Fred, Freddie, Freddy)

Wilhelm See **William**

Wilkes See **William**

Wilkie See **William**

Will See **William**

Willard [Anglo-Saxon]
'Resolute and brave'.

Willet See **William**

William [Teutonic]
'Determined protector'.
The strong guardian.
(Wiley, Wilkie, Wilkes,
Liam, Wilson,
Williamson, Willis,
Wilhelm, Willet, Will,
Willie, Willy, Bill, Billie,
Billy, Gwylim, Uilleam,
Uilliam)

Williamson See **William**

Willis See **William**

Willoughby [Anglo-Saxon]
'From the farmstead by the
willows'.

Wilmer [Teutonic]
'Resolute and famous'.
One renowned for his
firmness.

Wilmot [Teutonic]
'Resolute mind'. One who
knows his own mind.

Wilson See **William**
Also 'Son of William'
(Anglo-Saxon).

Wilton [Anglo-Saxon]

'From the farm by the
well'.

Winchell [Anglo-Saxon]
'The bend in the road'.

Windsor [Anglo-Saxon]
'The boundary bank'.

Winfield [Anglo-Saxon]
'From a friend's field'.

Winfred [Anglo-Saxon]
'Peaceful friend'.
(Winifred)

Wingate [Anglo-Saxon]
'From the winding lane'.

Winifred See **Winfred**

Winslow [Anglo-Saxon]
'From a friend's hill'.

Winston [Anglo-Saxon]
'From a friend's estate'.

Winter [Anglo-Saxon]
'Born during winter
months'.

Winthrop [Teutonic]
'From a friendly village'.

Winton [Anglo-Saxon]
'From a friend's farm'.

Winwald See **Winward**

Winward [Anglo-Saxon]
'From the friendly forest'.
(Winwald)

Wirt See **Wirth**

Wirth [Teutonic]
'The master'.
(Wirt)

Witram [German]
'Forest river'.

Witt See **Witter**

Witter [Teutonic]
'Wise warrior'.
(Witt)

Witton [Teutonic]
'From a wise man's farm'.

Wolcott [Anglo-Saxon]
'From the cottage of the
wolf'. *(Wulcott)*

Wolfe [Teutonic]
'A wolf'. A man of
courage.

Wolfgang [Teutonic]
'The advancing wolf'. A
warrior in the vanguard of
the army.

Wolfram [Teutonic]
'Respected and feared'.

Woodley [Anglo-Saxon]
'From the forest meadow'.
(Woodly)

Woodrow [Anglo-Saxon]
'From the hedge in the
wood'.

Woodruff [Anglo-Saxon]
'Forest bailiff'.

Woodward [Anglo-Saxon]
'Forest guardian'.

Woolsey [Anglo-Saxon]
'Victorious wolf'.
(Wolsey, Wolseley)

Wooster See **Worcester**

Worcester [Anglo-Saxon]
'Camp in the forest of the
alder trees'.
(Wooster)

Wordsworth [Anglo-
Saxon]
'From the farm of the
wolf'.

Worrall [Anglo-Saxon]
'From the loyal man's
manor'.
(Worrell, Worrill)

Worrill See **Worrall**

Worth [Anglo-Saxon]
'The farmstead'.

Worthington [Anglo-Saxon]
'Riverside'.

Worton [Anglo-Saxon]
'From the vegetable farm'.

Wray [Scandinavian]
'Dweller in the house on the corner'.

Wren [Celtic]
'The chief'.

Wright [Anglo-Saxon]
'Craftsman in woodwork; a carpenter'.

Wulfstan [Old English]
'Wolf stone'.

Wyatt See **Guy**

Wybert [Old English]
'Battle famous'.

Wyborn [Scandinavian]
'Warrior bear'.
(Wyborne)

Wycliff [Anglo-Saxon]
'From the white cliff'.

Wylie [Anglo-Saxon]
'The enchanter; the beguiler'.

Wyman [Anglo-Saxon]
'The warrior'.

Wymer [Anglo-Saxon]
'Renowned in battle'.

Wyndham [Anglo-Saxon]
'From the village with the winding path'.
(Windham)

Wynford [Welsh]
'White torrent'.

Wynn [Celtic]
'The fair one'.

Wystan See **Wystand**

Wystand [Old English]
'Battle stone'.
(Wystan)

Wythe [Anglo-Saxon]
'From the dwelling by the willow tree'.

Girls

Xanthe [Greek]
 'Golden blonde'.

Xanthippe [Greek]
 The wife of Socrates.

Xaverie [Aramaic]
 'Bright'.

Xaviera [Spanish]
 'Owner of the home'.

Xena [Greek]
 'Hospitality'.
 (Xenia, Xene, Zenia)

Xene See **Xena**

Xenia See **Xena**

Ximena [Greek]
 'Heroine'.

Xylia [Greek]
 'From the woods'.
 (Xylona)

Xylina See **Xylia**

Xylona See **Xylia**

Xanthus [Latin]
'Golden haired'.

Xavier [Spanish/Arabic]
'New house owner'
(Spanish) or 'Bright'
(Arabic). *(Javier)*

Xenophon [Greek]
'Strong sounding'.

Xenos [Greek]
'The stranger'.

Xerxes [Persian]
'The king'.

Ximenes See **Simon**

Xylon [Greek]
'From the forest'.

Girls

Yaffa [Hebrew]
'Beautiful'.

Yakira [Hebrew]
'Valuable'.

Yasmeen [Persian]
'Flower'.

Yasmin See **Jasmin**

Yasmina See **Jasmin**

Yasmine See **Jasmine**

Yasu [Japanese]
'Tranquil'.

Yedda [Anglo-Saxon]
'The singer'. One with a
melodious voice.

Yerusha See **Jerusha**

Yesima [Hebrew]
'Right hand; strength'.

Yetta [Anglo-Saxon]
'To give, the giver'. Also
dim. of Henrietta.

Yetta See **Henrietta**

Yevetta See **Yvonne**

Ynes See **Agnes**

Ynez See **Agnes**

Yoanna See **Jane**

Yolanda See **Iolanthe** or
Violet

Yolande See **Iolanthe** or
Violet

Yolanthe See **Violet**

Yosepha See **Josephine**

Yoshiko [Japanese]
'Good'.

Yovela [Hebrew]
'Rejoicing'.

Ysabel See **Isabel**

Ysabel See **Isabel**

Yseult See **Isolde**

Yvetta See **Yvonne**

Yvette See **Yvonne**

Yvona See **Yvonne**

Yvonne [French]
'Archer with the yew bow'.
*(Yvette, Yvetta, Yvona,
Yevetta, Yevette, Ivonne,
Von, Vonnie)*

Yale [Teutonic/Anglo-Saxon]
'The one who pays' (Teutonic) — the vanquished; or 'From the corner of the land' (Anglo-Saxon).

Yance See **Yancy**

Yancy [American Indian]
'The Englishman'. Name given to settlers in New England and subsequently became Yankee.

Yardan [Arabic]
'King; merciful'.

Yardley [Old English]
'From the enclosed meadow'.

Yarin [Hebrew]
'Understand'.

Yasir [Arabic]
'Easy, soft'.

Yates [Anglo-Saxon]
'The dweller at the gates'.

Yehudi [Hebrew]
'Praise be the Lord'.

Yeoman [Anglo-Saxon]
'The tenant farmer'.

Yestin [Welsh]
'Just'.

Ynyr [Welsh]
'Honour'.

Yorick See **York**

York [Latin/Anglo-Saxon/Celtic]
'Boar estate' (Anglo-Saxon); 'Sacred tree' (Latin) or 'Yew tree estate' (Celtic).
(Yorke, Yorick)

Yul [Mongolian]
'Beyond the horizon'.

Yule See **Yules**

Yules [Anglo-Saxon]
'Born at Christmas'.
(Yule)

Yves See **Ives**

Girls

Zabrina [Anglo-Saxon]
  'Noble maiden'.

Zada [Arabic]
  'Lucky one'. Fortune's
  favourite.

Zahra [Arabic]
  'Blossom'.

Zakira [Arabic]
  'Remembrance'.

Zamira [Hebrew]
  'Song'.

Zandra See **Alexandra**

Zaneta See **Jane**

Zara [Hebrew]
  'Brightness of dawn'. Also
  der. of Sarah.

Zara See **Sarah**

Zaria See **Sarah** or **Zara**

Zarifa [Arabic]
'Graceful'.

Zea [Latin]
'Ripened grain'.

Zebada [Hebrew]
'Gift of the Lord'.

Zelda See **Grizelda**

Zele See **Zelia**

Zelia [Greek]
'Zealous one'. One with a
true devotion to duty.
(Zele, Zelie, Zelina)

Zelie See **Zelia**

Zelina See **Zelia**

Zelma See **Anselma**

Zena [Greek]
'The hospitable one'.

Zena See **Zenobia** or **Zian**

Zenaida See **Zenobia**

Zenda See **Zenobia**

Zenia See **Zenobia**

Zenina See **Zenobia**

Zenna See **Zenobia**

Zennie See **Zenobia**

Zenobia [Greek]
'Zeus gave life'.
*(Zena, Zenaida, Zenda,
Zenna, Zenia, Zenina,
Zennie, Zenorbie)*

Zenorbie See **Zenobia**

Zephirah [Hebrew]
'Dawn'.

Zera [Hebrew]
'Seeds'.

Zerelda [Old German]
'Armoured warrior maid'.

Zerla See **Zerlina**

Zerlina [Teutonic]
'Serene beauty'.
(Zerline, Zerla)

Zerlinda [Hebrew]
'Beautiful as the dawn'.

Zerline See **Zerlina**

Zetta [Anglo-Saxon]
'Sixth born'. The sixth
letter of the Greek
alphabet.
(Zitao)

Zeva [Greek]
'Sword'.

Zia [Latin]
'Kind of grain'.

Zian [Hebrew]
'Abundance'.
(Zinah, Zena)

Zilla [Hebrew]
'Shadow'.
(Zillah)

Zilpah [Hebrew]
'Dropping'.

Zinah See **Zian**

Zinnia [Latin]
'The zinnia flower'.
(Zinia)

Zippora [Hebrew]
'Trumpet' or 'Sparrow'.
(Zipporah)

Zita See **Teresa** or **Zetta**

Zitao See **Zetta**

Ziva [Hebrew]
'Brightness'.

Zoë [Greek]
'Life'.

Zofeyah [Hebrew]
'God sees'.

Zohara [Hebrew]
'The bright child'.

Zona [Latin]
'A girdle'. The belt of
Orion.
(Zonie)

Zonie See **Zona**

Zora [Latin]
'The dawn'.
*(Zorina, Zorine, Zoran
Zorah)*

Zorana See **Zora**

Zorina See **Zora**

Zorine See **Zora**

Zosima [Greek]
'Wealthy woman'.

Zsa See **Susan**

Zsa-Zsa See **Susan**

Zuleika [Arabic]
'Fair'.

Zulema [Arabic, Heb
'Peace'.

Zach See **Zacharias**

Zachaeus [Aramaic]
'Pure'.

Zachariah See **Zacharias**

Zacharias [Hebrew]
'The Lord has
remembered'.
*(Zachariah, Zachary,
Zach, Zack)*

Zachary See **Zacharias**

Zadok [Hebrew]
'The righteous one'.
(Zaloc)

Zahid [Arabic]
'Pious'.

Zahir [Arabic]
'Evident, splendid'.

Zaloc See **Zadok**

Zane See **John**

Zared [Hebrew]
'The ambush'.

Zebedee See **Zebediah**

Zebediah [Hebrew]
'Gift of the Lord'.
(Zebedee)

Zebulen See **Zebulon**

Zebulon [Hebrew]
'The dwelling place'.
(Lonny, Zeb)

Zechariah [Hebrew]
'The Lord is renowned'.

Zeke See **Ezekiel**

Zelig [Teutonic]
'Blessed one'.

Zelotes [Greek]
'The zealous one'.

Zenas [Greek]
'Living being'.

Zeno [Greek]
'Stranger'.

Zeus [Greek]
'Father of the gods'.

Zimraan [Arabic]
'Celebrated'.